REALITY REVOLUTION

REALITY REVOLUTION

Return to The Way

by Erriel D. Roberson (Kofi Addae)

Kujichagulia Press

1996

Reality Revolution
Return to The Way

by Erriel D. Roberson (Kofi Addae)

KUJICHAGULIA PRESS ❖ Columbia, MD

ISBN: 0-9644932-1-7

Library of Congress Catalog Card Number: 96-75530

Cover Design by Larry Bradshaw of ONA DESIGN
9301 ANNAPOLIS ROAD, SUITE 204
LANHAM, MD 20706

For information on other titles from Kujichagulia Press, tapes and videos by Erriel D. Roberson (Kofi Addae), *Reality Revolution* T-Shirts or to arrange lecture appearances, contact:

KUJICHAGULIA PRESS
9506 Ridgeview Drive
Columbia, MD 21046
(410)880-4354

ACKNOWLEDGEMENTS

Praise is due to the Creator of the heavens and the earth in all her manifestations, as well as to the ancestors who are closest to her. Without Spirit, none of this would be possible. I also extend remembrance and mourning to all those Afrikan spirits who made the transition from this life in the most damaging disruption of humanity the world has ever seen, The Maafa; those who became Nsamanfoɔ. Thanks to all Afrikans who have struggled and still struggle for liberation.

To all of my family, there is strength in the love that has always been there through the best and worst of times. To my wife, Elisa, I respect and love you. To my beautiful baby daughter, Nandi Kira, a large part of my role in this struggle is for victory in your life and the lives of all Afrikan children, as well as those yet unborn. This world will be changed, Nandi, so that you do not have to walk through the madness as so many before you have.

To all who have personally assisted in making my previous book, *The Maafa & Beyond*, sucessful, especially Lucenia Dunn; Monica Walker and St. Paul Community Baptist Church; The Eye of Heru Study Group; Eso Won Books; Malik's Book Palace; Jamal Goree, The Good Life and KJLH radio in LA; Blacknificent Books, Mawiyah and Kamau Kambon; Nkiru Books; The Know Bookstore; Kassahun Checole and Red Sea Press; Inside Out Consortium; Dino and Freedom Found Books; U.B. & U.S. Books; Cheryl Wilkerson; Brendon Books; Afrikan World Book Wholesalers, Everyone's Place and Nati; WOL radio; Upper Nile Books; Jewels of Aton; Pyramid Books in DC; Afrocentric Pride; African American Book Center; Yawa Books; North Star Bookstore; WLIB radio; and all who I have failed to mention, but appreciate greatly.

To all with whom I have established friendships and from whom I've drawn inspiration in continuing this work, especially Nkosi Ato Diop; Dennis Rogers; Kimani Stancil; Gerald Smith and the Kwame Nkrumah Study Group; Da Real; The Organization of All Afrikan Unity and all members; Dr. Conrad Worril; Makini Niliwaambieni and Ankobia; Mutope; Abdul Aquil; Dwayne Adell; Samba Buri Mbuub; Demba Sarr; Larry Bradshaw; J.R. Fenwick; Stanley Crump; Darrell Butler; Justin Fenwick; Kim and Frank Jacobs; The Parker Family; Pat

McIntyre; Jerome Williams; Pam Joyner; Myrtis Bedolla; Lou Andrews; Malia Salaam; Kwaku Kushindana; Heru Ahki Seb, Ani Sa Merit and Shango; Nana Korantemaa; Lynn Collins; Kwesi; Lucrezia Esser; Sidney Thomas; Gary Williams and all who I have not named, but deserve mention. Many may not know their impact on my development, but I thank you nonetheless.

I also acknowledge all who have stood against me, as they have helped strengthen my commitment, thoroughness and resolve.

Thanks to all of the scholars who have done the work from which I and others have drawn. Special thanks to Mama Marimba Ani for all of her assistance in putting this book together, as well as for the phenomenal work she has produced, namely *Let the Circle Be Unbroken* and *Yurugu*. I am grateful to the commited Dr. Anderson Thompson for his encouragement and willingness to write the foreword for this book. Also, sincere appreciation for the help of Kwasi Odaaku in my understanding the Twi language of the Akan.

Hotep!

TABLE OF CONTENTS

PART 1: REALITY

Part 2: Revolution!!!

Part 3: Return To The Way

Part 4: Remembrance, Reverence, Closing Thoughts

reclamation

my ancestors
taught me
geodesy, astronomy,
geometry and
architecture,
so i built
the Pyramids
to display
knowledge...
my ancestors
taught me
hospitality,
generosity
and kind-heartedness,
so i welcomed
my foreign brethren
to display
righteousness...
my ancestors
taught me
perseverance,
pain, suffering
and spirituality,
so i became
enslaved
to display
strength...
my ancestors
taught me
equilibrium,
harmony
and the duality of
opposites, so i defeated
my enemy
to display
reciprocity...
my ancestors
taught me
humanity,
communality, and the Way, so i took my place
and reclaimed
my throne.

Nkosi Ato Diop © 1995

" When we get ready to create revolution we must redefine the world and redefine words; there's no way around it."

Amos Wilson, The Falsification of Afrikan Consciousness

"Liberation is a question of consciousness."

Marimba Ani, Yurugu

"Until African Americans are able to effectively define what is normal for our communities, we remain as subjects to an alien authority... The definition of normality and abnormality is one of the most powerful indications of community power. So long as these definitions come from outside of the community, the community has no ability to grow nor can human beings within those communities realize their full potential."

Na'im Akbar, "Mental Disorder Among African Americans" in Black Psychology.

"...we must consciously and unconsciously reorder the definitions of the world into their rightful frames of reference in order to function at all times in the best interest of Afrikan people;"

Haki Madhubuti, From Plan To Planet

FOREWORD

These are not the best of times for African people, nor are they the worst.

Out of the quagmire of the European slave industry, colonialism, and neocolonialism, we may see the triumphant rise of a New African World for a new century, or conversely we may very well witness the final demise of the black world and its people, leaving the field to Europe and Asia. Dr. Bobby Wright warned us in *The Psychopathic Racial Personality* that there would come a time when the African world would have to face "our moment of truth." That moment has arrived.

Indeed, these are not ordinary times. The next century can be the new century of hope for the black world. In the last two decades a new generation has sallied forth, breaking the dreaded cycle of historical and generational discontinuity referred to by Dr. Clarke as the battle over the history books. Today we are locked in a stratospheric "Star Wars" between white and black Defenders of Western Civilization and the fast, ever growing armies of the Defenders of African Civilization. What is at stake? The whole of Africa, African resources and African people themselves are at risk.

Faced with this challenge, as the African world plunges into the uncertainties of the next century, the Defenders of African Civilization and the black world in general must heed the query of our wise elder, Dr. John Henrik Clarke: "Can African People Save Themselves?" He answers with great reservations in the affirmative (*Notes for An African World Revolution: Africa At The Crossroads*).

The potentiality for a New African World is real. More than thirty million Africans locked inside of the United States make up the wealthiest, best educated, most technically trained, and potentially powerful African nation on earth. Approximately two hundred million Africans living in North, South, and Central America represent a regional Pan-African Community of unlimited potentiality. Together these components represent a powerful force for a New Africa for the new century. Complementarily, we have a generation of young Africans on the Continent, in the Caribbean, in South and Central America, and in Europe that forms a powerful armada in this era marked by the highest tide of African consciousness in modern times. The spirit of Black Power, self-determination, economic self-sufficiency, African nationalism, Pan-Africanism, and the call for the United States of Africa is in the hearts and on the minds of this rising contemporary fleet of black youth.

In Ayi Kwei Armah's novel *The Beautiful Ones Are Not Yet Born*, the hero regrets the colossal failure of the leaders in his country and their selfish betrayal of the ideals of the revolution. He also finds himself entangled in the reckless scramble for money, power, and prestige. Succumbing to the temptations too, he laments that in his time, "the beautiful ones are not yet born." I am so thankful that the Creator permitted me, a child of the traumatic events of the 30's and an activist of the 60's, to witness the timely rise of "the beautiful ones" of this decade, the 90's.

That "the beautiful ones *have* been born" is evident in the recent writings and activities of young Erriel D. Roberson (Kofi Addae) of Kujichagulia Press, author of *The Maafa & Beyond*. He now has presented us with his latest work, *Reality Revolution: Return to The Way*, a rich cornucopia of ideas of why and how we must completely restructure our thought processes, redefine our reality, and act accordingly. Protected by the guiding light of his intellectual ancestors and elders, Brother Kofi, through specific use of Twi, KiSwahili and other African languages, clearly demonstrates the power potential for the development of a universal African language system for the black world. In doing so, Erriel has built upon the challenges and assertions of both his elders and youthful peers.

In *Black Africa: The Economic and Cultural Basis For A Federated State*, the late Cheikh Anta Diop spoke of a common African linguistic background:

> The African languages constitute one linguistic family, as homogenous as that of the Indo-European tongue. Nothing is easier than to set down the values that allow transfer from a Zulu language (Bantu) to one of those of West Africa (Serer-Wolof-Peul) or even to ancient Egypt.

This assertion by Diop provides a technical rationalization and realizable basis for the development of a universal African language system.

In the political realm, a number of Defenders of African Civilization have made assertions that directly and indirectly pertain to an African lingua franca. Ngugi wa Thiong'o in *Decolonizing the Mind: The Politics of Language in African Literature* counsels the African writer to "take up arms against the use of his oppressor's language in speech and writing." Ngugi further asserts that "the choice of language and the use to which language is put is central to a people's definition of themselves in relation to the entire universe." In *Toward The Decolonization of African Literature*, Chinweizu, Onwuchekwa Jemie, and Ihechukwu Madubuike lead a formal assault on the tyranny of European domination of African literature.

Erriel's young generation of intellectual-activists has arrived at this moment in history, precisely when the battle lines have been drawn in what Dr. Jacob Carruthers calls "Intellectual Warfare." He commands us to start governing ourselves, and he challenges us to reject completely the twisted, perverted, insane Western Way and to return to the African Way. All praises are due to one so young, who has humbly sat at the feet of his elders and ancestors and dug way down to drink from what Dr. Carruthers so eloquently calls "the deep well of African Thought."

Dr. Asa Hilliard in his very instructive manner asks us, "What time is it? Where in the world am I? Who in the hell am I?" Iron willed African warriors in the last great battle of this century are attempting to address these and other questions. The liberation of time, space, memory, and identity from a culturally perverted Western World is one of the essential questions raised and answered in Erriel Roberson's *Reality Revolution: Return to The Way*.

Anderson Thompson
Department of Inner City Studies
Northeastern Illinois University

Note: Where we refer to Afrikans and Afrikan people or Europeans and European people in this text, it should be understood that these are broad generalizations that cannot, of course, apply to every single European or Afrikan in the various contexts where these generalizations are used. However, these generalizations have some utility within the context of this book and assume no absolutes or all inclusive meaning. The predominate use of the *asili* concept, i.e. European *asili*, provides a more specific identification of what and who is being addressed in this discussion. This concept, which is very specific, is made more precise as we reference European or Afrikan fulfillers of the respective cultural *asili's*. This makes it clear that when we speak of pathological orientations and behaviors, for example, we are speaking of those parties guilty of thinking and acting in a pathological manner or fulfilling the European *asili*. This text does not presume to make sweeping generalizations about people based simply on skin color or "race."

In addition, though there is no glossary in this work, there are numerous Afrikan language concepts that might be new to readers, i.e. *asili*. Sufficient amounts of text are dedicated to explaining these concepts, as each one generally has a section dedicated to its explanation.

Hotep!

INTRODUCTION

> Remember this: against all that destruction some yet
> remained among us unforgetful of origins, dreaming secret dreams,
> seeing secret visions, hearing secret voices of our purpose.
>
> Ayi Kwei Armah, <u>Two Thousand Seasons</u>

The words of Ayi Kwei Armah are prophetic. It is true that amidst the destruction and distorted reality of the Afrikan* existence, there are those of us who have remained resilient. There are those of us who have reclaimed our origins despite The Maafa**. We have dared to dream, maintain vision and hear the voices of our purpose telling us that it is time to move forward as a people on the road to true liberation.

So that we are absolutely clear, true liberation is defined here as self-definition, self-knowledge, psychological health, self-determination and self-sufficiency on the levels of both the individual and the collective. True liberation is a return to The Way. The Way is the return to origins that Ayi Kwei Armah wrote so cloquently about. It is a return to our ancestral sources and the reciprocity, balance, harmony, order, justice, compassion and truth that once governed the Afrikan existence.

> The way is not the rule of men. The way is never women
> ruling men. The way is reciprocity... The way is creation knowing
> its purpose, wise in withholding itself from snares, from
> destroyers.[1]

Our future as a people is true liberation, a return to The Way.

LANGUAGE

As we move, there are many challenges to face. Our struggle is one that of necessity must be carried out on many levels. Our psychological and spiritual health should be a matter of concern, as should be our forthright analysis of the world reality in which we live. Many of these levels of struggle will be discussed in this work. First, however, we might note the use of language in this discussion. Terms from the Twi language of the Akan are being used to describe the three general levels of struggle to be addressed later. This use of language is done with the express understanding that the concepts we use as a people moving toward liberation, and the language we use to understand them, play a major role in how we perceive of and define reality.

A "reality revolution" means we are speaking about completely restructuring our thought processes and redefining reality. We are redefining our terms and introducing new concepts for liberation and life purposes. This will be further developed as we move through this book. Our use of the Twi terms plays an extremely important role as a component in this reality revolution. In one sense, as mentioned in my previous work entitled *The Maafa & Beyond*, "What we say is the articulation of thought. What we say, or the language we use, is the bringing of thought into the realm of reality." [2] Therefore, using Afrikan language helps our thought processes to be closer to The Afrikan Way. It has also been stated as a sociological construct that,

> For people throughout the world, cultural heritage is rooted in language. Thus language is the most important means of **cultural transmission**, *the process by which one generation passes culture to the next.* Just as our bodies contain the genes of our ancestors, so our everyday lives are grounded in the symbolic system of those who came before us. Through the unique power of language, we gain access to centuries of accumulated wisdom. [3]

With this powerful construct in mind, we can then make the logical connection that if we are to return to The Way, our Afrikan source, our proper use of language in general is crucial. Additionally, our specific use of Afrikan languages to formulate new concepts also plays an important role in our return to The Way and gaining access to the Afrikan "centuries of accumulated wisdom." It activates the collective unconscious that connects us in Sacred Time to the ancestors, the living and the yet unborn. These centuries of accumulated wisdom are what we need as a foundation for our return to The Way. Our language tends to serve as a means of transmitting this wisdom and the cultural values of a people.

In this century there has been one--perhaps only one-- upsurge of popular interest in how language affects our lives. It began with the publication of Alfred Korzybski's *Science and Sanity* (1933)--or rather, with the popularizations of his work that appeared a few years later. Korzybski was a Polish-born scientist and philosopher whose interest in the continuity of culture led him to a study of the means of culture-transmission in modern society, which of course is language first of all. His laboratory was the failures of transmission, which he investigated in psychiatric patients. He was a pathologist of language; he probed the sane and insane ways of speaking and understanding, the social ills that result from certain forms of linguistic insanity, by no means confined to psychiatric wards. [4]

So we find that we are at a very important time in the history of Afrikan people, and of the world in fact. We have begun revolution- ary analyses of language and liberation that history sees infrequently. The conceptual nature of this revolution of reality calls into question the accepted norms and values of the present world reality, first and foremost by the use of language.

Just as Korzybski started a movement amongst European linguists that actually touched many disciplines outside of linguistics, Dr. Marimba Ani has done an even greater service to Afrikan liberation with the release of her book, *Yurugu: An African-Centered Critique of European Cultural Thought and Behavior.* Our sister is at the forefront of a movement that has galvanized Afrikan women and men. Her tools are redefinition and reconceptualization, which are first apparent in her use of language. The concept of Yurugu, and various other concepts she has developed which we will utilize, have been used by Ani to take our struggle out of the ideological domain of European culture.

Dr. Marimba Ani has crystallized the importance of ideological and cultural self-determination for many Afrikan people. Through her work, many have implicitly recognized that language is both a manifestation of an individual's thought and an influencer of thought. The language we use to frame our concepts influences the functioning of those concepts and their ideological thrust. We know that "...every language has a structure that must somehow influence the way its speakers view the world." [5] This is a realization articulated well in the following quote from Kwame Gyekye's book, *An Essay on African Philosophical Thought: The Akan Conceptual Scheme.*

> A number of philosophers have come to the realization that language, as a vehicle of concepts, not only embodies a philosophical point of view, but also influences philosophical thought. This observation implies that the lines of thought of a thinker are, at least to some extent, determined by the structure and other characteristics of his or her language, such as the grammatical categories and vocabulary. [6]

To take the impact of language on thought further, it can be suggested that European languages, especially English, influence or reflect European thought and behavior in very specific ways. In the next chapter as we look at various concepts utilized by Dr. Marimba Ani in *Yurugu*, one concept we will explore is "dichotomous logic." As this relates to language, we find the linguist S.I. Hayakawa explaining that,

> Korzybski argues that Indo-European language structure, with its strong sense of "is" and "is not," contributed much to our tendency toward the two-valued orientation. Benjamin Lee Whorf also argues for the recognition of the influence of language upon thought; if you spoke Hopi or Thai you would have difficulty having the same thoughts you have in English! [7]

Hayakawa goes further, regarding language and its relation to dichotomous logic, to share a quote by Stuart Chase, author of *Power of Words*.

> Linguists have also emphasized that Chinese is a "multi-valued" language, not primarily two-valued like English and Western languages generally. We say that things must be "good" or "bad," "right" or "wrong," "clean" or "dirty," "black" or "white"— ignoring shades of gray. When an economist talks about a middle road between "socialism" and "capitalism," both camps vie in their ferocity to tear him apart. (I have been that unhappy economist.)
> Speakers of Chinese set up no such grim dichotomies; they see most situations in shades of gray, and have no difficulty in grasping the significance of a variety of middle roads. As a result, Chinese thought has been traditionally tolerant, not given to the fanatical ideologies of the West... [8]

Dichotomous logic is directly related to the "fanatical ideologies of the West" and what is called here a "two-valued" language,
English. In the next chapter Ani's dichotomous logic concept will allow
us to see the manifestations of this logic in the European historical
reality. For now, it is sufficient to point out the role of language even in
this behavioral aspect of European culture.

Additionally, as we investigate language from the perspective
of linguistics and language theory, we find that language does indeed
impact all areas of life and language theory impacts many areas of
scholarship and intellectual investigation.

> Concepts in the theory of language are among the basic
> tools of thought in all intellectual inquiry. Part of the uniqueness
> of linguistic theory, then, is that no other field is likely to have so
> great an impact on so many other fields when new thought arises
> in it. [9]

Just as Korzybski surfaces as a point of departure regarding
language within the context of general semantics, in linguistics names
like Chomsky, Sapir, Whorf and Wittgenstein present themselves
frequently. For example, the Sapir-Whorf hypothesis surfaces in such
crucial fields of study as sociology and psychology. This linguistic
theory relates directly to our discussion as we find that in discussions
referring to the relationship between language and thought,

> Almost invariably we soon reach a viewpoint that is
> referred to as the "Whorf hypothesis" or the "Sapir-Whorf hypoth-
> esis," at which point a well known passage from Sapir's writings
> (rather than Whorf's) is often cited: "the fact of the matter is that
> the 'real world' is to a large extent unconsciously built up on the
> language habits of the group. No two languages are sufficiently
> similar to be considered as representative of the same social

reality. The worlds in which different societies live
are distinct worlds, not merely the same world with different labels
attached." [10]

All of this information regarding the work of European linguists is being shared as background to what this book submits and to
what Afrikan scholars have been saying for a long time. For example,
Dr. Marimba Ani's works, *Let The Circle Be Unbroken* and *Yurugu*,
are Afrikan linguistic theory in action. We shall witness this through
the course of this book as we deal with her Afrikan language concepts.
Amos Wilson focused on any number of areas, including the power of
language; his concepts heavily influence this book and are used in it.
Haki Madhubuti has spoken about language being a code that one can
use or be used by. Molefi Asante was very clear on the role of language
as he wrote about it in *Afrocentricity*, he dealt with "Language Liberation" in a chapter titled "Constituents of Power." Asante spoke about
redefinition and "systematic nationalism" requiring that we essentially
create language that is our own. Frantz Fanon dealt with the language
of colonizers and its impact on the colonized, from a cultural imposition and immersion point of view. Perhaps the major difference
between European language theory and linguistics and that of Afrikans,
is that Europeans have institutionalized and standardized these areas
to function in the best interests of Europeans. Europeans have
developed these areas as disciplines unto themselves, with various
schools of thought. We may need to look forward, in the near future,
to the development of Afrikan Language Theory and Linguistics, which
function in the best interests of Afrikan people. As will be seen through
the course of this book, this type of effort is a given when we speak of
a reality revolution and Afrikan scholarship is more than sufficient for
this task.

Many of these insights are profound ways of viewing language,
but despite their seemingly abstract nature, they are very powerful. This

is what lies behind the use of the term Maafa in *The Maafa & Beyond* and it is a linguistic restructuring expertly utilized by Dr. Ani as we have mentioned.

The attempt will be made in this book to relate ideas of naming and defining reality in the clearest, most easily understandable means possible. Hopefully we will be able to establish the practical and functional importance of language as it relates to naming and defining reality. It does play a significant role in the everyday lives of all people.

Again, I emphasize that we should not be mistaken and believe that no one has ever considered language in this light of Afrikan reality before. To the contrary, there have been many who have dealt with this aspect of liberation. James Baldwin wrote an article entitled "On Language, Race and the Black Writer," and stated that,

> For a Black writer in this country to be born into the English language is to realize that *the assumptions upon which the language operates are his enemy* {italics mine}... I was forced to reconsider similes: as black as sin, as black as night, blackhearted.[11]

This is clearly an articulation of the effect language can have in the lives of everyday people. Many Afrikan writers and scholars have pondered language, it is simply now that we have arrived at a time when we can act on it decisively and systematically, and are in fact doing so. Along the lines of Baldwin's comments it is important to highlight again the impact of language on the attitudes of unsuspecting citizens, especially the children. This is not limited to Afrikan people, but contributes significantly to European pathology as well.

> The language that white children heard taught them to despise their former slaves as surely as parades and band music taught them to respect the flag. The attitudes were implicit in the symbols. It was enough for the words and phrases to BE THERE.[12]

Additionally and more specific to life in general, we find that

> To understand how language works, what pitfalls it
> conceals, what its possibilities are, is to understand what is central
> to the complicated business of living the life of a human being. To
> be concerned with the relation between language and reality,
> between words and what they stand for in the speaker's or hearer's
> thoughts and emotions, is to approach the study of language as
> both an intellectual and a moral discipline. [13]

All of this should serve to impress upon us the importance of what is taking place in our day and time. This movement we are embarking upon that stands on the shoulders of previous movements, but is then grasped by the ancestors and set into flight from those shoulders, is profound. Language is being stressed because it is a starting point that highlights the impact of our movement in other areas and is in fact the vehicle for our movement in other areas.

Our movement has become a reality revolution. We are endeavoring to change the very nature of existence. Our footing must be sure and systematic because it will be challenged by the intricate apparatus of Amcrican propaganda and miseducation which serves to perpetuate the present oppressed status of Afrikans and marginalize efforts to change it. So that we clearly understand our mission and its tactics, we are being somewhat meticulous about our conceptions in this book.

To this end, we would be remiss in leaving the topic of language without quickly illustrating a few more essential points that make our need for a reality revolution clear. Because Alfred Korzybski seems to have been a major catalyst and point of departure for this century's European exploration into general semantics, we would fall short if we failed to address his work directly; not simply because it has insight to offer, but also because it shows us the serious degree to which Europeans have studied and put forth great effort to maintain their position in the world. Consequently, we must be more vigilant and persistent in putting an end to the madness and rising above it.

In the area of language and semantics, Alfred Korzybski is a reknowned European scholar as we have seen. In his work *Science and Sanity* he makes a profound statement regarding language which relates directly to a position that is held in this book. He speaks in the 1930's of the insanity of the present world reality, even though his European nationalism is still strong and he is not advocating what we are speaking of in this work.

> The system by which the white race lives, suffers, 'pros-
> pers,' starves, and dies today is not in a strict sense an Aristotelian
> system. Aristotle had far too much of the sense of actualities for
> that. It represents, however, a system formulated by those who, for
> nearly two thousand years since Aristotle, have controlled our
> knowledge and methods of orientations, and who, for purposes of
> their own, selected what today appears as the worst from Aristotle
> and the worst from Plato and, with their own additions, imposed
> this composite system upon us. In this they were greatly aided by
> the *structure of language* {italics mine} and psycho-logical habits,
> which from the primitive down to this day have affected us all
> consciously or unconsciously, and have introduced serious difficult-
> ies in science and mathematics. [14]

These words from Korzybski not only give us an indictment of the conceptual systems of a world dominated by Europeans (which we will carry further in this work), but also a glimpse into the value and impact he has assigned to language. And, although we will not completely analyze Korzybski, we must realize that his references to "non-Aristotelian orientations" and his criticism of the current world reality are not signs that he has escaped the conceptual framework of Europe. Within the context of his work, this is understood.

Through analogy Korzybski goes into the ways in which language can be a perpetuator of sanity or insanity. It can be therapeutic or damaging. In a particular pair of analogies, Korzybski articulates this belief.

The first analogy deals with machinery and the harmful, technology stagnating effects of "emery sand" in the lubricant of the machinery. In other words, dirty lubricant causes problems. Sand causes the friction that the lubricant is supposed to prevent. To connect this to the European cultural reality, sanity and the function of language, Korzybski goes on to say,

> Technically we are advanced, but the elementalistic
> premises underlying our human relations, practically since
> Aristotle, have not changed at all. The present investigation reveals
> that in the functioning of our nervous systems a special harmful
> factor is involved, a 'lubricant with emery' so to speak, which
> retards the development of sane human relations and prevents
> general sanity. It turns out that in the structure of languages,
> methods, 'habits of thought,' orientations, etc., we preserve
> delusional, psychopathological factors. These are in no way
> inevitable as will be shown, but can be easily eliminated by special
> training, therapeutic in effect, and consequently of educational
> preventative value. This 'emery' in the nervous system I call
> identification. It involves deeply rooted 'principles' which are
> invariably false to facts and so our orientations based on them
> cannot lead to adjustment and sanity.
>
> A medical analogy here suggests itself. We find a peculiar
> parallel between identification and infectious diseases. History
> proves that under primitive conditions infectious diseases cannot

be controlled. They spread rapidly, sometimes killing off more than half of the affected population. The infectious agent may be transmitted either directly, or through rats, insects, etc. With the advance of science, we are able to control the disease, and various important preventative methods, such as sanitation, vaccination, etc., are at our disposal.

Identification appears also as something 'infectious,' for it is transmitted directly or indirectly from parents and teachers to the child by the mechanism and structure of language, by established and inherited 'habits of thought,' by rules for life-orientation, etc. [15]

What Korzybski calls "identification" is similar to what we will refer to by Dr. Ani's term *asili* (explained in chapter 1). This is an important quote to remember for reference in later discussions in this book. Korzybski has not only recognized the pivotal role of language, but he has also identified the pathology of European culture, though his remedy might be different from ours.

As we embark on our reality revolution, we have established these linguistic foundations. And, we understand that,

> In other words, assumptions about the nature of reality and patterns of thinking are embedded in every language, and they do not necessarily correspond to equivalent assumptions and patterns of thinking embedded in other languages. [16]

Finally, before sharing the levels of struggle that will be addressed in this book, our late brother and former Professor of Psychology, Amos Wilson, shared with us that,

> Oppressors produce a consciousness in the oppressed not only by manipulating their ecological and sociological lifestyles and possibilities but also by naming the world in which both they and the oppressed exist. To name, to label, is to bring into con-

sciousness and therefore to transform consciousness. [17]

Perhaps this means that we shall have to change a common saying. Most people are familiar with "sticks and stones may break my bones but words will never hurt me." Knowing what we do about language, this shall have to be changed to *sticks and stones may break my bones but words transform consciousness.* How we refer to things, events, concepts, historical processes and people has never been inconsequential. Our naming and defining of reality is not only profoundly important, but will take concentration, dedication and intensive study.

LEVELS OF STRUGGLE

Of the many levels of struggle for Afrikan people moving toward liberation, there are three broad categories that this book will deal with. These general levels of struggle include a variety of areas in which Afrikan people must be concerned with the future, acting more or less as a framework for this book. They are as follows(note the Twi character, "ɔ," does not exist in the English alphabet. Its sound is like "ore.") :

1} *Nkoso ɔ* (Twi term meaning **"progress going on"** with the English conceptual equivalent of **movement or short-term action**): This level of struggle encompasses the practical, concrete, tangible activities of individuals within the collective of the Afrikan Global Community, as well as the unified activities of the collective.

2} *Daakye Abra B ɔ* (Twi term meaning **"life that includes struggle, the future"** or **"how you make up your life, plans,"** with the English conceptual equivalent of **long-term planning**): This level of struggle is one in which Afrikan people must be planning for 10, 15, 25 and many more years into the future. (Note: In the Twi language "ky" sounds like "ch" in English.)

3} *Nyansa Nnsa Da* (Twi term meaning **"wisdom has no end"** or **"wisdom is never exhausted,"** with the English conceptual equivalent of **naming and defining reality or thought without boundaries**): This is an important area which requires a larger vision and the ability to conceive of the future of Afrikan people on an entirely new level, on a grand scale.

While *Reality Revolution* will deal with all of these levels of struggle, *nyansa nnsa da* will be the major focus as we deal with many aspects of our struggle which require *nyansa nnsa da* and can be considered themselves to be the engagement of *nyansa nnsa da*. *Nyansa nnsa da* involves thinking on a grand scale which encompasses developing our own terms through which to define who we are, what we are, and how we, our concepts and definitions of reality are to be recognized. It involves Afrikan people establishing our own values, standards and norms. We must determine what behaviors, actions and ideologies are normal, desired and sane. In this sense, we will find that this book itself is *nyansa nnsa da*, in practice, as will become evident through the course of these pages.

We are at the genesis of a complete and systematic reworking of all the life-giving and life-sustaining institutions and concepts that guide individuals through life. We will write our own textbooks, develop our own understanding of life's purpose, determine how we will be defined, and develop institutions to support our definitions and direction.

Another very necessary and important conceptual area to be covered in this work deals with Afrikan people defining the nature of the current American society and the world. We must come to the very difficult and, for some, hard to swallow realization that we currently exist in a society that by deed or action, as well as ideology and philosophy, is abnormal and insane. By extension, since Europeans have subjugated, through physical, cultural and ideological means, the majority of the world's people, the world at large also exists in a state of abnormality and insanity. Amos Wilson said that "The most insane people on earth today are used as models for sanity." [18] He went further to suggest that,

> The possibility that what we call *normal* is itself *insane* is not questioned; that the organization of this society, the nature of its human relations, the structure of its economic systems, the values that motivate it, are the result of the madness of a people. [19]

The substance of these assertions will be thoroughly examined, not simply rhetorically stated in this book. Marimba Ani's concept of *asili* will be explained and utilized, in conjunction with her *utamawazo* concept, in order to identify and explore the pathology of the current European-dominated world reality. This will be done in the same fashion as in Ani's Yurugu, only in a brief emulation of her analysis technique. From this realization of the pathology we must look reality square in the face. If we are to move toward true liberation as Afrikan people, a component of which is psychological health, we **CANNOT** succeed operating within the framework of abnormality and insanity. In doing so we have failed before we've begun. We have attempted to become normal by imitating what positions itself as normal, but is abnormal. We have attempted to become sane and separate ourselves from insanity using the terms, concepts, epistemological frameworks and definitions of the insane, the European world reality.

To become truly liberated, we must exercise *nyansa nnsa da*, or thought without boundaries, to name and define our own reality of normality and sanity within which to operate. This is the only means of achieving our ultimate goal of upliftment; by sane and normal terms, concepts, values, norms, epistemology, definitions and desired behaviors which support our movement toward self-knowledge, self-definition, psychological health, self-determination and self-sufficiency.

In short, we must be able to conceive of and create an entire new reality, which our concept of *nyansa nnsa da* allows us to do. It allows us to see reality, not as a static and stagnant entity, but as a dynamic process; a process that can and has been shaped, molded, changed and systematically defined. Afrikan people engaging in the systematic redefinition of reality is a monumental undertaking that will require the best that Afrikan minds have to offer. We can re-create the world, or at the very least the parts of the world in which we must function. It will not be easy work nor entertainment. The proper mind-state will be required   because creating a new reality and returning to The Way is not a vacation, it is struggle and study.

There are many sisters and brothers who are already working and moving in this direction. Therefore, the time that we are currently living in is of paramount importance and, as we employ *nyansa nnsa da,* this time in history is comparable, only in significance and impact, to the Greek genesis of Western civilization; that time when individuals like Plato, Aristotle and Socrates were laying the epistemological foundations and articulating the vision that has led to contemporary Western civilization, albeit with the theft and misunderstanding of Afrikan philosophical concepts. Perhaps a more appropriate and positive comparison is to the thousands of years of intellectual and spiritual splendor of ancient Kemet (Egypt); we are quite possibly approaching that splendor again within the context of modernity as we return to The Way. *It is the obligation of all Afrikan people to participate on some level,* so as you read find your place or create one. It is clearly time to move.

The information that is provided in this book will by its very nature be considered controversial and disturbing to many. Still others will attempt to suppress and dismiss this work as invalid. This is expected since we are questioning and criticizing the very fabric and conceptual foundations of contemporary society on the most basic and yet the deepest levels, while beginning to illuminate a new standard. These foundations we are criticizing support not only Europeans, but so many Afrikans who only know the reality created for them by European people. This is a reality founded in conquest, enslavement, colonialism and other ills. This is a reality I propose we reject, a foundation we intend to destroy; the foundation upon which many European and Afrikan feet are standing.

With this in mind, it is anticipated that there are many, even amongst the Afrikan community, who will have an unsettled, negative, critical reaction to the tenants of this book. Despite this anticipated reaction, this work must be done. It is truth, it is justice, it is a beginning of our return.

This book is only preparation for the coming reawakening. It is to participate in outlining the foundations for a return to The Way and to prepare the minds of Afrikan people to make the journey. It is a preview of what is already coming. It is up to you to be a part of what will happen or to be left to destruction. I prefer creation to destruction. I hope we all do.

---

* Throughout this text we will be using the word Afrika spelled with the "K."

> The K symbolizes to us a kind of Lingua Afrikana, coming into use along with such words and phrases as Habari Gani, Osagyfo, Uhuru, Asante, together constituting one political language, although coming from more than one Afrikan language.[20]

In addition, although we are using the term Afrika in this text, we recognize the term "Alkebu-lan" as another way to refer to our mother continent. Yosef ben-Jochannan shares that "'Alkebu-lan' is the oldest, and the only one of indigenous origin. It was used by the Moors, Nubians, Numidians,

Khart-Haddans [Carthagenians], and Ethiopians." [21]

** The term "Maafa" will be used throughout this text. The explanation for
this can be found in a quote from my previous book, *The Maafa & Beyond*.

> The precise use of words is powerful and critical. The very term,
> "Afrikan Slave Trade," is inadequate for the remembrance and
> memorialization of our great tragedy. Slavery is a generic term that
> describes a condition of bondage that has existed in various forms
> throughout recorded history. As a generic term, it is not an adequate
> descriptor for our great tragedy, which was different and more devastating
> than any form of slavery in the history of the world. Trade is an equally
> generic term which implies business or bartering and the selling of
> commodities. It is blasphemous to regard human suffering and death as
> selling commodities or doing business. Perhaps this was the degrading
> attitude of slavers, and even some of those who write on the subject today,
> but we must REFUSE to cast it in such a callous and disrespectful light.
> This use of words insures that the impact of the so called "Afrikan Slave
> Trade" will be viewed more in terms of commerce and just another event
> in the age old tradition of bondage, rather than the horrific and uniquely
> significant event that it was. It would be akin to calling the Jewish
> Holocaust something as crass and inappropriate as "The Great European
> Cleansing Project." This book will, from this point, cease to refer to the
> "African Slave Trade" except where it is necessary for citing sources or
> clarifying quoted text. Instead, the term coined by Marimba Ani in her
> book *Yurugu* will be used. Ani, who thoroughly understands the use of
> language, used the Swahili term, "Maafa." Maafa is defined as a disaster,
> calamity, damage, injustice, misfortune, catastrophe, etc. Ani referred to it
> as "The Maafa, the great suffering of our people at the hands of Europe-
> ans in the Western Hemisphere." [22]

The original conceptualization of The Maafa can be found
in Dr. Marimba Ani's book, *Let The Circle Be Unbroken*. One should add to
this all that has been said about the power of language thus far.

PART 1

REALITY

Chapter 1

ooooooooo

The Nature of the Problem: Revolution Against What?

In order to properly grasp the significance of a reality revolution and a return to The Way, it is necessary to take a cursory glance at contemporary Western society and the history of Western civilization. If we do this from a sane, Afrikan, culturally and spiritually grounded perspective, we establish the foundation of our assertion that this present standard-bearer of a society and worldview is flawed and abnormal. It is what Dr. Marimba Ani describes symbolically as "Yurugu."

Yurugu is a figure from Dogon mythology characterized by incompleteness and "When Yurugu, 'the pale fox,' reaches his final form of development, he is 'the permanent element of disorder in the universe,' 'the agent of disorganization.'" [1] This is a view of pathological orientations in European cultural and ideological foundations that Ani thoroughly examines in *Yurugu: An African-Centered Critique of European Cultural Thought and Behavior.* We shall see that this is a fair characterization of the conceptual systems of Western civilization. However, Western society, and by connection the European collective, have named and defined reality. They have exercised the power to label and name the world in which we live, and consequently have positioned themselves and their conceptual systems as the standard by which all else is measured, despite the flawed nature of their conceptual systems.

The logical place to begin examining the current flawed and

abnormal world reality is with its *asili*. *Asili* is a concept developed by Marimba Ani that might be called "the ideological matrix of the culture." [2] Although this is a concept that cannot be easily explained, we should view it as the conceptual system of this European-dominated world, understanding that,

> *Asili* allows us to recognize culture as a basic organizing mechanism that forges a group of people into an 'interest group,' an ideological unit. This is the case even when the descendants of an original culture and civilization have become dispersed in other areas of the world; as long as they are connected through a common *asili*, they constitute a diaspora, manifesting the continued life of the civilization. *Asili* allows us to distinguish the peripheral, the anomalous, and the idiosyncratic, and at the same time *asili* allows us to interpret patterns of collective thought and behavior (in terms, of the cultural *asili*). *Asili* is both a concept and a cultural reality. If we assume it (the concept), then it helps to explain a culture in terms of the dominant and fundamental principle of its development (its reality). [3]

Not only will we use this tool developed by Ani, but we will also replicate on a small level the extensive work Ani has done in analyzing European cultural thought and behavior. The substance of this chapter and its goal in establishing the pathological character of European conceptual systems has already been done in *Yurugu* to a far greater degree than we could hope to achieve in one chapter. What I have done is taken Ani's framework of analysis in *Yurugu* and substituted some different examples to illustrate the same points. And, of course, while the analysis being done in this chapter is necessary for the continuity of the ideas we hope to cover in this book, it is recommended that the reader see *Yurugu* for a more complete understanding.

So, using this concept of *asili* as a starting point in establishing our basis for reality revolution, we are able to do two things. [1] We are able, as an Afrikan Global Community, to hold people accountable for their role in the destructive impositions of the present reality and [2] we can go back in history and look at how principles established in antiquity relate directly to the abnormal, insane and flawed reality that presently dominates the world. We can do both of these things precisely because the *asili* represents the germinating principles of the culture; those underlying aspects which guide and determine patterns of collective behavior and thought. The *asili* operates on a level that transcends the expressed beliefs of the individual. This is an extremely important point to remember.

Accountability

To first deal with the issue of accountability, the European *asili* or the ideological matrix of European culture, provides the framework for addressing and answering a paradox that W.E.B. DuBois articulated and many still have problems formulating an answer to. DuBois expressed the still prevalent frustration and confusion that comes when it appears that "A group, a nation, or a race commits murder and rape, steals and destroys, yet no individual is guilty, no one is to blame, no one can be punished!" [4]

Typically, the answer to this paradox has been expressed by those who maintain that contemporary Europeans benefit from "institutionalized racism" and the perpetuation of those institutions established during The Maafa. However, using the concept of *asili*, we find that the accountability of contemporary society runs much deeper than the perpetuation and benefit from institutionalized racism. The guilt of contemporary society is more than the continued legacy of The Maafa. The European *asili*, which we will examine, is to be held accountable for the perpetuation of a reality and conceptual systems that make such things as The Maafa and institutionalized racism, the continued legacy of The Maafa, possible. Individual and collective accountability can be directly related to an individual or collective adherence to the European *asili.* It is adherence to the flawed ideas and concepts of a society responsible for the enslavement of Afrikans and a long list of other pathological ills, which determines accountability.

Incidentally, for the sake of analyzing the destructiveness of European culture, it is preferred that we avoid the confusion of simply analyzing the merits of individuals for our application of accountability, so that we might clearly hold accountable the destructive thought and behavior guided by the *asili.* However, for those who choose to look at individual Europeans and their personalities, friendships, etc., the *asili* is still a way to assess accountability.

Because of Ani's concept we are able again to look at individual adherence to the *asili,* though not a desired point of departure for analysis. Even when we look at individual Europeans with our current imbalance between compassion and reciprocity; i.e., too much compassion, forgiveness and complicity with European pathology and a failure to exact a sufficient proportion of reciprocity for the criminal/pathological orientations of Europeans within European culture, we can place these individuals in the context of adherence to the *asili.* In other words, is a particular European individual an active participant in the perpetuation of the European conceptual framework and worldview, or is this person open to seeing the flaws in the ways of their culture; and in seeing these flaws are they as persistent about ending the destructive aggression of European culture as are those of us Afrikans who are fighting for liberation? Rather than letting our emotions and acquaintances with European individuals cloud our holding the culture and its constituents accountable, do we see the subtle aspects of how individuals, sometimes unknowingly and often knowingly, participate in and perpetuate the destruction of the European *asili* by adhering to its conceptions of normality, sanity, desired behaviors, etc.?

Now, to minimize confusion it is much preferred that we avoid the mind-trap that intentionally leads us to the false belief that we cannot lump individual Europeans into a collective accountability. We accomplish this by our analysis of the culture's behaviors and thoughts on the conceptual grounds of the *asili*. In this type of analysis we clearly see the historical record of European destructiveness. The historical record and a critique of European thought and behavior speak for themselves. We need not waste time confusing the issue by looking *solely* at individual relations to inform our analysis.

Individuals have always expressed their abhorrence of enslavement, brutality and destruction, yet these things continue to happen. This will always be the case unless we go deeper and look at the *asili* as a tool of accountability, which can then be applied secondarily to an understanding that individuals make up a culture and can be held accountable. Collectives or cultures are not abstract entities that have no individuals to comprise them and carry out their will. We must understand the interrelationship of the individuals who make up the collective, to the *idea* of the collective or culture. This interrelationship is most clearly seen through the overall driving force which is the *asili*.

This perspective allows less room for contemporary attempts, by the dominant European world reality, to escape accountability for crimes committed; this being the paradox DuBois wrote about. Every European today can claim, however a feeble defense it may be, that they have "never owned slaves," in their attempt to dismiss Afrikan people seeking reparations, reciprocity or simply an acknowledgment of the continued legacy of The Maafa. However, every European cannot say they haven't adhered to the epistemology, norms and conceptual framework, the *asili*, of the present European world reality. So, in fact we *can* answer the paradox and someone can be punished. Yurugu can be punished and that is the reason for reality revolution; an all out assault on Yurugu. Some may ask why attack the European world reality and how? We answer the first question of why by saying that it is precisely because this reality dominates the world and is a manifestation of a destructive *asili*. If we choose not to attack the people, we must at least attack the ideas and concepts that guide their actions and behaviors. The actions and behaviors of Europeans cannot be denied. So, the "how" of this attack is what this chapter will focus on. (We should note as an aside that this concept also allows us to understand and hold accountable those Afrikan people who have become fulfillers of the European *asili*. Dealing with them from this perspective offers more substance than "sellout" or "uncle tom.")

This assault or reality revolution requires us to understand the nature of Yurugu, something that can best be accomplished by intensively studying (the only way to approach Marimba Ani's work) the book *Yurugu*. However, in taking a cursory glance at the European *asili*, we can follow Ani's example by looking at those who expressed, fulfilled and articulated the *asili*; this includes people like Plato, Aristotle, Socrates, Darwin, etc.

UTAMAWAZO AND ACCOUNTABILITY

Within the context of the *asili*, its expression in culturally structured thought is called the *utamawazo* by Dr. Ani. The concept of *utamawazo* allows us to look at the specifics of the culture's ideological thrust, an area in which accountability can be exercised. Dr. Ani shares that,

> *Utamawazo* is like 'world-view' in that it stresses the significance of metaphysical assumptions and presuppositions about

the nature of reality, and the way in which the culture presents its members with definitions and conceptions with which to order experience. *Utamawazo*, however, places more emphasis on conscious mental operations and refers to the way in which both speculative and nonspeculative thought is structured by ideology and bio-cultural experience. *Utamawazo* allows us to demonstrate the ideological consistency of the premises of the culture and to identify those premises as they tend to be standardized expressions of a single cultural entity. [5]

Specifically as it relates to Plato and the others we will examine, "the character of the *utamawazo* is expressed most obviously in literature, philosophy, academic discourse, and pedagogy..."[6] Thus, in looking at Plato, Aristotle, Socrates, Darwin, etc., we see that these types of individuals and their philosophies have had an admittedly overwhelming impact on the development of Western civilization. They have been fulfillers of the *asili*. This is attested to in such writings as the following:

> In the golden days of Greek civilization, four hundred years before the birth of Christ, the philosopher Plato wrote DIALOGUES which, to this day, comprise the most influential body of philosophy of the Western world. [7]

Rather than an exhaustive study here, it will be sufficiently informative to share examples of ideological foundations as expressed in the works of some of the individuals mentioned above and put them within the context of *asili*. Again, as we look at these examples, we should keep in mind that the *asili* transcends the stated beliefs of individuals. It operates on a subconscious level in many instances and most often is a part of the "rhetorical ethic" Ani describes, where a group of people practice "Hypocrisy as a Way of Life." It allows

Europeans to name a ship, carrying enslaved Afrikans during The Maafa, *The Jesus.* It allows a society to sing the star spangled banner and glorify the constitution of the United States, while contradicting these expressed beliefs in blatant ways, including the enslavement of Afrikans and the annihilation of Native Americans. These are overt and simple manifestations of the ethic, but the rhetorical ethic is much more complex.

In a work by Gunner Myrdal, a Swedish scholar brought into the United States to study the American "Negro problem" in the 1940's, it is stated regarding the "American Creed" that "While the Creed is important and is enacted into law, it is not lived up to in practice. To understand this we shall have to examine American attitudes toward law." [8] Regarding law, Myrdal says that "Another cultural trait of Americans is a relatively low degree of respect for law and order." [9] This is a description of the rhetorical ethic. It is expressed in this analysis of the culture. As far as explaining this contradiction Myrdal related that,

> The *popular* explanation of the disparity in America between ideals and actual behavior is that Americans do not have the slightest intention of living up to these ideals which they talk about and put into their Constitution and laws. Many Americans are accustomed to talk loosely and disparagingly about adherence to the American Creed as 'lip service' and even 'hypocrisy.' Foreigners are even more prone to make such a characterization.[10]

Although Myrdal may not agree with this "popular" explanation, the weight of evidence is strong for it, just as it is strong for hypocrisy being accepted as the norm. It is also a possibility, or rather a LIKELIHOOD, that there is some deep-seeded psychopathology accounting for the "schizophrenia."

With the rhetorical ethic, expressed ideals are actually

abstractions that do not function in the overall human interactions of the culture. Consequently, this reference to the rhetorical ethic is being shared so that we realize that although Europeans may say or state an ideal such as brotherly love or world peace, this does not sway our accurate assessment of the *asili* as we are about to briefly view it.

THE EUROPEAN *ASILI*

It is helpful to travel far back in time to begin drawing on examples from those who help form the articulated foundations and culturally structured thought (*utamawazo*) of the European *asili*. This approach is confirmed to be valid by European scholars constantly, one of whom says, "As heirs of the Judeo-Christian and Greco-Roman traditions, we have a common core of principles and values..." [11]

We can first take a look at Plato's *Symposium* and a part of it which, after dealing with the mythical nature and origins of man and the deity Love, a masculine deity interestingly, is describing the male product of this divine origin. This starts us on the road to looking at some of the ideological underpinnings that are affecting the present abnormal and dysfunctional reality. Specifically, we can begin to understand the imbalance that exists currently between masculine and feminine principles, as well as disparities between the value assigned men and women in Western society.

> But those which are a cutting of the male pursue the male, and while they are boys, being slices of the male, they are fond of men, and enjoy the lying with men and embracing them, and these are the best of boys and lads because they are naturally bravest. Some call them shameless, but this is false; no shamelessness makes them do this, but boldness and courage and a manly force which welcomes what is like them. Here is a great proof: when they grow

up, such as these alone are men in public affairs. And when they become men, they fancy boys, and naturally do not trouble about marriage and getting a family, but that law and custom compels them; they find it enough themselves to live unmarried together. Such a person is always inclined to be a boy-lover or a beloved, as he always welcomes what is akin. [12]

We also gain insight into the way in which the above beliefs are acted out in the sexuality of Socrates, in the *Symposium.*

Then Socrates said, "Agathon, won't you defend me? I find that this person's love has become quite a serious thing. From the time when I fell in love with him, I am no longer allowed to look at or talk with a handsome person, not even one, or this jealous and envious creature treats me outrageously, and abuses me, and hardly keeps his hands off me. Then don't let him try it on now, but do reconcile us, or if he uses force, defend me, for I'm fairly terrified at his madness and passion. [13]

The lover of Socrates, Alcibiades, goes on to say:

... so I got up, and without letting this man say another word, I threw my own mantle over the man and crept in under this man's threadbare cloak—for it was winter—and threw my arms round this man, this really astonishing and wonderful man, and there I lay the whole night! You will not say that is a lie, either, Socrates! [14]

One should notice here that this is not simply conversation about homosexuality. Likewise, it is not our goal to enter discussion on the morality of homosexuality. There are several other issues here. Homosexuality in the Platonic context is directly related to some of the pathological constructs of the European *asili.* First, there is an obvious affinity for sexual relations with children, as seen in the first quotation, since it makes a clear distinction between men and boys; this is a distinction made throughout *Symposium* and much is made of boy-love and lovers. It even goes so far as to mention that men of public affairs "fancy boys." This has very real implications as to how this Greek outlook manifests an *asili* that, as is the nature of *asili*, is still affecting the present reality.

Presently, there is such a thing as a "pederast," which is a man who has sexual relations with a boy. Interestingly enough, this present day practice relates directly to ancient Greek practices. The following is the written testimony of a professed "boy-lover" from his contribution to a book entitled *Varieties of Man/Boy Love: Modern Western Contexts.*

Because of themes in the writings of early advocates of homosexuality, the best-known form of pederasty has often been called "Greek Love," the relationship between tutor and pupil, mentor and youth. Private schools, the Boy Scouts, Big Brothers, and of course the Catholic Churches are contexts for this form of pederasty. Though this has long been known and a subject of locker-room humor, only recently has there been a systematic attempt to wipe it out. Educators have long realized that there is an erotic element in good teaching and that many good teachers, priests, and others who work with boys are drawn to their profession precisely because it allows access to intimate man/boy relations. As a judge commented in a case where a man was accused of kidnapping a working-class boy, but where no sexual act or intent was alleged, "why else would a sane adult want to hang around a junior high school boy?" There are currently so many lawsuits against the Roman Catholic Church alleging sex between priests and altar boys or other adolescent believers that some observers fear it may bankrupt even that wealthy institution.

Greek-love proponents generally attribute positive, integrative, socializing aspects to these relationships. They see their sexual relationships as being in the service of socialization, sexual education, and the proper development of adolescence into mature, responsible adulthood. The literature about Greek Love has often blurred lines between children and adolescents, though it has always been a homophilic relationship, almost never including girls. [15]

The carryover of ancient Greek ideological foundations is most obvious in this type of not often spoken of fact that there is a serious problem with pedophilia in Western society, from religious leaders to children's pornography to the highest levels of government ("men in public affairs"). This problem is highlighted by government subcommittees on child pornography and pedophilia.

The American Association for Protecting Children, a subsidiary of the American Humane Association, noted a ten-fold increase in the number of children reported to be sexual abuse victims from 1976 to 1983, but it was not until the following year that the problem was presented to the general public as a 'crisis'. [16]

Perhaps a more clear issue regarding this manifestation of the European *asili*, through its *utamawazo*, is in the connection of these sexual attitudes to the way in which women are viewed. The observation made in the quotation regarding the absence of girls from the pederastic relationships is not a mistake or odd, within the context of the Greek origins of this behavior. In Plato's *Symposium*, there is a description of the two types of "Love," which reveals the connection between the Greek homosexuality and the devaluation of women. There is the inferior Common Love and the superior Heavenly Love.

The Love, then, which belongs to Common Aphrodite is

really and truly common and works at random; and this is the love
which inferior men feel. Such men love firstly women... for this
Love springs from the goddess which is much younger than the other,
and in her birth had a share of both female and male. But the other
Love springs from the Heavenly goddess, who firstly has had no share
of the female; next she is elder, and has no violence in her: consequently those inspired by this love turn to the male, because they feel
affection rather for what is stronger and has more mind. One could
recognise even in boy-love those who are driven by this Love pure
and simple... [17]

Now it is clear here that the homosexuality being expressed
has a direct relationship to what might be called a divine belief in the
unworthiness of a woman to provide "Love pure and simple" to a
man in the same way that another man or boy could. It is expressed
that "inferior men" feel the kind of love that draws them to women.
The male is seen to not only be stronger, but have more mind. The
quote also serves as an admission of Yurugu's incompleteness. The
Superior Love "had no share of the female." Thus you have the basis
for Yurugu, void of spirit and the feminine principles that are
necessary for cultural, personal and cosmological balance. That love
which is considered superior is completely male or masculine. Therefore, superior love is out of balance.

Again, these are expressed ideological constructs, the European *utamawazo*, coming from what the Western world has held up
to be their foundations. In fact, Plato's works are among the works
considered "Classic" and being taught today in colleges, universities,
high schools, etc. More specifically, some modern day defenders of
pederasty use the "Platonic model" as a direct reference point to the
relationships that only "intellectuals and artists" are suited to have
with boys. [18] Such individuals as Gustav Wyneken in the early 1900's
with his Free School Community "introduced the erotic bond

between a leader and a boy as an educational principle, in this way accommodating the boy's desire..." [19]

It is granted that every aspect of Plato's work is not dealing with homosexuality, nor is every aspect of it an outright manifestation of the pathological *asili*. In fact, there are some works of Plato which seem to contradict his enthusiastically homosexual and pederastic writings. He deems the only natural intercourse to be between men and women in *Laws*, but,

> While framing a law of almost monastic rigour for the regulation of the sexual appetite, he remains an ancient Greek. He does not reach the point of view from which women are regarded as the proper objects of both passion and friendship, as the fit companions of men in all relations in life... [20]

So, even when contradicting himself Plato gives us examples of the pathology and unbalanced nature of the European *asili*. He has had a major impact on the articulation of the culturally structured thought (*utamawazo*) and fulfillment of the *asili*. And, as Alfred Korzybski is quoted as saying in the introduction to this work, much of the worst of Plato and other European philosopher/scholars has been that which the West has adopted.

So, it can be seen in the ideological core of European society why the female is afforded a demeaned, devalued, subservient role in life. It is more than subservient actually; it is almost a position where women are the standard victim of male aggression. It is also as deep and profound as religion and the removal of the woman from what is referred to as "the holy trinity" in Christianity. Women in various cultures have occupied the image of the Supreme Being and other key manifestations of the Creator. In addition, predecessors of European Christianity and the "holy trinity" contained the Father,

Mother and Child. Now, the woman has been replaced by the Holy Spirit. Even ancient Gnostic Christians, who were Afrikan-influenced and non-political unlike the European-centered Church that is still functioning, are said to have acknowledged the feminine principles and the female in the "holy trinity." [21] In some cultures, women are still key figures, maintaining positions as High Priestesses, etc. Today in the "industrialized," European-dominated world, women fight to be allowed positions of spiritual leadership in contemporary religions. Thus, these pathological aspects of the European *asili* are of concern especially because they continue to seriously impact Western society, which is abnormal, flawed and insane.

Another aspect of this gender pathology is found in *Symposium* with references to males being pregnant as a result of their relationships with other males. While it is a symbolic pregnancy, it is problematic because it is valued above the birth of real human beings!

> But much the greatest wisdom,' she said, 'and the most beautiful, is that which is concerned with the ordering of cities and homes, which we call temperance and justice. So again a man with divinity in him, whose soul from his youth is pregnant with these things, desires when he grows up to beget and procreate... For by attaching himself to a person of beauty, I think, and keeping company with *him* {italics mine}, he begets and procreates what he has long been pregnant with... [22]

What is expressed here is men being with men and begetting and procreating virtue and all of the other intellectual values that come with two men educating each other. It goes further to say that the man who attaches himself to another in this way,

> ... with him fosters what is begotten, so that as a result these

people maintain a much closer communion together and a firmer friendship than parents of children, because they have shared between them children more beautiful and more immortal. *And everyone would be more content to have such children born to him rather than human children* {italics mine} ... [23]

The woman has symbolically been removed even from the process of procreation. This is a clear statement of the devaluation of women even to the depths of their divine manifestation of creating life and bringing children into the world. The implications of this are of course seen today as there is a necessity for women's rights, feminism and even affirmative action for European women in Western society.

The rape of women is another serious problem in the world and the United States of America. Approximately 2 out of every 1000 women between the age of 12 and 15 are raped annually according to Department of Justice Statistics. The number peaks to 5 out of every 1000 between the ages of 16 and 19, translating to 1 out of every 200 women; the numbers declined slightly to around 4 out of every 1000 between the ages of 20 and 24. [24] Other figures suggest that we are living in a "rape culture" with perhaps more than 600,000 women raped per year. Haki Madhubuti comments on rape in his book, *Claiming Earth*, sharing that,

> One can safely assume that no woman wants to be raped. And if men were raped as frequently as women are, rape would be a federal crime rivaling that of murder and bank robbery. If carjacking can command federal attention, why are we still treating rape as if it is a "boys will be boys" sport or a "woman's problem" (as in "blame the victim")? In the great majority of the sex crimes against women in the United States, the women are put on trial as if they planned and executed their own rapes.

Male acculturation (more accurately, male "seasoning,") is anti-female, anti- womanist/feminist, and anti-reason when it comes to women's equal measure and place in society. [25]

In response to such a distorted ideological matrix as relates to women, Oba T'Shaka shares, in *Return To The African Mother Principle of Male and Female Equality*, that,

A philosophy centered around **"just males and females being equally empowered to govern every phase of the family, community and society,"** is the philosophical thrust that will protect our youth and adults from a spiritually empty society where anarchy rules male-female relationships, and the Euro-American culture is dysfunctional and out of control. [26]

As alluded to by T'Shaka, the problems in the current American society, and the European *utamawazo* expressed in the work of Plato go further as relates to children. It is stated that this symbolic procreation that Plato writes about between men is valued even above "human children!" This is an incredible statement and its fruits, as perpetuated by the European *asili*, bear out in the fact that we have to have "children's rights" activists, there has had to be legislation in the past against child labor abuses in America and homeless children make up a large portion of the country's homeless today. In Plato's *Republic* there is also talk about children being servants and even more disturbing references to children in the establishment of Socrates' utopian republic.

The children of the good, then, they will take, I think, into the fold, and hand them over to nurses who will live in some place apart from the city; those of the inferior sort, and any one of the others who may be born defective, they will put away as is proper in some mysterious, unknown place. [27]

Certain children are to be stashed away and hidden if they are not born "perfect" or born to the right people. There is additional reference to children who are "begotten" out of the proper circumstances prescribed by the State and outside of the proper State prescribed conditions, saying that "... if a child is born, if one forces its way through, they must dispose of it on the understanding that there is no food or nurture for such a one." [28] This cruelty and lack of value assigned to children is tied into theories of social control expressed in *The Republic.* The control of "breeding" and the discarding of children who do not fit into the development of a superior race provides the seeds of Hitler's Nazi Germany with the European Jewish Holocaust, as well as things such as Eugenics and the types of pseudo-scientific racist theories espoused by people like William Shockley who advocated the sterilization of Afrikan people in America. It is precisely the spiritual emptiness and masculine/ feminine imbalance, that T'Shaka writes of, that leads to Plato advocating "disposing" of human beings. With regard to yet another disturbing contemporary manifestation of this attitude toward children, we find that,

> Brazil has one of the world's highest numbers of children who live or survive on the streets. The numbers are in the millions. Between 1988 and 1991 about 5,664 children between the ages of five and seventeen were murdered. The perpetrators of the crimes, including off duty policeman and official death squads, justify their actions by claiming: killing a Black child today will prevent having to kill an adult criminal in the future. This behavior is sanctioned by many Brazilians in the middle and upper classes. [29]

Of course, like America, Brazil was established by European

Maafa criminals carrying on and fulfilling the European *asili*, only they were Portuguese instead of English. In *The Republic* it is also conceded that "the rulers will have really to use falsehood and deceit for the benefit of the ruled..." [30] and "there must be some clever kind of lots devised, I think, so that your worthless creature will blame his bad luck on any conjunction, not his rulers." [31] Not much needs to be said about deceit and the above mentioned manipulation of the populace, since it is acknowledged reality with politics today. The masses of United States citizens are manipulated and tricked by the government in numerous ways and Plato has laid this down as a paradigm and necessity. The problem is that this country's propaganda machine is so strong that not only do many Afrikans not recognize its nature, but the masses of poor and even so called middle class Europeans are being deceived in the exact way Plato prescribed it.

The Republic does give some hint of approaching equity for women in the utopian city, but we find that this is only in as much as women are "useful" to the city. This hint of equality is negated by the true nature of the Grecian sexism, however, in such references as it being "mean and greedy to despoil a corpse, and a sign of a petty, womanish mind to think the dead body of an enemy..." and there being no difference between this "womanish" behavior and "dogs which worry the stones that strike them and never touch the thrower."[32] Women are degraded and unimportant because of their so called "petty" behavior. Additionally, it is related in Plato's work that marriage is compelled by law and custom, but men who had found boy-love would rather live their lives together than bother with marriage. In the modern context, it is this disdain of the female principle which is unbalanced and pathological.

Plato may be a beginning point in looking at the *asili* of the present world reality, through the European *utamawazo*, in all of its abnormality, insanity and flaw, but he is not alone. Plato's student

Aristotle has had a significant impact as well. It has been written that "The success of Aristotle's endeavor may be measured by the enormous impact of his *Ethics* on Western moral philosophy through the centuries." [33]

With Aristotle we begin to see the rise of what he considered "scientific knowledge," and the compartmentalization of the soul. Aristotle's approach contributed to an ideological matrix that allows for all scientific knowledge being teachable, the existence of "first principles" and the consequent existence of "universal knowledge." First principles are moral values which may be deduced and aid a person achieving scientific knowledge. Scientific knowledge is demonstrable. In other words, according to Aristotle, you do not have scientific knowledge if you cannot demonstrate what you know or its truth. In this line of thought, the material begins to take a prominent role in establishing "universal truths." Additionally, "... the intellect is the highest thing in us, and the objects that it apprehends are the highest things that can be known." Objects, or material things apprehended, are the highest things that can be known according to this manifestation of the *asili*. This speaks to Marimba Ani's perception of European science which states that,

> The concept of cause is the basis of a tradition of European science that deals exclusively with the physical and in which the metaphysical is debunked as mystical and antiscientific... European science is predicated solely on the predictability of the relationship between cause and effect and treats this relationship in a totally mechanistic way. It is a science that has attempted to materialize a spiritualistic concept, just as from an African-centered viewpoint, it has attempted to materialize a spiritual universe. [34]

It is not only in science where Aristotle's influence has been felt, but in the tradition of Greek philosophers, he has touched other areas of "being" as well. He and his Greek cohorts had a rather supremacist, European national stance that undoubtedly has played a role in the germination of white supremacist ideology. This may seem like a stretch, but we are told that "The ethnocentric teachings of Aristotle and others cast most of these peoples [other cultures] in bestial modes as people without civilization, social order, or religion."[35] It is generally safe to say that Greek and Roman culture in general, were generators of this type of thinking. In *Clash of Cultures*, by Fagan, this influence is further elaborated upon with regard specifically to the birth of Europe, its consciousness and its identity. This is important in that it articulates the bridge from Greek civilization to European culture at large, given from the perspective of a European scholar.

> This consciousness was born of Greek civilization, nurtured on the battlefields... The philosophies and thoughts of the Greeks had spread from the meditteranean deep into Western Europe, creating a European spirit that was opposed to Asia, but looked towards it. Part of this philosophy was Aristotle's famous notion that the world was divided into Greeks and barbarians, those people who were by nature free, and those who were destined to be slaves.
>
> This attitude toward other societies was one of the forces that gave Europeans a curious ambivalence about the outside world. One part of their psychology filled them with a sense of hostility and rejection towards foreigners, and a need to project themselves against intruders. [36]

Again we see Aristotle's influence. The contribution of Aristotle to the fulfilling of the European *asili* is further witnessed in his impact on the European philosophers and thinkers in the many generations to follow; this can be expected as the nature of *asili* is to manifest the continued life of the civilization. Aristotle and other

Greeks are quoted and referred to in the vast majority of writings dealing with European scholarship and thinking. The expanse of his influence is as wide as the many European nations themselves. It is even said that "...the more sophisticated justification for exploitation employed by the Spanish jurists who adopted Aristotle's definition of 'barbaric' peoples as natural slaves." [37] Of course we know the influence the Spanish were to have in terms of their invasion of the Americas and their fulfillment of the European _asili._

Aristotle was born around 384 B.C. and there were later philosophers such as Boethius, who was a Roman philosopher born around 480 A.D., and Thomas Aquinus, born around 1225 A.D., solidly grounded in Aristotelian philosophy.

It is said of Boethius, for example, that "The historical importance of his work was immense, because it was only through Boethius's translations that the knowledge of Aristotle survived in the West." [38] With Boethius, whose writing had a religious bent, you find knowledge being compartmentalized to inferior and superior.

> The point of greatest importance here is this: the superior manner of knowledge includes the inferior, but it is quite impossible for the inferior to rise to the superior. The senses cannot perceive anything beyond matter; imagination does not consider universal species; and reason does not comprehend simple form; but intelligence as though looking down from above, first perceives form and then distinguishes all things that are under it, but in such a way that it comprehends the form itself which could not be known to any other.[39]

We see in this quote from Boethius a real splitting of the "soul," or the aspects of the soul concerned with knowledge. The senses have become the most inferior knowledge capable of perceiving only the material, with intelligence being the superior knowledge.

The implications of this is that the despiritualizing of reality is still being furthered as the wholeness of the soul and reality has been disrupted. Even though Boethius believes the intelligence to be divine and of God, God is materialized in as much as the God concept is abstracted from senses, imagination, reason and placed as an entity apart from these other types of knowledge. In a sense, God is materialized as yet another, although supreme, compartment; an entity separate and by itself.

Similar to Boethius, Thomas Aquinus was renowned for his scholarship in Aristotelian philosophy. Aquinus spoke of "self-evident principles" contained within all people. These principles are akin to divine seeds of knowledge put in place by God. The connection to Aristotle becomes very apparent as we find out that these divine principles form the basis for scientific knowledge and therefore science is divine and certain. These principles are assumed to be immutable and the building blocks of science. This circular thought has found a way to make science, which according to Aristotle must be demonstrable, an absolute and divine entity based on what we recognize as non-demonstrable assumptions. These assumptions do not have their origins in the material world, yet are being used to make the material divine. In other words, the material, which can be demonstrated, becomes divine and the despiritualization inherent in the European *asili* is articulated through the maze of "first principles," "supreme intellect," "self-evident principles," etc., which help eliminate the need for spiritual insight. Thus, the material is justified and exists without the spiritual. Science takes the place of the spiritual, unseen cosmos which is not material. Therefore, according to the European *utamawazo,* spirit is non-demonstrable, non-scientific and not divine. The necessity, in this thought process, of "first principles," and similar constructs, represents a conflict between the value being assigned to material science and the intuitive spiritual realm from which these "first principles" would theoretically emanate. Despite the spiritual, intuitive nature of such principles and assumptions, these same spiritual and intuitive aspects of science, and by connection existence, are discredited. This is a continuation of the inner conflict and denial of spirit inherent in Yurugu.

It is on the basis of the European worldview's determined certainty and divinity of science that absolutes and universals of knowledge, science and the divine, or God, are established. By the nature of the European *utamawazo* establishing what is divine, true, absolute, universal and certain, they also implicate that everything else is other than divine, true, absolute, universal and certain. This is the dichotomous logic of the European *asili*. Things are good or evil, right or wrong, true or false, European or uncultured, pro-European or anti-European and so on. Incidentally, we can recall that the Greeks referred to people who were not Greek by using the term "barbarian," another manifestation of this logic.

The clearest manifestation of the way in which this outlook has been pathological is the way in which the European *asili* has identified and related to the "cultural other," or what the Greeks would call barbarian. The "cultural other" concept is one developed and elaborated on by Marimba Ani. Essentially, since Europeans have identified what is divine, everything else is evil. They have identified what is refined, so everything else is barbaric. European culture becomes the panacea and therefore all *other* cultures are to be submitted to the whims of the superior European culture.

This translates into the ability of those who operate within this *asili* to refer to people who display a different belief system and *asili* as savages, as was the case with Native Americans who could then be annihilated because they were other than the European *asili's* divine, absolute, true and certain European reality. Thus, we can see that many Europeans during the annihilation of Native Americans who,

...drew on eulogistic accounts of the Incas and other Indian
societies, agreed with Bartolome de Las Casas that the Indians were
people of natural superior goodness. All the Indians needed was
conversion to Christianity to become the most blessed of souls. [40]

Despite the recognition of the so called "natural supreme
goodness" of Native Americans, the European dichotomous logic
still made it necessary for conversion. This is because the logic
dictates that you are either Christian or heathen, Christian or a
necessary convert. A sane person, on the other hand, would
acknowledge this goodness and see no reason to change these
naturally good people, especially at the cost of annihilation if there
was not compliance.

This logic has not only been played out by Europeans against
others, but also against themselves within the context of the Spanish
Inquisition. It is also witnessed in the ability of the Pope to sanction
the barbarity of The Maafa, which entailed the enslavement,
psychological mutilation, kidnapping, rape and murder of millions
of people. This was sanctioned because the European *utamawazo*
embodied in religious dogma was able to convince the adherents of
the European *asili* that the "cultural other" represented the opposite
and antithesis of the divine, absolute, true and certain European
reality. Consequently Afrikans, being "other" than Europeans, were
considered other than divine; this meant Afrikans could be declared
"soulless" and The Maafa justified.

We can even see the extensions of the "cultural other" mindset in European scholarship that is attempting to address cultural
conflict.

Encounters between different cultures are instances of a
more extensive problem which has received considerable attention

recently: that of relating to whatever group one's society defines as other than onesself. Most societies define women as other than men; many define children as other than adults; while medical, ethnological, sexual and religious classifications produce such groups as 'madmen,' 'blacks,' 'homosexuals' and 'heretics.' This classifying process gives us a map of our society and provides us with stereotypes in terms of which we approach other individuals. [41]

It is difficult to tell whether the revelation of how Afrikan people are perceived in the same breath as madmen and heretics was intentional or a subconscious slip of the pen. It is revealing of the "cultural other" mentality as it specifically relates to Afrikan people, whatever its intention. In addition, why must we see encounters between cultures as inherently problematic? Our answer is found in Ani's "cultural other" concept of the European mentality and the dichotomous logic which bread aggression and cultural imposition. Why would women be considered as "other" than men in this context, when they should be considered complementary opposites? Shouldn't children be considered *of* adults and not *other* than adults?

These are brief examples of the manifestations of the European *asili,* generating and being fulfilled by its *utamawazo,* which can be identified in the works of some of the scholars and philosophers we have discussed. Additionally, the *asili,* aside from the aspects of its *utamawazo* we have analyzed, was also fulfilled through many other processes which include the fact that, according to Ani in *Yurugu,* "cognitive styles were being molded or at least anticipated" [42] and people like Plato "...created a reality. Hypothesis became theory." [43]

A more contemporary manifestation of European *utamawazo* is found in the works of Charles Darwin. While some argue that Darwin altered the course of European thinking by changing and challenging existing philosophical notions, his fulfilling of the European *asili* and his continuation of it in the same pathological direction cannot be denied. We are told that "perhaps the single most important influence on pragmatism from the standpoint of science, however, was the work of Charles Darwin." [44] Darwin's "major work, *On the Origin of Species* (1859), rocked the intellectual and religious communities of the Western World." [45] What is usually never related to most people about Darwin is the complete title of his most famous work. It is *On the Origin of Species by Means of Natural Selection, or The Preservation of Favoured Races in the Struggle for Life.* Considering that we are not left to wonder who *the* "Favoured" cultural group or "race" is, Darwin helped drive the aggressive, "cultural other" aspects of the European *asili.* Dr. Marimba Ani outlined a statement of Darwin's, which we will use here to give a bottom line, indisputable example of how men such as Darwin fit into and help further European *utamawazo,* fulfilling the *asili.*

> At some future period, not very distant as measured by centuries, the civilized races of man will almost certainly exterminate and replace, the savage races throughout the world. At the same time the anthropomorphous apes... will no doubt be exterminated. The break will then be wider, for it will intervene between man in some more civilized state... than the Caucasian, and some ape as low as a baboon, instead of as at present between the negro or Australian and the gorilla. [46]

This statement speaks for itself. Amongst the numerous pathologies of an abnormal, insane and flawed worldview that Darwin's, and the other philosopher's, articulated beliefs represent, we must realize that [1] Darwin's views "helped foster an examination of many areas of intellectual inquiry, and the cosmology of development, spurred by Darwin's efforts, has become more widely applied in fields that even Darwin himself never envisioned" [47]; and [2)] all of the individual philosophers and scholars we have examined so far are taught intensively in schools and universities, as well as being highly regarded by the present society and its institutions.

****

What has been discussed thus far represents only a glance at some of the foundations of European thought and behavior; the ideological matrix or *asili*. The ways in which this *asili* manifests in actual behavior and thought, once we understand the *asili* itself, becomes all the more clear. This chapter not only helps us better understand the basis for a reality revolution, but also highlights the tremendous import of the work Dr. Marimba Ani has done in *Yurugu*. It is this work and its continuance that allows for our clearest possibilities for liberation since we are able to purge ourselves of the European *asili* once we recognize it and subsequently identify it as the enemy. Thus identified, demystified and destroyed, Afrikan people can leave European conceptual frameworks and begin our re-creation.

Some might say that this type of harsh critique of the European cultural and ideological foundations is "racist." To them we say that if we can't even attack the *ideology* of a culture that has pillaged and conquered the world, how do we ever expect to be free? We are only attacking pathological ideas and behaviors, which is logical and absolutely necessary. There can be no apology for the *victim* of a violent criminal criticizing and analyzing the mind of the criminal that has wreaked havoc and destruction.

Others may ask the question of whether the European *asili* simply represents a *different* worldview, instead of a pathological, abnormal, insane reality. The answer is **NO!** The reason for this answer is not because we are being like the European *asili* and declaring the "cultural other" mentality, but instead there are two very different reasons. First of all, the European *asili* has been destructive to itself and the world it currently dominates (see next chapter and section entitled "The Case Against the European *Asili*: The Rapist, The Murderer, The Thief"); this is whether the *asili* manifests in European thought and behavior, or in the thought and behavior of others who have attempted to assimilate into this *asili*. Secondly, this *asili* is not parallel to the world's majority of cultures. It is deviant from the cultural norms of the world's majority of people.

Keep in mind what the *asili* concept is and that it may not include small deviations from the behavior and thought that currently facilitates world domination, nor in many cases the *stated* beliefs of individuals. Again, the concept of *asili* refers to the ideological matrix and conceptual systems of a group of people, not simply a list of crimes they have committed nor the color of their skin. Consequently, this allows us to recognize the interconnections of cultural groups and of individuals, while holding firm to our analysis of the insanity of the present European world reality.

For example, the ancient Afrikans in Kemet (Egypt) had interaction with the ancient Greeks. In fact, the Greeks were students of these ancient Afrikan ancestors of ours. We might note here that despite what opponents of "Afrocentricity" have to say, this teacher-student relationship between the Afrikans and Greeks is not fantasy, conjecture, "reverse academic racism," or a conclusion based solely on the writings of Herodotus. It is sufficient to say that all of the major Greek philosophers spent time learning in Kemet (Egypt) and the testimony of so many sources and so much evidence proves this to be true. The medical community's continuing use of the Hippocratic oath is one example of a multitude. This oath is one that many medical practitioners must take and is named for Hippocrates, a Greek physician.

A survey reported in 1966 indicated that twenty-one of
eighty-four medical schools reporting in the United States still
administer the Hippocratic Oath to their graduates, or exactly 25
percent of the total number. The ancient oath however was not taken
by graduates but by *beginning* students of medicine. [48]

In the oath, the name Asclepius is mentioned. Asclepius is
the Greek name for Imhotep, the ancient Afrikan physician of Kemet
(Egypt), thought of as the first physician and multi-genius in recorded
history. However, Europeans walked away with incomplete
knowledge of their Afrikan teachers in this instance and used it to
fulfill their *asili.* Evidence of the Greek's removal of spirit from this
practice of medicine can be found in *The American Heritage
Dictionary of The English Language, 3rd Edition* under
"Hippocrates."

> Called "the Father of Medicine." 460? - 377? B.C. Greek
> physician who laid the foundations of scientific medicine by freeing
> medical study from the constraints of philosophical speculation and
> superstition. [49]

There is the assumption here in a modern dictionary that
medicine had to be freed from the "constraints" of "philosophical
speculation and superstition." What is considered by the European
worldview to be philosophical speculation and superstition tends to
be the spirituality and higher level consciousness of Afrikan and other
peoples. Thus, you have the dichotomous logic again of either
European science or superstition. So, this definition in the dictionary
speaks directly to the process of despiritualization. Interestingly
enough, one of the most popular movements at present is the
investigation of the spiritual aspects of medicine and healing; the
movement is evidenced in the best-selling and very popular author/

lecturer Deepak Chopra, M.D., who is enlightening many on the necessity of spirituality in the healing process. Dr. Chopra, to a degree, brings the worldview of his Eastern Indian origins to medicine and healing.

As one more example of the interaction and student role Greeks had with Kemet (Egypt), Aristotle, whose authority and authenticity is not questioned by Europeans, claims that the mathematical arts originated in Kemet.

Thus realizing that the Greeks learned much from Afrikans, the question arises as to how European *utamawazo* came to be so drastically different and pathological? The first answer to this question is that the *asili* guides *utamawazo*. Additionally, we already have the example of medicine and the removal of spirit from its practice. Greeks altered the knowledge they gained to meet their own needs and fulfill their own *asili*. With this in mind, a logical second answer to the question is found in a closer look at the history of this interaction. In short, the Greeks who studied in Kemet (Egypt) did so for a relatively short time in the larger scheme of things, even though most of them spent many years there. For example, a Greek who spent 20 years in Kemet (Egypt) only received a very incomplete education.

This can be best illustrated by a look at the Dogon knowledge system, since "The Dogon process of education through initiation to different levels, involving years of study, is similar to that of Kemet."[50] The Dogon have degrees of knowledge. The first is the "word at face value" or "fore-word" knowledge called *Giri So*. The second is the "word on the side" or "side word" knowledge called *Benne So*. The third degree is the "word from behind" or "back -word" called *Bolo So*. Finally, there is the "clear word" knowledge called *So Dayi*, which consists of 8 levels itself. [51] After 16 years amongst the Dogon, two French anthropologists named Marcel Griaule and Germaine Dieterlen had only reached the "slight acquaintance" level of the "clear word" system. Needless to say, their knowledge was far from complete after 16 years.

With this in mind, we can appreciate the years the Greek students spent in Afrika as being nowhere near adequate to walk away with the knowledge of Afrikan people; a proposition compounded by the fact that Afrikan knowledge includes that of the collective unconscious or the wisdom of the ages passed on from the Afrikan ancestors. Consequently, with insufficient study time and no access to the ancestral memory of Afrikans, the Greeks left with an incomplete understanding of what they learned. They probably returned home thinking their knowledge was complete, evidenced in the plagiarism of Afrikan concepts and knowledge, the results of which lacked the spirit and cosmological understanding of the originators and teachers of the knowledge. This is just one possibility as to contributing factors to the pathology of European *utamawazo*, despite its interaction with Afrikans of whom history records high civilization and a lack of this pathological behavior and ideological core.

There have been theories advanced as to the reasons for this pathology and Marimba Ani, who gives one the most critical and meticulous examinations of the European *asili*, suggests,

> The value of any theory of White Supremism, from an African-centered perspective, lies in its ability to lay bare the dynamics and centricity of the power relationship in European ideology and behavior. Whether it is the "anal personality" theory of Joel Kovel, the "genetic inferiority complex" theory of Francis Welsing, the Northern Cradle theory of Cheikh Anta Diop, the psychopathic racial personality theory of Bobby Wright, or the historical analysis of W.E.B. DuBois and earlier Pan-Africanists—in each case their value lies in the fact that they place white supremism squarely within the matrix of European ideology and biocultural development. [52]

Although some may be uncomfortable with what has been expressed so far; which is largely due to the fact that Europeans have established a clear paradigm for the study of the "cultural other" and the negativity of studying or criticizing the European, a brief glance at aspects of the historical record in the next chapter confirms what has been expressed concerning the European *asili*. It also confirms the necessity for a reality revolution, as even people of color in this world dominated by the European *asili* act out the madness.

CHAPTER 2

○○○○○○○○○

THE RECORD, THE MADNESS

There is a large body of historical and contemporary evidence which suggests uncompromisingly that something is very wrong with the world today. This fact is articulated constantly by people in all walks of life, including scholars and religious leaders. One can always hear expressions along the lines of "what is the world coming to" and "things are getting real crazy." There is perplexity in the voices of people who call Afrikan radio talk programs and European programs alike. There is frequent discussion about the killing that is taking place amongst the youth and adults as well. The government shuts down on what seems like a regular basis now days and countless scholars voice their opinions on what the problems are.

A very significant part of Christian religious expression is directed toward warning individuals not to be "of this world," not only in the biblical sense, but from the realistic perspective of encouraging people to separate themselves from the chaos of the world that surrounds them. Part of this religious commentary can be seen in books such as *Living in Hell: The dilemma of African-American survival*, in which the voices of Afrikan ministers are brought together to speak of our existence. Without having to get into the substance of the book itself, one encounters the reality of the current world right in the preface.

> If living in America is hell for me, an African-American
> man possessing a few trappings of success, then there can be no
> doubt concerning the pressures experienced by the majority of

African-Americans existing at the bottom of the American ladder
of success. This defines the burden of blackness in our time.
Here's the truth of the matter: For African-American men and
women, living in America is like living in hell. [1]

This is the type of recognition of the problems of the world
that is common amongst people everyday. You would be hard pressed
to find many who don't agree that there is an intolerable level of
madness in the world (Such people would at least be hard to find
amongst those who are not completely delusional). What is
uncommon is the carrying out of this problem recognition to its logical
conclusions. People seem to have difficulty employing cause-effect logic
and coming up with an operational completion of the phrase "if the
present world reality is crazy, then it follows that..."

This book will attempt to logically end that phrase by expressing the pathology of the European cultural *asili* that creates the
madness while dominating the world and the need to separate from it
in consciousness, ideology and philosophy, thus creating something
sane, normal and desired: a new reality. This chapter will attempt to
systematically lay out some of the signs and symptoms of this
pathology so that they are readily available in one place and can be
compared to the analysis of the European *asili* and *utamawazo* in the
previous chapter. After reading this chapter, one is urged to come to
the conclusion that if this world is crazy, we must create a sane one.
We can change reality. Too often, even those who recognize the
insanity of the present world reality have no better strategy than
figuring out how to better maneuver within an insane culture. They
develop program after program, so called solution after solution which
rely culturally, ideological and philosophically on the same cultural
reality they have determined to be crazy. They are trying to use
insanity to look at how to avoid being insane. I would hope that we
can be a little more creative than working within an insane ideological

and cultural matrix once we have recognized it. WE CAN CREATE A NEW REALITY! In chapters to come we will examine how this can be done. As for now, we need to examine the historical record and the madness.

THE CASE AGAINST THE EUROPEAN *ASILI*: THE RAPIST, THE MURDERER, THE THIEF

> President Roosevelt defined U.S. war aims as freedom of speech, freedom of worship, freedom from want, and freedom from fear. This appealing rhetoric helped maintain cohesion in the war against fascist powers, but it had as much reality as most state propaganda. In reality, as the documentary and historical record show with great clarity, U.S. policy has been guided by what we may call "the fifth freedom," the freedom to rob, to exploit, and to control.
>
> **Noam Chomsky**

There is no pride in being the most proficient rapist of the world's people and resources. There is no pride in being the best thief. There is no pride in being the most prolific serial killer, living well off of the belongings of many victims. Who can feel pride in having the highest standard of living amongst fellow criminals and languishing victims?

America is a European society which currently dominates the world and is itself dominated by the people who fulfill the European *asili*. Consequently, we must view this society within the context of its flawed nature, rather than the propagandized presentation of "America the beautiful," "the greatest nation in the world," or its hypocritical Creed of freedom, justice and equality. Its greatness and beauty are only relative to a world which the people fulfilling the European *asili* have done a great deal to destroy and drive mad. In its proper context, America is a rapist, thief and serial killer, as are European societies around the world and through history who fulfill and have fulfilled the

European *asili.* Europeans have not been able to get along with any culture they have encountered on the face of the earth. What's worse is that they have systematically wiped out civilizations and societies, arrogantly imposing their culture and values upon others. The case for this assertion follows.

THE AMERICAS

The landing of Europeans in the Western Hemisphere meant that aggression would visit Native Americans in the form of barbaric annihilation. The existence of so called "reservations" in the United States as we close the 20th century remains an affront to the indigenous inhabitants of this land and a reality check for conscious individuals who believe in humanity. These reservations represent the last remnants of destruction.

To ascertain the decline of the American Indian population following the European arrival, it is necessary to establish the size of the population before the first European contacts. There is no question that the Native American population was decimated afterwards; the issue is the *magnitude of the destruction.* {italics mine} [2]

Keep in mind that with the estimates of the Native American populations before European destruction, there are many of the same problems that we saw with estimates of the numbers of Afrikans kidnapped and murdered during The Maafa. (Refer to *The Maafa & Beyond*) Some estimates of Native American populations prior to the destructive arrival of Europeans vary from 8.4 million to 112.5 million.

Dobyns, in contrast, examined population histories of

American Indian peoples following European contact, particularly
in Central and North America. He concluded that, on the average,
aboriginal populations declined to depopulation ratios about 1/20
or 1/25 of their original size before reaching nadir, that is, the low
point from which they started to increase in size. [3]

The list of horrors that lead to this depopulation is not well
known by the general public. While European diseases played a large
role, outright aggression and savagery on the part of Europeans also
contributed to the annihilation of Native Americans.

❖   The official colonial doctrine of Spain and Portugal
defined the inhabitants of other continents as people who had had
the misfortune not to share the Christian revelation: by promising
to convert them, one gained the right to conquer their territories. [4]

❖   That the Indians were idolaters provides one of the
principle justifications for what Spanish historiography continues
to call the 'just titles' of the conquest of the New World. [5]

❖   This was the determination of the Spaniards in all the
lands they conquered: to commit a great massacre that would
terrorize the tame flock and make it tremble. [6]

❖   Captain John Smith, a hardened campaigner with no
regard for human life, bombarded the Native Indians and reduced
their dwellings to ashes... The case of Virginia was to demonstrate
that such ruthless behavior at the outset contained the seeds of the
subsequent collision. [7]

There are records of babies' heads being smashed against rocks,
women being raped, people being burnt alive, mutilations and

decapitations. These are but a few of the instances, and mild ones, that allow us to peak into the savagery of the European arrival in the Americas.

SOUTH PACIFIC ISLANDS

Speaking of the English, French and Spanish, it has been written that,

❖   All these visitors—perhaps intruders is a better word—
were going to make their separate contribution to the transformation of the Tahitians, whether by firearms, disease or alcohol, or by
imposing an alien code of laws and morals that had nothing to do
with the slow, natural rhythm of life on the island as it had been
lived up till then. It was perfectly true that the Europeans were also
going to import the antidotes to their poisons and diseases—the
doctors, the priests, the administrators and the policemen—but the
Tahitians had had no need for these people before; if they had been
left undisturbed they might have gone on forever without them,
and at the time of Cook's arrival they were probably happier than
they were ever to be again. [8]

As is the European tradition of conquest, the attempt to justify the destruction is in the form of suggesting that Europeans brought "antidotes to their poisons." The responses to this justification should be that the destruction had no business being there in the first place; what is an appropriate antidote; and is there any justification possible at all?

Certainly, it can be said that the destructive marauding of Europeans around the globe should neither have happened, nor is there a justification for it. As for the so called antidotes, what had been called antidotes for the poison of European destruction, i.e. priests, police and administrators, were actually additional poison. To wreck the lives and worldviews of a people and then bring in unnatural replacements and maintainers of that destruction cannot be considered an antidote. Priests, police and administrators each played strong roles in further usurping the culture and religion of the people Europe was destroying. Even the doctors, as part and parcel of the European *asili*, perpetuated cultural imposition and a backward misunderstanding, even physiologically, of peoples who were not European.

❖   The population of Tahiti and Moorea declined from about 35,000 to around 8,000 between 1769 and 1800. [9]

Again, as a general rule, the estimates of European destruction are most often skewed to the interpretation that best meets European needs. The point is, however, that in the South Pacific Islands as in the rest of the world, Europeans pillaged and destroyed. Even in an area of seeming tranquility such as Hawaii, the rape and conquest was just as pervasive.

AFRIKA

To most of the readers of this book, the destruction of the European *asili* in Afrika is perhaps the best known of all. For those who are unaware, the presence of the vast majority of Afrikans in the Western Hemisphere is Exhibit A of the destruction of Afrikan people. Afrikans kidnapped during The Maafa from their respective home societies on the continent of Afrika are the primary reason for the existence of Afrikan people in the United States, Central America, South America and the Caribbean. It is also very easy to look to the continent and take note of the number of Afrikan countries in which English and French are the main languages or the languages of government and commerce.

The general course of destruction was and is so expansive and pervasive across the entire continent that it would be impossible to get an actual picture in one book, not to mention in one section of a chapter. However, what follows gives an inkling of the nature of the destruction.

Earlier this century in invaded, or what is usually called colonial Kenya...

❖   Of the 225,000 square miles in Kenya over half is desert. Of the rest, 3,000 white settlers own 16,700 square miles of the most fertile land and 5,250,000 Africans occupy, without owner ship rights, 52,000 square miles of the poorest. [10]

Additionally,

❖   In the legislature the 29,000 whites have 14 elected representatives; the 90,000 Asiatics have six, and the 24,000 Arabs one elected and one appointed; the 5,251,120 Negroes have no elected representatives but the Governor nominates six to speak for them. The natives pay three different kinds of direct taxes, and indirect taxes are placed on their necessities instead of on luxuries. [11]

In the Kongo,

❖   Each village was ordered by the authorities to collect and bring in a certain amount of rubber—as much as the men could bring in by neglecting all work for their own maintenance. If they failed to bring the required amount, their women were taken away and kept as hostages in compounds or in the harems of government employees. If this method failed, native troops, many of them cannibals, were sent into the village to spread terror, if necessary by killing some of the men; but in order to prevent a waste of cartridges they were ordered to bring one right hand for every cartridge used. If they missed, or used cartridges on game, they cut off the hands of living persons to make up the necessary number. The result was, according to the estimate of Sir H.H. Johnston, which is confirmed from all other impartial sources, that in fifteen years the native population was reduced from about twenty million to scarcely nine million. [12]

❖   Then came centuries of invasion from the west and northeast, and finally this valley fell into the claws of Leopold II of Belgium, with Stanley as his press agent. The two inveigled the Congress of Berlin to let Leopold hold the Congo as a sort of great Christian enterprise where "Peace and Religion" would march hand in hand.
        The result in theft and sheer cruelty astounded even Europe... [13]

In South Afrika or Azania, the criminal institution of enslavement called "apartheid" was not officially ended in its overt and government sanctioned murder, brutalization and rape of Afrikan people and Afrikan land until 1994. In the time period that apartheid was being criminally practiced, by what can only be called barbaric and murderous "Afrikaaners," neither thc U.S. nor any so called developed country went to war with Azania's European invaders to end the slaughter and murder of Afrikan people.

❖   Peaceful demonstration resulted in the shooting of four high school students by the police and shortly after this Soweto became embroiled in battle; a battle between the armed whites and unarmed blacks... After the smoke cleared in Soweto hundreds of Blacks were dead and thousands more injured. [14]

❖   The Native is to be treated as a child and denied the franchise. We must adopt the system of despotism such as works well in India in our relations with the barbarians of South Africa... These are my politics and these are the politics of South Africa. [15]

The list of atrocities against the Afrikan people in Azania, is extremely long. The tortures, kidnapping and psychological mutilation could fill volumes.

In Nigeria,

❖   Between August 1987 and May 1988, almost 4,000 tons of toxic wastes were dumped in Koko, Nigeria. As a result, the people of this small port town have seen a corresponding increase in the number of cholera patients and premature births. [16]

The type of destruction that has been outlined was and is carried out throughout the Afrikan continent. Perhaps what is worse than this physical brutalization is the mental/psychological and cultural   mutilation that took place alongside the physical brutality. European missionaries undermined Afrikan religion and culture and promoted Christianity as the universal and *One* religion. They therefore justified their assault on people not practicing Christianity. In addition, as we recognize the ways in which religion is bound and undergirded by culture, this religious imposition was a cultural imposition and destruction in every way.

INDIA

The British were to establish a brutal and savage reign in India that continued the pattern of European aggression and pathology.

❖   William Howitt (1792-1879), an English Quaker, visited Australia and the East early in the nineteenth century and has left us a record of what he saw. Of the treatment of women in India he wrote: "The treatment of the females could not be described. Dragged from the inmost recesses of their houses, which the religion of the country had made so many sanctuaries, they were exposed naked to public view. The virgins were carried to the Court of Justice, where they might naturally have looked for protection, but they now looked for it in vain; for in the face of the ministers of justice, in the face of the spectators, in the face of the sun, those tender and modest virgins were brutally violated. The only difference between their treatment and that of their mothers was that the former were dishonoured in the face of day, the latter in the gloomy recesses of their dungeon. Other females had the nipples of their breasts put in a cleft bamboo and torn off..." [17]

❖   India was occupied and brought under firm British authority during the years 1760-1858, coinciding with the period 1760-1840 when the industrial revolution was being pioneered in England... The British established themselves over India not merely to control its trade, or to displace the natives and settle on their land, but to rule them and to reorganize and exploit their toil for the benefit of an industrial Britain. [18]

CHINA

❖   ...let them consider that the British, from 1839 to 1842, waged war on China to buy opium which her Britannic Christian Majesty's imperial agents grew in India. Victory in the Opium War earned the British the "right" to addict so many Chinese to opium that much of the population, nodding and half asleep all the time, was supinely amenable to western cultural aggression and imperialist manipulation. [19]

AUSTRALIA (NEW SOUTH WALES) AND TASMANIA (NOW PART OF AUSTRALIA)

❖   For nearly eighteen years after Cook's departure the
aborigines of New South Wales remained undisturbed, and would
have continued so even longer but for the American war of independence. The British defeat in 1781 meant that the American
colonies could no longer be used as a convenient dumping ground
for criminals, and in order to relieve the overcrowding in the
British gaols it was necessary to set up a penal settlement in some
other country. As early as 1779 the matter was considered by a
committee of the House of Commons. New Zealand was rejected
on the grounds that the Maoris there were too ferocious, but Banks
came forward with the suggestion that Botany Bay on the Eastern
coast of Australia might be the answer to the problem... the
committee agreed, and Lord Sydney, the Secretary of State for the
Home Office, submitted the plan to the Treasury for its approval.
          Botany Bay had obvious attractions. The natives were few
in number, and being of a timid disposition were not likely to cause
trouble. The land was there for the taking; no other European
nation claimed it, and it was also commendably distant from
England; once landed in New South Wales the criminals would not
have much chance of getting home again. [20]

In this unleashing of European convicts and their equally
criminal keepers upon the indigenous people of Australia, it is interesting to note the role of the American colonies as a dumping ground for
European convicts as well. We also get insight into the European
nationalist mindset when the land was supposedly there for the
"taking," because no other European had claimed it, as if to say
Europeans were the only people on the face of the planet and never
mind those who were living on the land already. This is in fact the
mindset that was at work; Europeans are the only true and civilized

beings on the planet and all else are barbarian, savage, etc. Thus, it would follow that conquest was justified, encouraged and seen not as conquest, but as "manifest destiny" and other sorts of madness.

The indigenous inhabitants of Tasmania were systematically destroyed by the British. The decision to destroy was voiced by a young Englishman.

❖   ...the only alternative now is, if they do not readily become friendly, to annihilate them at once. [21]

The disgusting thing about this comment, made by an invader, is that the so called aborigines were expected to become friendly as their land and life-style was being stolen and destroyed.

❖   So the moment had started, and it grew more savage as it went on. In 1830 Tasmania was put under martial law, a line of armed beaters was formed across the island, and an attempt was made to drive the aborigines into a cul-de-sac. They succeeded in slipping through the net, of course, but by now the heart had gone out of the tribe, and their terror was greater than their desperation... In 1835 the last survivors, only a couple of hundred of the original 5,000, were shipped away. If there had ever been any intention of preserving the race it was now too late; they could not sustain life away from their tribal hunting grounds and the instinct to survive very quickly flickered out. Within seven years their numbers were down to fifty. The last pure-blooded Tasmanian died in 1876. [22]

❖   Phillip had estimated that there were about 1,500 aborigines around Sydney when he first arrived in 1788. By the eighteen-thirties only a few hundred remained. Darwin, in 1836, found them still trying to live their tribal lives among the colonists' farms on the outskirts of the settlement, but there were practically no wild animals left for them to hunt. A few years later even this last remnant had disappeared, and all that was left were a few beggars in the Sydney streets. 'Wherever the European has trod,' Darwin wrote, 'death seems to pursue the aboriginal. We may look to the wide extent of the Americans, Polynesia, the Cape of Good Hope and Australia, and we find the same result...' [23]

****

The aggressive, destructive nature of the European *asili* is decisively clear in these relatively few and mild descriptions of their activities around the globe. It is absolutely imperative that this type of activity, and the mindsets that perpetuate it, be analyzed regardless of who makes the faulty claim of this type of analysis being "racist" or "hate-mongering." There could be nothing further from the truth. Such analysis of history is not being done simply for the sake of pointing the finger or "playing the blame game," but because to ensure the survival of Afrikan people into the next millennium, we must study and correctly interpret history. To fulfill and realize what Dr. Kobi Kambon calls the Afrikan Survival Thrust, we must understand history. The aggression and destructive nature of the European *asili* must be properly understood in order to understand its present manifestations and still active destructive potential. The late Dr. Amos Wilson told us that history is functional and operational for Afrikan people when properly understood and correctly interpreted. It is not and cannot be a simple celebration of personalities and heroes. Its misinterpretation and/or lack of interpretation could mean the contemporary destruction of Afrikan people, without a fight, because we are not prepared. Dr. Wilson also asserted that the manipulation of history causes real changes in the individual personality and is development arresting when it is denied. Those who suffer will be unable and unwilling to challenge those who dominate the world in the manner we have seen so far in this text.

****

Finally, the aspect of Europeans using America and Australia as dumping grounds for criminals during colonial times brings forth another aspect of the case against the European *asili*. That is the European's violence within the European *asili* and against one another.

EUROPEAN VS. EUROPEAN: HISTORY OF PATHOLOGICAL WHITE ON WHITE VIOLENCE

We should not be mistaken to believe that because this European vs. European aspect of the European reality exists that somehow Europeans are simply destructive regardless of whom it is directed towards. There clearly exists a European nationalism, even as enemies come together in solidarity to oppress the world's people of color. The European *asili* dictates the functioning of the European collective as one destructive worldview which happens to bite its own tail rather fiercely on occasions when this behavior does not threaten the loss of believed supremacy over others.

Whether we are viewing the evidence that exists in the Spanish Inquisition, the Italian Inquisition, the European Jewish Holocaust, World Wars, the Cold War, the Peloponnesian War, the American Revolution, the American Civil War, the Bolshevik Revolution, the French Revolution, the Thirty Years War, the War of the Spanish Succession, the War of the Austrian Succession, the Seven Years War, countless "civil wars," or the endless other examples of "tribal" warfare amongst European groups, there is a definitive record of pathological destructiveness on very large scales. This "tribal" warfare includes continuous in-fighting such as that going on in Bosnia, in the former USSR, between Ireland and Britain, and so on. Only very proficient propaganda machines, the fact that warfare fulfills the European *asili*, and the ability to name reality allows Europeans to have their collective self seen as anything other than brutally savage and aggressive nations of people. At the same time, conflict that is often created by European nations in other lands between indigenous peoples is used to show why these "third world" people need Europeans to intervene and to govern them.

It is no wonder that Europeans have become quite proficient at death, destruction and oppression, because they have practiced on one another through history, before using their mastery of destruction on the world.

❖　　　　Even when one remembers the precariousness of life in the eighteenth century, the universal poverty and the great difference between the rich and the poor, one is still hard put to it to understand the callousness and ruthlessness of the authorities in dealing with lawbreakers. They had advanced beyond the stage of cutting off hands and feet, but not very far. Three hundred lashes, more than most men could bear, was not uncommon punishment for the theft of a sheep, and it made no difference if the culprit was a boy of twenty or even less; he was a criminal, the curse was in blood, and that was that. It was almost as if the society was in a state of permanent civil war, the haves against the have-nots, and it hardly needed the French Revolution to remind the English gentry that the mob at home could be just as menacing as any enemy they might encounter in a foreign war. [24]

Torture is another particular aspect of the Europeans' interactions with one another which is noteworthy because of its institutionalized and systematic nature in European societies.

❖   Since Roman law, shaped by some Greek influences,
constituted the greatest body of learned jurisprudence known to
Western tradition, its doctrine of torture influenced strongly the
two revivals of torture that the Western world has experienced—
those of the thirteenth and twentieth centuries. [25]

❖   Torture with red-hot metal, flogging, close constriction of
the body in confinement (the mala mansio, or 'evil house')—some
of these techniques borrowed from the Greeks—constituted
additional forms of torture... Greek methods of capital punishment had included beheading, poison, cruxifiction, beating to
death with clubs, strangling, stoning, hurling from a precipice and
burial alive. [26]

❖   Torture was also generically divided into the *question
ordinaire* and *extraordinaire*—a rough classification to proportion
the severity of the infliction to the gravity of the crime or the
urgency of the case. Thus, in the most usual kind of torment, the
strappado, popularly known as the Moin de Cain, the ordinary
form was to tie the prisoner's hands behind his back with a piece of
iron between them; a cord was then fastened to his wrists by
which, with the aid of a pulley, he was hoisted from the ground
with a weight of one hundred and twenty-five pounds attached to
his feet. In the extraordinary torture, the weight was increased to
two hundred and fifty pounds, and when the victim was raised to a
sufficient height he was dropped and arrested with a jerk that
dislocated his joints, the operation being thrice repeated. [27]

This simply shows, in a few brief examples, the ways in which
European culture has practiced insanity on one another before using it
on the entire world. The lashes, red-hot irons, lynchings, burnings, and
even such things as thumb- screws and the cutting off of hands and

feet, were insidiously mastered at home on European criminals (a relative term) before they were expanded, systematized and intensified on the rest of the world. It is heinous. It is the European *asili.*

These are the facts that we must not be afraid to look at, that we must look at if we are to survive. This is the analysis that must be made. There is no way around this reality because we only have two choices. We either make the proper analysis and move toward true liberation, or we fail to analyze the truth and move toward both prolonged captivity and the slow, or for many the immediate, destruction of ourselves and our children.

THE CONTEMPORARY RECORD

The general madness of the world dominated by the fulfillers of the European *asili* is very evident not only in the historical reality we have examined, but also in the day to day observance of what takes place around the world.

PROTECT AND SERVE?

❖   The 'Good Ol' Boys Roundup', a gathering of law enforcement personnel that has been gathering as long as 15 years and has included FBI, CIA, IRS, DEA and other federal agents, has the racist nature of its activities revealed.

Even Afrikan police officers are not safe from law enforcement.

❖   *"Police officer Reggie Miller felt the barrel of a .38 caliber hand gun pressed against his temple."

*"Miller, who is Black, was operating an undercover prostitution sting assignment on Dec. 14, 1992. He was alone in a government-owned, police department

issued truck. About 8:40 p.m., he was pulled over by the White officer, and suddenly his tour of duty became a nightmare. The six-year veteran of the Metro Nashville Davidson County Police Department didn't have a chance to identify himself."

*"Within minutes, Miller found himself using his body to cushion blows from five White uniformed police officers who had surrounded him. 'There was some choking and some gouging of eyes,' Miller recalls two years after the encounter."

Undercover officer Miller had been stopped only for expired tags. [28]

**"As harrowing as Miller's experience was, *it is not unusual.* [italics mine] Oakland, Calif., police officer Derrik D. Norfleet's 1988 beating at the hands of three of his fellow White officers is similar to Miller's experience, except that his attackers knew him." [29]

There are also two heinous incidents involving New York City transit police officers, Derwin Pannell and Desmond Robinson.

***"On Nov. 18, 1992, while he was attempting to arrest a farebeater in a darkened subway station in the Canarsie section of Brooklyn, N.Y., Pannell was fired upon 21 times and critically wounded in the neck." This was at the hands of White officers. [30]

*** "Evidence in the Robinson case, including forensic accounts by an independent pathologist, suggests that on August 22, 1994, off-duty NYPD Officer Peter Del

Debbio, who is White, approached on-duty Officer Robinson
as he lay on a subway platform, stood over him and shot him
at least four times in the back—a fifth slug was lodged in his
waist pouch.

Robinson, 31, was undercover on the lookout for
pickpockets. He was in a pursuit of a suspect with his gun
drawn, and Del Debbio, also 31, was on his way home to
Long Island when he shot Robinson." [31]

There are many more incidents of undercover
Afrikan police officers being shot or beaten by fellow European officers. Because these Afrikans know the law, they are
able to share with us just how their situations represent gross
violations of police procedure and racism. Their positions as
officers also mean that we know and hear at least a little
noise about their experiences. This is not the case with the
thousands (or millions) of Afrikans who are undoubtedly
brutalized and never heard from.

❖   *"Here in the former 'Cabbage Capital of the World'
(pop. 854), word that the Federal Bureau of Prisons was
shopping for a central Florida site for a new $134 million
prison sent local boosters into overdrive.

' We were on the phone with Washington morning,
noon and night' to snare the 3,200-inmate prison says Jack
Pae, a former Sumter County economic development director.

In a year when the nation's prison population topped
1 million for the first time, Coleman's jockeying is typical of
a vast rush to cash in on the booming incarceration business." [32]

There can be no question about the insanity, abnormality and unsafe nature of the present world reality, especially for Afrikan people. As we see 'Good Ol Boys Roundups', overt hostile and racist attitudes toward Afrikans coming from police and other "law enforcers," disproportionate numbers of Afrikans being incarcerated, and unequitable sentencing based on "race" for the same crimes, we must begin to wonder about how all of this is connected to the business of incarceration. The United States is spending billions of dollars to build new prisons and train new people to incarcerate prisoners. The private and public sector is also making a fortune from prison business and slave labor from prisoners doing everything from making license plates to blue jeans to preparing farmland for agricultural production. Given this scenario of profit, based on the numbers of people incarcerated, there is the very real *probability*, not simply a possibility, that instead of trying to lower crime and incarceration this country will either increase it or keep it steady.

> But so far, the explosive growth in prisons has "not made much of a dent" on crime, says Morris Thigpen, director of the National Institute of Corrections, a Justice Department research arm.
> Meanwhile, there's evidence some social service programs, such as community crime prevention programs, can help reduce crime. [33]

With all of the evidence of the money making function of incarceration as a billion dollar industry, we cannot expect anyone in positions of power and wealth in this country to seriously attempt to stop crime and incarceration. In addition to this, we realize the racist and white world supremacist nature of this country and those who currently dominate the world, as seen by the evidence in this chapter. Therefore, Afrikan people are the most expendable population to be locked away for profit. It is The Maafa all over again. **Wake Up!**

With regard to the nature of the incidents in which Afrikan police officers undercover have found that even they are not safe, people are beginning to try and take action.

> Because of what they see as a fatal trend and not isolated incidents as claimed by police authorities, many Black law enforcement officials have been clamoring for reform of training methods, closer scrutiny of police culture and investigations by federal authorities. [34]

The problem with the demands of Afrikan officials upon recognizing that these are not isolated incidences is that, as was seen with the "Good Ol' Boys Roundup," federal authorities are as much a part of the destructive law enforcement culture as anyone. Afrikans cannot expect to get much relief from insanity from the insane.

Yurugu has a hand in virtually every point listed in this record of madness.

EXTRA! EXTRA! READ ALL ABOUT IT!

The following quotes are a small sampling of what can be seen in the nation's newspapers. These qoutes represent a portion of 9 days in the life of the country, from only a handful of the nation's thousands of newspapers. These are only quotes from newspaper articles, which leads us to only imagine how much more of such information is offered on the radio stations, on television, etc. The pathology is clear.

❖   "In radical feminist enclaves at American colleges and universities, the age old idea of two polarized sexes is dim... Depending upon the classroom and the curriculum, the five "reimagined" genders are, besides the traditional male and female, hermaphrodites, merms—or male pseudo-hermaphrodites—and ferms—or female pseudo-hermaphrodites.

Some feminists teach that the five 'reimagined' genders are female, male, homosexual, bisexual and transsexual." [35]

❖ *"A racially offensive gathering of about 300 local police and federal agents in Tennessee was condemned Wednesday" [36]

*"Officials at the Bureau of Alcohol, Tobacco and Firearms learned of the controversial 'Good Ol' Boys Roundup' soon after the annual gathering of law enforcement officials began in 1980 and have long been aware of allegations of racist activity, the agency's director said yesterday." [37]

*"In testimony yesterday, the chiefs of the ATF, DEA and FBI each admitted that members of their agencies have attended the roundup in the past years..." [38]

*"Committee Chairman Orrin G. Hatch (R-Utah) said his staff had obtained three affidavits from a retired law enforcement official and two women who had attended past roundups and who alleged that 'multiple rapes' and the use of illegal drugs took place at the gathering." [39]

*"According to reports first published in the *Washington Times*, T-shirts were sold at the retreat that showed Rev. Martin Luther King Jr.'s face under a target..." [40]

❖ *"Ignoring President Clinton's declaration on

Wednesday that affirmative action "has been good for America," the governing regents of the University of California voted last night to stop admitting students, hiring professors and awarding contracts on the basis of race and sex."

*"'We cannot tolerate university policies or practices that violate fundamental fairness, trampling individual rights to create and give preferences to group rights,' he said in urging the board to dismantle the university's affirmative action programs." [41] This was said by California's governor.

❖   "A Baltimore Circuit Court Judge sentenced Michael Edward Joseph Reirtz yesterday to two consecutive life terms for bludgeoning his grandparents to death with a baseball bat as they slept in their Guilford home nearly a year ago." [42]

❖   "A 26-year-old Baldwin man received a life sentence yesterday for sexually attacking a Towson-area middle school student in a parking garage stairwell at Towson Town Center last year." [43]

❖   *"Two children walking to school yesterday found the body of a man who had been stabbed at least 50 times lying near a side entrance to a Northwest Baltimore elementary school."

*"It is the fifth time this school year that a body has been found on school property, and the third time that students have made the discovery." [44]

❖   "A local Alaskan government has filed a $428 million claim against four federal agencies on behalf of 70 Inupiat

Eskimos exposed to radiation in government medical experiments, officials said." [45]

❖   "Robert Young, 34, and Stanley Rich, 29, both of Jacksonville, Fla., face up to 17 years in prison if convicted of federal charges they burned a cross in April 1992 to intimidate white business owners who hire blacks. The wooden cross was stolen from an Easter display." [46]

❖   "Authorities have gone public with a nationwide search for New York high school teacher Glen Harris, 33, and a 15-year-old student known as Christina. The pair fled March 7 when the girl's mother found a love letter the teen had written to Harris." [47]

❖   *"A pregnant scientist and 25 co-workers unwittingly consumed contaminated food or water and have been exposed to radioactive materials at the National Institutes of Health."

*" It is under investigation, but the nature of what we know suggests that it was not accidental' said Anne Thomas, an NIH spokeswoman." [48]

❖   "Three days after the New Jersey Supreme Court ruled that Alan Gubernat could not force his son Scott to take his last name, police say the father shot the $3^{1/2}$-year-old boy to death, and then killed himself." [49]

❖   "Eric Star Smith, 34, was ordered held in Torrance County, N.M., in lieu of $500,000 bail on charges he decapitated his 14 year-old son on a road-side. Smith, of Parker,

Ariz., was arrested Saturday after several motorists saw him hacking at his son's head. Smith's older son, age 13, escaped. Investigators still are searching for the weapon. Prosecutor Ron Lopez said Smith has been 'delusional' and 'thought his child was the devil.'" [50]

❖   *"Secret documents show researches for Phillip Morris gave electric shocks to college students to see if stress would increase smoking, and studied hyperactive schoolchildren as potential future customers, a congressman said Monday."

*"Research from 1974-78 in which scientists collaborated with the Chesterfield County, Va., school system to identify hyperactive third-graders to see if they were likely as teens to 'discover the advantage of self-stimulation via nicotine.'" [51]

❖   "Smoking among eighth-graders surged 30 percent between 1991 and 1994." [52]

Not only is there madness in the events captured here in the nation's newspapers, but we must be able to understand the demoralizing and incapacitating effect this has on the people who live in such a nation. Afrikan people are especially susceptible to a double edged sword. First there is the physical danger of being Afrikan in America; vividly reconfirmed by the 'Good Ol' Boys Roundup' where virtually every law enforcement agency (FBI, DEA, Customs, IRS, city police forces, etc.), supposedly designed for our protection, had representatives involving themselves in a gathering that had "nigger hunting licenses" among other things. Secondly, for Afrikan people there is also the mental strain of existing in such a hostile environment, combined with the bombardment of psychological attacks. And, despite what people would like to believe, the myriad examples of madness that we witness and experience, for example the madness of the 'Good Ol' Boys Roundup', are not aberrations or isolated instances. They represent the functioning of the European *asili*, an *asili* that allowed and perpetuated The Maafa, the European Jewish Holocaust, lynching, rape, colonialism, imperialism, the annihilation of Native Americans and any number of abnormal and insane behaviors, none of which were happenstance or unusual for the European *asili*.

The people who call others paranoid and crazy for speaking about conspiracies are actually themselves having an unhealthy denial reaction to a world of conspiracy and madness. At the same time, those they criticize are at least questioning the madness that cannot be denied by a healthy, conscious individual. Regardless of the angle from which you view this, this madness, conspiratorial and otherwise, represents a tremendous problem for the psychological health of the human beings subjected to it.

It might be helpful to look at the schematic on the following page outlining the possible impact of the aforementioned mental and physical strain.

TRAUMA CYCLE

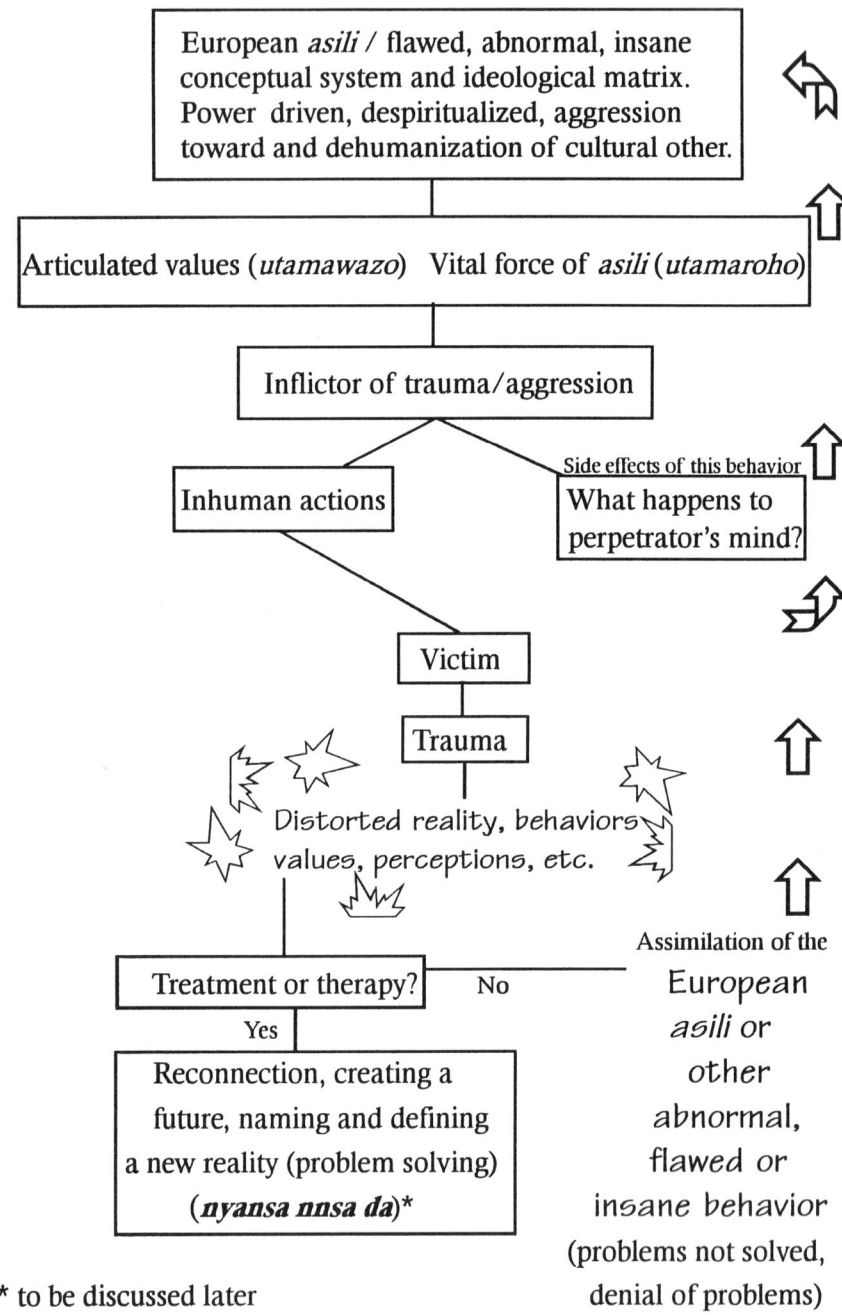

There are many implications and inferences to be drawn from the schematic presented on the previous page. We have examined the cause of the distorted reality seen in the schematic and will address the nature of this distortion later in this work. We can see the European *asili* as the capstone and generator of a culture that inflicts trauma and aggression upon others. The *utamawazo* and *utamaroho* extend from this *asili* and lead those in the culture into the fulfillment of the *asili*. Dr. Marimba Ani's *utamaroho* concept is one that has not yet been dealt with in this work. It represents a culture's will, vital force, or energy to collectively move and be inspired to fulfill the *asili*.

So, you have a culture's people under the influence of the *asili*, its *utamawazo*, and *utamaroho*. These individuals go on to manifest the thought and behavior that is generated by these aspects of the *asili*. Subsequently, Europeans have institutionalized aggression, imperialism and the infliction of trauma upon other people. This trauma is often manifested in inhuman actions on the part of Europeans. History has an enormous amount of evidence to this effect, whether we look at The Maafa; the slaughter, mutilation and devastation of Afrikans in the Belgian Kongo and elsewhere on the continent during colonization; the decimation of Native Americans and the colonization of the few who remain on reservations; and the list goes on and on as we have seen in this chapter.

The victims of these inhuman actions are traumatized and their reality is distorted as a result. The mental and physical oppression and brutality of the aggressive fulfillers of the European *asili*, manifested in such inhuman actions, alters the behaviors, values, perceptions, etc., of the victim. This trauma is of course compounded by the denial of the victim's suffering and justification of the actions of the perpetrators. The victim is chastised and denied the right to the normal behavior of resistance and crying out from the pain of trauma. Therefore, as we move down the schematic and look at treatment, a very real and important question is, what treatment? For many victims, including Afrikan people throughout the world, the trauma isn't even acknowledged and the victim's distorted reality is deemed normal by the perpetrator. Any severely problematic behaviors are blamed on the victim.

In *The Maafa & Beyond*, the framework was laid for the usefulness of historical memory, as well as naming and defining our own experiences, as therapeutic measures to begin the restoration of Afrikan people to health. However, that is only a beginning. The concept of *nyansa nnsa da*, which will be discussed in the next chapter, also represents a conceptual beginning for the healing process and there is more work to be done as to specific structural frameworks and sociotherapeutic models that will represent treatment and therapy for Afrikan people. (See chapters, "Spiritual Dimensions of *Nyansa Nnsa Da* and Afrikan Catharsis" and "Healing As A Process: Healthy Coping Mechanisms, Expanded Conceptions of Treatment and Sociotherapy for a People," chapters 4 and 5) We thus begin to recognize our trauma, deal with the pain of it, recognize our distorted behaviors and perceptions, and revolt against the madness to create a future for ourselves.

However, as we look further at the schematic we see that one of the consequences associated with Afrikan people not receiving treatment or therapy from the insanity and pain of the current world reality is that many of them become fulfillers of the European *asili* or express manifestations of inadequate coping measures, both of which can lead to an inability to *accurately* address and solve the problems we face as a people. The effects of this scenario are also cyclical as we can see on the schema; where the end product of not receiving therapy or treatment leads us back to where we began with the European *asili*. Thus, you have Afrikan people, and others, who have historically been the victims of the European *asili*, becoming its supporters, perpetuators and biggest cheerleaders, manifesting this by expressing European *utamawazo.* Hence, the syndrome known as "selling out" is really a pathological reaction to the trauma of oppression and mental incarceration when one goes without treatment or therapy. As we shall see later, Kobi Kambon categorizes these phenomena excellently by using the concept of Cultural/Psychological Misorientation.

Also, it should be noted that if the victim of the European *asili* becomes severely misoriented, then the aggression toward the "cultural other" is actually going to be aggression toward self and people like self. For example, when the "cultural other" that the fulfillers of the European *asili* act aggressively toward is Afrikan, then an Afrikan who goes through the trauma cycle, and becomes a fulfiller of the *asili,* will act aggressively and/or devalue Afrikan people, including his or herself. This is what we have long called self-hatred. Self-hatred is an unavoidable consequence of Afrikan people adopting the European *asili.* This cyclical effect of trauma, such as in The Maafa, that leads ultimately to an adoption of the European *asili,* obviously also has other consequences such as materialism, power drive, devaluation of women, etc.

This brings us to an interesting point. In dealing with the concept of *asili* we can begin to understand that Europeans are not bound to a certain conscious expression of a behavioral pattern simply because of skin color, just as Afrikan people are not bound to any conscious expression of behavior because of skin color; this is apparent especially in the number of Afrikans whose actions have deemed them enemies of their people. The question is, what is the *asili* or ideological matrix that a person is functioning within? Or, more precisely, what *utamawazo* has been the foundation of a person's development. It is more the *asili* than the ambiguous "race" concept that determines thought and behavior, although the complexity and power of Melanin might lead us to consider the effects of its relative absence in Europeans. This is an area in which we can gain further understanding by looking at Kobi Kambon's concepts of Afrikan

Self-Extension Orientation (ASEO) and Afrikan Self-Consciousness (ASC).

Kambon asserts that Melanin and its dominant presence in human beings is a determiner and vital part of the Afrikan Self-Extension Orientation. The Afrikan Self-Extension Orientation is similar to Ani's *asili* concept. It also represents the seeds and germinating principles of a culture, and is an undergirding and immutable part of the Afrikan personality. Kambon also defines it as being biogenetically determined and present in all Afrikan people, due in large part to Melanin dominance. It is the Afrikan Self-Consciousness which is the consciously expressed aspect of the Afrikan personality. It is determined by and interconnected with the Afrikan Self-Extension Orientation, but also determined to a degree by environmental factors. Thus, although Kambon asserts that all Afrikans possess the Afrikan Self-Extension Orientation, he also says that their conscious day to day behavior, the Afrikan Self-Consciousness, can be determined to a degree by the environment. Therefore, coming back to the original point, those Afrikans we view as sellouts have had the Afrikan Self-Consciousness interfered with and influenced by the European *asili* and its *utamawazo*. The confusion and mental instability of such Afrikans, using Kambon's model, could possibly relate to the conflict that is occurring between their Afrikan Self-Extension Orientation and their corrupted Afrikan Self-Consciousness. (The implications of this imbalance will be dealt with in Chapters 4 and 5)

With this understanding, we do not have to have consternation when we find that "every brother ain't a brother." Linda James Meyers, in speaking about the assumptions and principles of the Eurocentric view, explains that,

> These assumptions and principles are at the roots of
> racism and other societal "isms" and are thus sub-optimal—less

than the best to achieve harmonious interpersonal relationships.
To the extent one internalizes the conceptual system, security and
well-being is external to the individual and one is perceptually
looking outside oneself to find someone to be "better than." *This
realization does not mean that all people acknowledging European
descent are racist, but rather anyone buying into the conceptual
system is at risk of its natural consequences, which are the segmen-
tation and self-alienation fostered by the separation of the material
and spiritual.* [Italics mine] [53]

Though our analysis and language are somewhat harsher
regarding the Eurocentric view or *asili*, we utilize Meyers' emphasis
on those who buy into the conceptual system being at risk of its
consequences and extend this to all people immersed in European world
domination that might buy into the *asili* or more precisely its
utamawazo. The key is whether you buy into the conceptual system or
not; that conceptual system outlined earlier in terms of the European
asili.

Now, it is true that individuals are much more likely to be
attached to the *asili* of their cultural group, but the resultant behavior is
not solely determined by the ambiguous and faulty nature of the "race"
concept, as the concept of *asili* clarifies. (This concept will be dealt
with later in the chapter, "The 'Concept' of Race") Thought and
behavior patterns are more accurately based on the *asili* that is
generated by a particular cultural group to which an individual belongs.
Individuals within a particular culture subsequently adapt the *asili* of
that culture as a natural consequence of membership in the cultural
group. Therefore Europeans, whom we tend to classify as "white" are
more than likely to exhibit the thought and behavior of the European
asili, as a result of socialization, education, cultural values
transmission, etc. Additionally, existing in this European-dominated
society of the U.S. and the world, many Afrikan people also adopt

aspects of the European *asili* through these same means, as well as through the trauma cycle. Many other Afrikans in the U.S. exist within this society as a culture within a culture, adopting something different from the European *asili* in many ways and similar in others, while either denying or only partially fulfilling their own *asili*. However, Europeans typically and expectedly fulfill their European *asili*.

Given these facts, questions can be asked and answered. Can European people extricate themselves from the European *asili*? Marimba Ani says that,

> A European who understands the nature of her culture,
> but does not share the *utamaroho* of her culture (a highly improb-
> able circumstance, since it contradicts the *asili*), must act to
> change the culture's *utamaroho*, to get rid of its "carriers": That is
> her only recourse, if she is honest. [54]

Dr. Marimba Ani answers the question, explaining that it is possible, although unlikely, for a European to oppose their *asili*. Hence we have an understanding of the *asili* as not being an interchangeable concept with that of "race," which is predominantly based on skin color. This also explains why, *despite* skin color, we have such people as Supreme Court Justice Clarence Thomas who have had the European *asili*, via the *utamawazo*, imposed upon them and of course Kambon's concepts also help us to better conceive of this phenomenon. Thomas's Afrikanness has not changed in terms of pigmentation, but the European ideological matrix he adheres to is detrimental to Afrikan people in his expression and acting upon the European *utamawazo*. We might even explain his opposition to things such as affirmative action, which he himself has benefited from, as logical according to the schematic we have presented. As an Afrikan victim of the European *asili*, Clarence Thomas has gone through the cycle and is now fulfilling the *asili* which has victimized Afrikan people, subsequently allowing him to be aggressive toward the "cultural other" or Afrikan people. This is manifested in his attack on an affirmative action program that he benefited from as an Afrikan. His adoption of the *asili* was inevitably aided not only by his being Afrikan in America and enduring that trauma, but ultimately by his matriculation in some of the more prestigious institutions in this country that perpetuate and fulfill the European *asili*. One of the most significant examples of Clarence Thomas' infection with Yurugu was found in a *USA Today* article speaking about the recent stands, by Thomas, against affirmative action and his comments to long time friend Armstrong Williams.

> In a syndicated column written by Williams, Thomas added a religious dimension to his views: "You cannot embrace racism to deal with racism. Its not Christian," Thomas is quoted as saying. "If I type one word at my word processor in one opinion against them (whites), I break God's law." [55]

Clarence Thomas, while attacking Afrikan people in his decisions, has declared it would be against God's law to write a decision against Europeans. Having adopted the European *asili* and expressing the *utamawazo*, Thomas has become a European nationalist and despite the criminal behavior of Europeans against Afrikans, he will not write a decision against the criminal. He is ill. He is a delusional victim of the European *asili*. So, is what we have traditionally referred to as a "sellout" simply someone who has chosen a different path or is ambiguously "acting white?" The answer is in fact no, because the European *asili* is extremely damaging to Afrikan people and choosing it is not simply personal choice. It really isn't a choice at all, it is a pathological denial of the Afrikan self. On the other hand, if we see people like Thomas as simply "acting white" or "selling out" which are arguably a matter of choice, they are more difficult to deal with and hold accountable. Using the concept of *asili*, we have a much better means of holding "sell outs" accountable and articulating exactly why they are absolutely detrimental to their people and not just exercising choice, mainly because of the nature of the European *asili*.

Now that we understand what white world supremacy, manifest in the European *asili*, actually is, we can act upon it. Yurugu is not mystical and incapable of defeat in the way that many people view white world supremacy. You often hear people coining phrases such as "that's the way of the world" or speaking about how crazy the world is. More often than not they are saying these things not realizing that the world can be changed and in fact this is not the way the world is supposed to be. Many have never known anything other than the present madness and consequently think madness is the norm. However, we intend to do away with this limited view of reality.

SYSTEMATIC ENEMY ANALYSIS

Given the pervasiveness of destruction and distortion imposed upon the Afrikan existence, there is a need for constant vigilance and decoding of our present world reality. This constant vigilance and decoding is what I call Systematic Enemy Analysis. It is an analysis of the enemy, which is the European conceptual and ideological system or *asili* and its fulfillers, on a continuous basis. Once we understand how to utilize the concepts of *asili* and *utamawazo* to identify Yurugu in thought and behavior, our decoding must be of everyday images, institutions, language, people, behavior, media, etc. As tedious as some may see such an exercise, it is essential for consciousness transformation and sanity. We must be persistent in questioning and analyzing every aspect of our existence, including our own behavior and thought, in order to identify and purge the enemy (European *asili* and its fulfillers) from our consciousness and our lives. When we seem to be overdoing it and "always talking that black stuff" when it comes to daily analysis of white world supremacy and distorted images, we are most likely only beginning to approach a satisfactory level of efficiency and consistency for a liberated existence into the 21st century.

Systematic Enemy Analysis is absolutely essential due to our inundation with the imposition of the enemy in the body of propaganda. Noam Chomsky is a European who has adequately described the American propaganda machine as "the most awesome propaganda system that has ever existed in world history." [56] Chomsky goes further to offer commentary that substantiates the need for persistent and constant analysis of Yurugu.

> Terms like "the free world" and "the national interest" and so on are mere terms of propaganda. One shouldn't take them seriously for a moment. They are designed, often very consciously, in order to try to block thought and understanding. For example, about the 1940's there was a decision, made in public-relations circles to introduce terms like "free enterprise" and "free world" and so on instead of the conventional descriptive terms like "capitalism." Part of the reason was to insinuate somehow that the systems of control and domination and aggression to which those with power were committed here were in fact a kind of freedom. That's just vulgar propaganda cxcrciscs. We are inundated with this every moment of our lives, and to the extent that many of us internalize it, one has to defend oneself against it, but once one realizes what's going on it's not very hard to do. [57]

Systematic Enemy Analysis is for us a defense against Yurugu and the propaganda machine of white world supremacy. It has as an end result, the detection of pathology and threats to true liberation, as well as the purging of these pathologies and threats from our lives. The way in which we carry out this Systematic Enemy Analysis is to apply Ani's critique of Yurugu and the European *asili* to all areas of our lives. As we mentioned, we must consistently analyze images, institutions, language, people, behavior, media, etc. The European *asili* as the overall guiding framework of European culture touches all of these areas and many more, and is in fact reinforced by the behavior and thought it generates.

Dr. Marimba Ani laid out several areas of the European *asili* we might pay attention to in *Yurugu*. These areas include institutionalized religion—christianism, ideology and values, aesthetic, self-image, image of others, intracultural behavior, and behavior towards others.

Institutionalized Religion

According to Dr. Ani, institutionalized religion is characterized by proselytizing, its anti-nature perspective, hierarchy, white supremacist nature, patriarchal orientation, and non-spirituality. In this book I have not dealt specifically with religion because of its complexity and overriding problematic position in the lives of Afrikan people in America. It is a topic that deserves a complete analysis in a volume of its own. However, it is sufficient to say that religion has had many undesirable, destructive and pathological implications for Afrikan people who have adopted the religious practices of other cultures.

For an individual conducting Systematic Enemy Analysis, the question should be asked as to the nature and context of their faith and/or place of worship. Does one's place of worship embody white supremacist values by continuing to depict Jesus as a "fair skinned" European male for example? Not only does this represent an accepted lie (something that should have no place in Sacred space and time) that flies in the face of all evidence, logic and biblical description, but it is also white supremacist (and therefore psychologically damaging to Afrikans) from a symbolic point of view. The symbolism of a

European Jesus imposed upon people who are not European does a great deal to subconsciously deify Europeans in the eyes of those who are not European. This can be seen in numerous ways from the Afrikan throughout history who fails to see their enslaver as a mortal enemy to contemporary Afrikans whose religious ideology of turn the other cheek tends to only apply to European oppressors; the cheek is seldom if ever turned when a wrong is committed by another Afrikan. In an extreme case we may witness a Clarence Thomas claiming it to be against God to write a decision against Europeans, as we witnessed earlier in this chapter.

The bottom line is that if one's chosen faith is antithetical to liberation, self-preservation, or clear thinking and enemy identification, it is subject to Systematic Enemy Analysis. The end result, then, should be the rethinking of one's faith and/or place of worship. This is difficult for many people to do, but it is absolutely necessary if the faith and/or place of worship is a fulfiller of the European *asili* and functionary of oppression. The degree to which we fail in this type of analysis is directly proportionate to our failure to achieve sanity and liberation. What kind of statement are we making to ourselves psychologically if we have never even thought to return to the spiritual systems of Mother Afrika, instead of clinging to the systems we have adopted while in exile? This is a question that deserves further analysis because I'm sure we would find that this is an area that affirms our lack of confidence in our Afrikanity and our real belief in the spiritual and conceptual systems of Yurugu.

So, in our Systematic Enemy Analysis we would call into question any faith that expresses the need to save (convert) others from their own faiths. This is the proselytizing Dr. Ani mentioned. Other questions should center around the culturally destructive practice of missionary work, as well the exclusion of women from positions of governance and spiritual guidance within religious hierarchy. These things have manifested pathology in the Western need to control and impose itself upon the world.

Ideology and Values

Dr. Ani gives as characteristics of this area of the European *asili*, things such as money = symbol of value, materialism, universal dominance, white supremacy, and devaluation of spirit. As we engage in Systematic Enemy Analysis there is the need to identify these characteristics as they are manifest throughout the culture. Our consistency and persistence must span from the largest institutions to what we might view as the most insignificant of influences. For example, are we aware of the role of cartoons and animated features in cultivating the ideology and values of Yurugu in our children?

The animated feature "Pocahontas" as an example, this is a children's film which used animation and music to capture the hearts and minds of America's children and many adults. At the same time, "Pocahontas" represented a film which perpetuated gross historical inadequacies which served the interests of European cultural memory and white supremacy. The character of John Smith was idealized in physical appearance and philosophy. He was made to be the "ideal" blond haired, blue eyed, square jawed, European hero; this is an image that is not close to the historical man. His molestation and rape of the historical adolescent Pocahontas was fabricated into a mutual love affair between adults standing on equal footing. Equally, his historical complicity and leadership in the rape of Native American people and land was transformed into this movie "hero" being a mediator between two hostile camps each filled with hate; the role of Europe in aggression and destruction was trivialized and diluted as the false perspective was given of two peoples, Europeans and Native Americans, being equally guilty of hatred while Pocahontas and John Smith represented the voices of peace and reason. This "cartoon" served the ideology and values of European culture, while redefining history in the interest of that culture.

Systematic Enemy Analysis dictates that we see through the pomp and circumstance of a Disney animated feature film to identify "Pocahontas" as a film insulting to Native Americans and serving the interests of white world supremacy justification and maintenance: the enemy. Systematic Enemy Analysis compels us to apply such critiques across the board and to purge this type of influence from the lives our children and ourselves.

Aesthetic

In *The Maafa & Beyond* we addressed the importance of the Afrikan Cultural Aesthetic as a component of liberation struggle and Afrikan identity/mental health. Dr. Ani gave several characteristics of the aesthetic within the European *asili* in *Yurugu*. Some of these characteristics are that it is artificial, non-spiritual, white, pristine, rational. Engaging in Systematic Enemy Analysis we should identify and perpetuate our own aesthetic, while eliminating the vehicles of the European aesthetic from our own physical and psychological space, i.e. our institutions, homes and minds. The reader is referred to The Maafa & Beyond for the discussion of the Afrikan Cultural Aesthetic.

These are just a few areas in which we can illustrate the applicability of Systematic Enemy Analysis rather easily. The analysis will not always be so simplistic and straight forward. It will require critical thinking and scrutiny more often than not. There are many, many more areas that we will necessarily have to address as well. In Chapter 7 of this book, the discussion is extended in terms of offering areas of the present world reality that need to be examined. This too is Systematic Enemy Analysis in practice.

****

In the next chapter we begin to look conceptually at how to *attack* the current "way of the world" and utilize the dynamic quality of reality (The word "attack" implies an offensive position as opposed to a reactionary or defensive one). We should understand that reality is dynamic and not a stagnant, unchangeable entity. Essential in this attack is the realization that we cannot achieve liberation, which is a return to The Way, operating within the ideological and cultural matrix which is the European *asili* or Yurugu. We have lost the war before we have begun, even if we do win a battle here or there in our struggle to be a liberated people. We must shape an old/new Afrikan conscious-ness and emerge from the trauma and devastation that Yurugu has subjected Afrikan people to. This is unfortunately even applicable to many of our Afrikan nationalists and Pan-Afrikanists who have not yet reached the point of waging their revolutionary struggle on their own conceptual terms. Even Pan-Afrikanism will fail when grounded in the ideological and cultural core of Europe, using their terms, definitions, constructs and deep-consciousness level thought processes. We must wage a revolution of reality, changing paradigms and concepts. We must return to The Way.

PART 2

REVOLUTION!!!

CHAPTER 3

○○○○○○○○○

PREPARATION FOR THE RETURN

In order for Afrikan people to become truly liberated and return to The Way, it should be clear that we must create an old/new Afrikan *consciousness* as our means of fulfilling the Afrikan *asili* within which our activities should originate. This means that the concepts we utilize and the language used to express them must be developed by and for Afrikan people. Put simply, if we are to build our own institutions, we must determine for ourselves how they will operate, what their ideologies will be and not be dependent on the bankrupt ideologies of Western society currently claiming to be the standard. If we are to aspire to become better human beings, we must define what a good human being is for ourselves according to a tradition of harmony and order in the universe, which means we do not aspire to the current power driven, despiritualized, material, individualistic European standards. We cannot use the concepts and constructs of an abnormal, flawed and insane European *asili* as a means for our struggle toward sanity and liberation: a return to The Way. This is why it is necessary to create an old/new Afrikan consciousness to fulfill our *asili*. Afrikan people have been *systematically* destroyed and must therefore systematically reconstruct themselves. We must reconstitute Afrikan *utamawazo* to return to The Way.

When I say old/new in reference to a consciousness, I am using Oba T'Shaka's term to convey the fact that in order to extricate ourselves from the present madness, which includes inactivity and a lack of resistance on the level of the masses of Afrikans, we must use our Afrikan historical and ancestral consciousness to aid us in the creation of a NEW reality. We must employ Sankofa, looking back to move forward, in order to successfully name and define a new Afrikan reality after so much destruction and devastation.

For example, Sankofa in my previous book, *The Maafa & Beyond*, in one instance was manifested, in this context, as the chapter entitled "The Ancient African Model," where we looked back to the genius of the Afrikan past as a model for where we should be going. Sankofa was also evident with the general theme of ancestral connections in the book.

In addition, we should understand that the concept of Sankofa aids us in implying that there is an existent order that we are going back to fetch. There is a natural order of the universe, a natural balance of Afrikan consciousness and connectedness that has never left our people. We must simply reclaim and summon that which has remained in us. In creating a new reality, we are simply returning to the natural order. We are essentially not creating, except in the sense that we create conditions that allow us to be more receptive to our spirit and the natural order of the cosmos.

The creation of a new reality is not necessarily a task that each individual must perform, but those of us dealing with creating new conceptions of reality must develop these in a way that they can begin to impact the masses. The process will be one in which we first establish the theoretical and conceptual constructs and then develop the institutions that will serve as vehicles for a new reality to begin impacting the lives of sisters and brothers everyday. This is the second stage of how we reconstitute Afrikan *utamawazo* that fulfills our *asili*. The first stage of identifying Yurugu has already begun.

In this chapter we will begin to lay the *foundations* for concepts which *prepare* us to move along the road to liberation, to return to The Way. Twi words are used to describe the concepts or levels of struggle to be discussed, because along with the discussion of language in the introduction of this work,

Language skills not only put us in touch with the past, they free the human imagination. Connecting symbols in new ways, we can conceive of life other than it is. Language—both spoken and written—distinguishes human beings as creatures aware of our limitations and ultimate mortality, yet able to dream and hope for a future better than the present. [1]

This statement on language concisely outlines and re-emphasizes the profound nature of our use of Twi terms, or any Afrikan languages we may choose to use for that matter. In one sense they connect us to the Afrikan past that many of us don't physically know. Also, any time we are trying to create a new reality, we must free our imaginations to wander beyond the European *asili*. The use of the Twi terms *nkosoɔ* and *daakye abra bɔ* allows us to communicate two very important concepts in the next chapter that will make this reference to language functional in the most basic, grassroots applications. And, perhaps most important is that we can conceive of life other than it is simply by using language and then moving on from there! Language allows us to move beyond our so called limits to first *think* about a better future. This is of paramount importance to the concept of *nyansa nnsa da*, or thought without boundaries, which will be dealt with in this chapter. As we shall see, *nyansa nnsa da* is a concept that will guide everything we do as we move to create a new reality in our fulfillment of the Afrikan *asili* and return to The Way. *Nyansa nnsa da* will guide and frame the activities of the other two levels of struggle to be discussed, *daakye abra b ɔ* and *nkosoɔ*, as well as allowing us to create an old/new Afrikan consciousness. *Nyansa nnsa da*, thought without boundaries, is the big picture. It is the vision within which we can begin to move. It is like a flashlight that lights the way as we walk through the darkness of this world. So it is with *nyansa nnsa da* that we begin.

NYANSA NNSA DA (THOUGHT WITHOUT BOUNDARIES)

Nyansa nnsa da means "wisdom is never exhausted" in Twi. This term was chosen to refer to the concept of Afrikan people naming and defining a new reality by thinking beyond the limits of our present reality, thought without boundaries. In other words, our thoughts must know no limits, so that our actions will know no limits until we return to The Way. *Nyansa nnsa da* will be required to break the mental fetters that make us believe that "the world is just the way it is and we must learn how to navigate within it." It is a concept that in the simplest terms will allow us to change the world we know into the world we want to exist; one where there is peace, harmony, balance and all of the other things that   indicate sanity. From the perspective of health, Dr. Deepak Chopra shares that,

> ... there is incredible liberation in realizing that you can change your world—including your body—*simply by changing your perception.* How you perceive yourself is causing immense changes in your body right now. To give an example: In America and England, mandatory retirement at age 65 sets an arbitrary cutoff date for social usefulness. The day before a worker turns 65, he contributes labor and value to society; the day after, he becomes one of society's dependents. Medically, the results of this perceptual shift can be disastrous. In the first few years after retirement, heart attack and cancer rates soar, and early death overtakes men who were otherwise healthy before they retired. "Early retirement death," as the syndrome is called, depends on the perception that one's useful days are over; this is only a perception, but for someone who holds it firmly, it is enough to create disease and death. By comparison, in societies where old age is accepted as part of the social fabric, elders remain extremely vigorous—lifting, climbing, and bending in ways that we do not accept as normal in

our elderly. [2]

Although the quote from Dr. Chopra is speaking about health, it is significant because it speaks directly to the ability of thought processes and perceptions to impact and change reality. *Nyansa nnsa da* will be required to first **conceive** of upturning a rotten, insane world reality and then acting upon the conception and creation of a new reality; for if we cannot conceive of something, chances of it ever happening are slim. To speak about the ultimate liberation of Afrikan people without ever conceiving of Afrikan people being truly liberated or envisioning our triumph and control of our own destinies in this lifetime, is self-defeating. You really have got to believe and be able to see it happening in your mind's eye. There must be no doubt in our minds that these things can happen, not simply because of faith, but on the ability to foresee liberation and then initiate whatever action is necessary to fulfill the vision and make it a reality.

Again, Deepak Chopra gives a validation of this from the perspective of health.

There exists in every person a place that is free from disease, that never feels pain, that cannot age or die. When you go to this place, limitations which all of us accept cease to exist. They are not even entertained as a possibility.

This place is called perfect health.

Visits to this place may be very brief, or they may last for many years. Even the briefest visit, however, instills a profound change. As long as you are there, the assumptions that hold true for ordinary existence are altered, and the possibility of a new existence, higher and more ideal, begins to flower. [3]

Nyansa nnsa da, thought without boundaries, allows us to have pride and take great comfort in the FACT that true liberation and the destruction of white world supremacy are both within our control and influence as Afrikan people. It is for us that place inside that is free of Yurugu and in which limitations do not exist. We simply must make liberation happen by visiting that place inside that is limitless thought. The same *nyansa nnsa da* that allows us to actually SEE these eventualities will also play a pivotal role in bringing these things to fruition. The assumptions of our ordinary existence are altered as *nyansa nnsa da* empowers us to see the world in a completely different way. A future of freedom, peace, sanity, self-determination, self-sufficiency, self-knowledge, harmony, prosperity, reciprocity, justice, compassion, balance and order is possible if we name that future, define that future and move toward creating it.

Nyansa nnsa da is the breeding ground for ideas. It is the breaking and shifting of paradigms. It allows the mind to be free of narrow thinking, constricted realities and dogmatic concepts. Limitless thought is the ability to conceive of things that, to some, would be considered the "wildest dreams."

Nyansa nnsa da also explains another reason why it was necessary for us to examine and castigate the European *asili*, above and beyond glancing at its still detrimental and destructive impact on Afrikan people and the world today. The mere recognition of the insanity inherent in the European *asili*, Yurugu, allows us to begin to think outside of it. If you're speaking about liberation yet you cannot step back and recognize Yurugu for the sickness that it is, you will not be able to think outside of Yurugu, which is necessary for liberation. In fact, you wouldn't necessarily want to think beyond the limits of a reality you perceive as normal and valid, as is the case with many Afrikans who have yet to identify Yurugu. If you cannot move outside of the European *asili* then you are not going to achieve true liberation (self-knowledge, self-definition, psychological health, self-determination and self-sufficiency: a return to The Way), because the nature of the European *asili* is diametrically opposed to these goals. It turns out in truth that it must either be liberation or the European *asili.* This is a case where you cannot have your cake and eat it too. There is no complementarity between the two.

We must take only the best that European people have been able to create, and no doubt they have achieved many things. However, we can only integrate what accomplishments can be separated from the European *asili,* i.e. some of the technological advances. We say some technological advances because we recognize that much of what the West has been able to accomplish technologically has been based on *nyansa yereketse,* which is an Akan phrase meaning "distorted wisdom." Progress for the sake of progress is distorted wisdom. In *Yurugu,* Dr. Marimba Ani writes about "Progress as Ideology," and quotes from Henry Skolimnowski's article "The Scientific World View and the Illusions of Progress." Skolimnowski believes that "Progress has been a cover-up for Western man's follies in manipulating the external world." [4]

In this we find that one may say progress is the fact that in the West we have better medical care, but the West has stolen from, destroyed or attempted to destroy every culture it has come in contact with. This theft and savagery contributes to the advantages the West may seem to have in areas such as medical care. One may say that in the West we live better, but have also caused ecological imbalances; "Our superior scientific understanding did not prevent us from radically misreading the behavior of Nature." [5] One might ask, does the West possess superior scientific understanding at all if it cannot create without destroying?, a feat which many other ancient traditional cultures mastered.

It definitely has taken wisdom for the West to achieve much of its accomplishments, but it is distorted wisdom that figures out how to split atoms and then creates weapons of destruction; that aquires an understanding of molecular biology and then spends billions on biological and chemical warfare. This is *nyansa yereketse* and should be avoided as *nyansa nnsa da* helps us conceive of a new reality. And, had the West not traveled the world "spreading civilization" what might traditional cultures have been able to achieve for the past 500, and more, years in harmony with nature and humanity. Although all cultures have had conflict, none has roamed the earth with the anti-human, anti-nature, destructiveness of the European. *Nyansa Yereketse* is the progress of Europe.

So, avoiding *nyansa yereketse*, we can take some of the technological achievements of Europeans. Having done this, we weave these elements into an old/new Afrikan consciousness and reality informed by the Afrikan past and developed in the Afrikan present to create an Afrikan future. This must be done while discarding the European *asili* itself.

Nyansa nnsa da allows all of our activities to be concerted, creative, relentless, strategic, ingenious and wise. It dictates that we occupy a place in history capable of changing the course of history itself. Our ability to employ limitless thought means we can change the world, just as Plato, Socrates and Aristotle altered the course of European thought. The difference is that we will create a balanced, spiritual, sane reality. We can make a more appropriate comparison to the time when Imhotep achieved such a high level of humanity and God-force in Kemet (Egypt) that we still struggle to comprehend his genius and that of those who would follow him.

With the concept of *nyansa nnsa da* in place, there are obligations and directives for Afrikan people. We have already mentioned that there are many levels at which individuals will contribute to true liberation, namely *nkoso ⊃and daakye abra b⊃*. On the level of *nyansa nnsa da*, where we are naming and defining reality, the task is to begin establishing a framework within which all of our activities and creative thought can function. We can thus approach the deepest reaches of conceptual systems to establish our framework. The deepest reaches of conceptual systems are found in a system's *asili,* or ideological matrix. We must examine the nature of the Afrikan *asili* so that we might fulfill it by creating a new consciousness and reality.

While the masses can take part relatively easily in *nkoso ɔ* and *daakye abra bɔ* , those who have identified Yurugu (i.e. studied   Marimba Ani's work, *Yurugu*) will be responsible for at least beginning the critical work of *nyansa nnsa da*. As we have mentioned, *nyansa nnsa da* is the framework that directs *nkoso ɔ* and *daakye abra bɔ* and allows the articulation of Afrikan *utamawazo*, while being a catalyst for the creation of an old/new Afrikan consciousness (See figure 1)

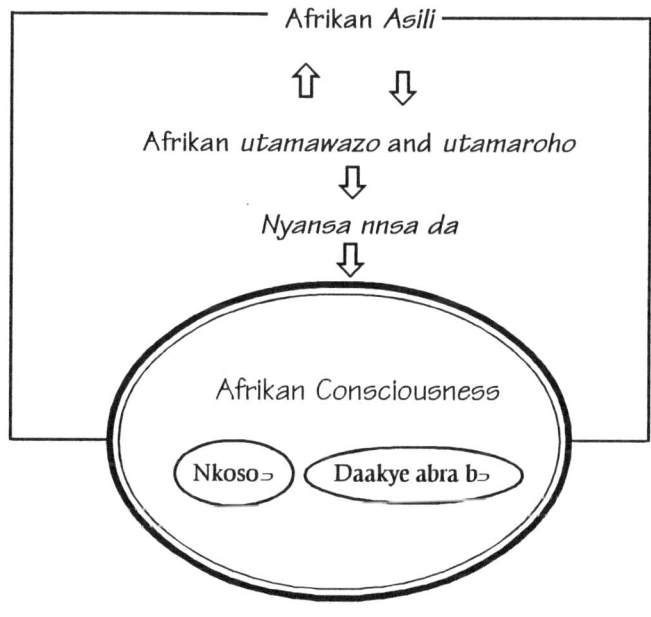

Fig. 1

Individuals who have identified Yurugu will have to further develop and articulate what *nyansa nnsa da* will mean to Afrikan people and Afrikan consciousness, shape the Afrikan consciousness, and begin to build the institutional vehicles to support an old/new Afrikan consciousness once it is clearly articulated and developed. The bringing of an old/new Afrikan consciousness to fruition represents what Akoto, in his book *Nationbuilding*, called the "Re-Afrikanization Process." (See chapter 8, "Return to The Way: The Nature of an Old/ New Afrikan Consciousness ")

The nature of our current predicament is that we have had an entire conceptual system **imposed** upon us as Afrikan people. It has involved the imposition of philosophies, ideology and worldview through physical abuse and psychological terrorism. It has involved the disruptive force of Yurugu.

Accepting this as true, we have to be able to assess how we will move from a culture that has been the most inhuman and cruel culture that the world has ever seen, to something new. *Nyansa nnsa da* is not just a term to be tossed around in intellectual or pseudo-intellectual circles and then forgotten as we "return to the real world." *Nyansa nnsa da* is a concept to be internalized and moved upon. It should become a functional part of our conscious thought processes and values. We should be reminding ourselves several times a day that the current world reality is not the way it should be and "I" can play a vital role in changing it as "We" move toward true liberation. Conscious and determined efforts need to be made to cease using oppressive language once we understand the power of language and have been given new concepts and language to utilize. For example, once an individual knows the inadequacy of terminology such as "Afrikan Slave Trade" and has been introduced to The Maafa, a conscious effort must be made not to continually revert to old language and habits. It might be hard at first to stop saying "slavery," but the reasons for using terminology like The Maafa are serious and impactful, not trivial.

Conscious effort needs to be made in the little areas of our existence in order for us to even approach *nyansa nnsa da*. This, however, seems to be a problematic area for Afrikan people, which is why it is important not only to develop the concepts but also to build the institutions that validate them.

When people have ideas, feel a certain way about issues in general or need to make conscious behavioral changes, it is much easier to be strong on such ideas and issues if there are institutions or groups of people saying and doing the same thing. An Afrikan in America who resists the psychological mutilation of the European *asili*, may be made to feel as if they are wrong for doing so. They may be called militant, radical or a trouble maker, as well as being ostracized. They may be made to feel abnormal because they resist. Such resistance, and all of the negative reinforcement that goes with it, can make for a lonely and alienated existence. However, if there are other people who say that resistance is sane, normal and desired, it becomes easier to resist. If those people also have clearly articulated evidence to back this up, such as books and scholarly works, then resistance becomes even easier. If organizations and institutions back up and validate the people, the books and the scholarly works, then resistance becomes the norm. The loneliness, alienation and doubt that often accompanies those who struggle for the masses need not be. Through *nyansa nnsa da* and institution building, these sisters and brothers are seen as normal, valued, sane members of the Afrikan community.

There is another aspect of institution building as relates to individuals. As Afrikan people we often find ourselves cognizant of the proper values, concepts and realities without being committed to living them. This is the case for a number of reasons. One such reason is that many of our concepts and values don't have sufficient back up. We may speak of self-sufficiency, but without self-sustaining institutions we are *only* speaking. An individual is presented the fact that resistance is sane and necessary in a few books, while an entire society says otherwise with educational, cultural, social, legal and financial institutions and systems that say otherwise. Although this is not an excuse for the Afrikan who chooses not to resist and, instead, maintains status quo, it is an explanation as to why this might happen.

Another reason for the importance of institutions on the level of the individual is that many Afrikans have become comfortable and accustomed to just talking and not *doing*. Merely talking is relatively safe, while action involves risks. We don't tend to perceive much danger in simply talking or griping about our condition as a people and what needs to be done. However, becoming a doer involves a certain amount of risk and danger that engenders fear amongst many Afrikans. It is often fear of losing a job, fear of being alienated or ostracized, fear of disturbing a perceived comfortable status quo and even fear of physical harm or death. Afrikans have a long history of being physically brutalized and killed for moving toward liberation and this is a real fear in the minds of many. Francis Cress Welsing wrote a chapter in *The Isis Papers* called "Black Fear and the Failure of Black Analytical (Ideological) Commitment." Welsing asserted that a "high level of fear and a profound sense of vulnerability..." might eventually lead to

> ... moving from problem perception, *away* from problem solution (down a diversionary path), and back again to problem perception. This may be followed by worrying and obsessive complaining. There is never consistent motion towards problem *solution* because to do so would challenge and alter the power dynamic of oppression. Thus, high-level fear is set in motion. [6]

Many of us have seen the pictures of our ancestors hanging from trees and realized that it was a consequence of "stepping out of place." We have seen the assassinations of Dr. King, Malcolm X, and Medgar Evers. We have read about or experienced COINTELPRO and other government sponsored terrorism against Afrikan people.

Rodney King's beating was etched in many of our minds and we saw it as symbolic of the vulnerability of all Afrikan men and something that happens frequently when there is no camera to record it. We see Assata Shakur in exile for her strength in fighting for liberation. Geronimo Pratt remains in prison and Mumia Abu Jamal had been sentenced to die. Eddie Conway, another former Panther, has been in prison 26 years. Fear is real, given all the trauma that Afrikan people have endured. It is easier to just talk and not become a doer like Malcolm X, Dr. King, Assata Shakur, Mumia Abu Jamal, etc.

However, becoming a doer is made much easier for the masses when there are institutions and groups of people to back them up. You will always have the courageous among us who step forward and stand up regardless, but the masses need some support and validation. This is especially true in a time when Yurugu has elevated oppression to an art form not easily identified by many sisters and brothers who have not studied or reached some level of consciousness. In the 60's, Yurugu was exposed in all of its brutality, white sheets, black robes and blue uniforms. However, today many Afrikans wear the same uniforms and robes, and the enemy is not so clear as it used to be. It is there though. Conscious people, books, scholarly works, grass roots activists and Afrikan institutions help to identify the enemy in a systematic and clear manner. This organization, institution building and nation building is what is necessary to alleviate some of the fear and move Afrikans from the understanding of what the problems are, to problem resolution and action.

Yet another facet of the often times problematic lack of commitment and lack of problem resolution on the part of Afrikan people involves the way in which many people perceive certain aspects of our liberation movement. For example, many Afrikans understand the concepts espoused by our scholars as simply theory with no clearly discernible real life application. Recognizing this as a legitimate problem, some very practical and everyday examples of *nyansa nnsa da*, or thought without boundaries, are in chapter 7 along with their complete opposite European-centered thought processes and obstacles presented by the present world reality. In addition, it must be understood that this work, *Reality Revolution*, is preliminary work to be followed by scholars and grassroots sisters and brothers who develop specific areas of our reality, utilizing *nyansa nnsa da*. For example, as this book is being written there is a compendium in progress, entitled *To Heal A People: Afrikan Scholars Defining a New Reality*.

With an understanding that *nyansa nnsa da* is a functional concept, we can begin to act on the concept. Since our limitless thought involves the naming and defining of reality, we as Afrikan people are responsible for defining what normal, sane and desired behaviors and constructs are. As we reclaim and reconceptualize our historical experiences, we see in the example of The Maafa that resistance is normal and we come to the understanding that self-knowledge, self-definition, rejection of Yurugu, self-love, etc., are all normal, sane and desired in our old/new Afrikan consciousness (new reality). For an Afrikan sister or brother to be lacking in the knowledge of themselves, embracing Yurugu and seeing no reason to resist is no longer acceptable. We define such Afrikans as abnormal and insane. Ignorance, once recognized, is not an excuse. Those sisters and brothers consciously resisting and nation building are "mainstream" in our Afrikan reality. Put bluntly, everyone else is crazy to some degree. Those Afrikans who exhibit the qualities of assimilation, delusion, self-destructiveness and adoption of the European *asili*, who are often considered normal and "good Blacks," are in fact not normal at all. As definitions and conceptions change, some who have been considered models and "pillars" of the Afrikan community will be seen in a different light. The things we aspire to be and the people we aspire to be like will drastically change. Our neurotic wants will be distinguished from our survival and liberation needs, and even our wants will cease to be pathological. This is the nature of *nyansa nnsa da*.

CHAPTER 4

○○○○○○○○○

SPIRITUAL DIMENSIONS OF NYANSA NNSA DA AND AFRIKAN CATHARSIS

As Afrikan people, even in a *seemingly* disconnected existence in the Western Hemisphere, we have maintained a profound level of spirituality. We have maintained a belief in the validity of emotion, intuition and God-force within human beings; even though this has been one of the areas that we have been faulted for by the European *asili*, manifested in its *utamawazo* which describes these qualities as irrational, superstitious, childish, and overly emotional, with all of these conveyed with a degree of condescension. Reasoned, analytical, cold, calculated, material thinking has been positioned as the ideal and the opposite of the spirit of Afrikan people. Though many Afrikans have bought into this thinking, we must reject such a worldview.

Our spirituality is a valuable quality and is not the opposite and less desired quality in relation to reason or intelligence or the ability to think critically. This is what the dichotomous logic of the European *asili* dictates. We in fact realize that Afrikan people possess the inseparable ability to think spiritually and materially, analytically and intuitionally, etc. Dr. Marimba Ani comments in her book, *Let The Circle Be Unbroken*, regarding spirituality, that,

> To deny it is a tactical error, which results in a plethora of impotent organizations and "leaders" with no roots. The African

experience in America must be used to turn spirituality into a political strength rather than the political deficit it has been historically. Our spirituality must be anchored to sharp political analysis and critical thought. In this way we can achieve the balance necessary for creating a healthy new society of revolutionary implications. [1]

So we must not deny our spirituality. Afrikan people exist in Sacred Time, where there is no beginning and there is no end. We exist in a spherical arrangement in which the ancestors, the living and those yet unborn can commune together at the same time. Again, from *Let The Circle Be Unbroken* we understand that,

Through sacred time, life and time are continually regenerated. Space is expanded; the Eternal is achieved! What is called "past," "present" or "future" in   lineal terms, is not separated but is joined together in a phenomenal and special unity. This is made possible through the extraordinary mechanism of ritual drama.

Spirit does not die. If we continually make that religious and philosophical statement through ritual; if we "remember," then the physically deceased members of the family continue to be part of that family, and we are assured of immortality. In order for the family to be healthy, its continuity and wholeness must be continually experienced, and it is through the ancestors that we keep in touch with our sacred origins. [2]

So, our communion with the ancestors in Sacred Time is not only possible but essential to our health and wholeness as a people. The Maafa represented a tremendous rupture in the existence of Afrikan people; a rupture in which the harmonious spiritual development of Afrikan people has been arrested, especially in the Western Hemisphere. In large part, we've lost the practice and/or understanding of our need for rituals.

The connection of Sacred Time and ritual to *nyansa nnsa da*, is that thought without boundaries is a concept that reopens Afrikan eyes to the spirit, to The Way. We see Sacred Time, the ancestors and ritual as necessities and our thought is free and limitless, allowing our re-creation of ritual. We must reclaim and create Afrikan ritual drama.

> In ritual drama we "die" and are "reborn," just as youth "die" and are "reborn" as adults, and as elders "die" and are "reborn" as ancestors, or as ancestors are given new life as they "become" new members of the group. In ritual we are energized and revitalized. Values and beliefs are redefined, reaffirmed and reinterpreted, at once giving them added viability and sacralizing their new form. [3]

We have spoken in this text about true liberation and given its definition. It is inherent in true liberation and a return to The Way that we become balanced again and in touch with spirit. We cannot achieve liberation as a people without spirit! Spirit is psychological health. Spirit is our self-knowledge and self-definition. We understand true liberation to be self-knowledge, self-definition, psychological health, self-determination and self-sufficiency. Spirit and our spirituality are essential! Ritual is essential!

In our present predicament, not only do we need to be energized and revitalized, but our values and beliefs must be redefined, as occurs through ritual. As I made clear in *The Maafa & Beyond*, we have neither properly remembered nor mourned our experience of enslavement, The Maafa. Not only has this rendered us off balance psychologically, but spiritually as well. We are not in tune with spirit, our ancestors and the yet unborn, as a people. Because of this we do damage to our mental and spiritual health. We have also consequently failed the ancestors miserably and have done them harm. The spiritual damage caused by our lack of remembrance and mourning of the **over**

100 million Afrikans engulfed by The Maafa is complex and sad in a sense.

> Death is not seen as an ending but rather as an opportunity for a person to take off these ragged clothes we call a body, and walk naked. Even though this is a view commonly held by the Dagara, death still produces a kind of sudden vacuum and loss of attachment that requires grief in order to heal. Without grief, the separation between the living and the dead never actually shifts into that stage in which the living accept the fact that a loved one has become a spirit. The departed loved one consequently never arrives where death commands him or her to go and, therefore, becomes angry with the living.
>
> If there is no expression of grief, it will affect the dead and the living detrimentally. The dead cannot then go free from their earthly consciousness. [4]

So, with this understanding of the Dagara spirituality, we recognize that we not only suffer from the distorted reality of The Maafa's physical and mental trauma, but we are spiritually off balance and have not healed the rupture of spirit, since we haven't mourned; many of our ancestors have not been allowed to undergo the peaceful journey of transition because they are not remembered and we, as a people, do not commune with them. And, because ancestors become spirits to be reborn in our children, we have damaged generations of youth as well. All of these things are clearly evident today, especially the emptiness and pain of many of our youth and the unhealthy state of the masses of Afrikan people.

A return to The Way must include a return to our true spirit, not simply what we have been able to maintain and adapt through the intense destruction we have faced. We must create ritual dramas that remember the ancestors, while giving spirit to the yet unborn and healing the living.

Nyansa nnsa da allows us to embark on this spiritual re-creation as a people. Afrikan people must return to ritual drama and Afrikan spirituality, old and new.

> Our rituals, our songs, our music and dance, became vehicles through which to contact the divine, media through which we reached the spiritual source and so received sustenance and energy, from the knowledge of our specialness.
>
> Ritual Drama in African society is a multidimensional mechanism of cultural expression. It can be understood on metaphysical, religious, communal, and psychological levels simultaneously. Ritual Drama involves the repetition of a sacred act performed in a prescribed manner. It is religiously understood, therefore, as an imitation of divine beings or of our revered ancestors. Events are placed within the context of a harmonious order and so are sacralized. We "understand" them better because they are placed within a familiar mode. That is the function of ritual. [5]

In addition to the repetition of a sacred act, described above by Dr. Marimba Ani, Malidoma Somé shares that ritual involves several elements.

> 1. Invocational. Humans call on non-humans for a specific purpose. To meet as a group without invoking the spirits means that you are on your own.
>
> 2. Dialogical. We enter into a kind of solemn dialogue with the spirit and with ourselves. When we call in somebody who doesn't have a physical form, then we are giving a different contour to the place we are sharing with our people.
>
> 3. Repetitive. The actions (structures) in ritual are the same. When you pour a libation, the pouring stays the same.
>
> 4. Opening and closure. The ritual space is opened

whenever the spirit is invoked. The ritual space is closed when the spirit is sent away. The spirit is sent away symbolically, not dismissed. And this happens when we tell the spirit that what we embarked upon is over and we are ready to resume normal life. We don't call people and then just leave them as if we had forgotten them. They will invent a way to remind us of their being there... In ritual, *openings and closures are very important.* Whatever happens between these two extremes must be coming from the "pit of your belly," as village people say. This spirit structure is what is basic to indigenous ritual. [6]

Understanding our current predicament and the seminal role of The Maafa in shaping the current insanity and pain of the masses Afrikan people, we must deal with it. It is of extreme importance to deal with the spiritual damage and chaos of The Maafa. And again, ritual drama is one of the means of doing this. Whether we are pouring libations to begin any endeavor we enter into, symbolically reclaiming our Afrikanness through a ritual oath or ceremony, extending prayer to the Creator, celebrating unity, mourning the ancestors lost in The Maafa or whatever we are doing, ritual is a way to ground us again in health. Understanding this we must realize that though we exist in Sacred Time, a large part of ritual is dependent on where we are in time and space; our present reality is important. Because our reality has so drastically changed from what it was before the severe ruptures we have experienced, our new reality demands new rituals. Just as we must create in so many other areas, we must create in this one as well. We can use some of the rituals passed to us from our ancestors, but we must also adapt new rituals that deal with our present reality and to which we can relate.

In our rituals, music is also a key element. Our brother elder Kelan Phil Cohran has related his profound wisdom in a story about the "Sun Drummers" who once played in Chicago. He shared how Afrikan traditional drumming could bring a gathering of people into harmony with one another to the point where heartbeats and even the blinking eyes, of those gathered at events where the Sun Drummers were playing, were in sync. This is profound. Music is spirit. It moves us on levels that the spoken word cannot reach. Music helps us repair the rupture of spirit caused by The Maafa and actually commune together again spiritually with one another.

Ritual is actually already everywhere. In the Catholic Church when the priest takes the incense and walks around the altar, surrounding it with the incense, this is ritual. The call and response in the Catholic Church is ritual; where the priest utters words and the congregation has a response which is repetitive and always the same. The "call to altar" in the Baptist church is ritual, as is the taking of communion in all Christian churches, when the symbolic ingestion of the blood and body of Jesus is performed. If there was no power or meaning behind this, it would not be done. The ways in which practitioners of Islam pray can even be called ritual in its sacred and repetitive nature. The way in which Allah is called upon and dialogue carried on, with the use of the prayer rug and the repetitive bowing in supplication to Allah, is ritual. So ritual has an importance that has never faded. We as Afrikan people have simply lost the conscious recognition of its power and its Afrikan expression.

We must put power and meaning in rituals that ground us in who we are, where we are going, what our duties are and so on. Afrikan people must reclaim themselves.

As we recognize these spiritual ruptures, we also realize that Afrikan spiritual healing cannot be separated from the physical and mental trauma of Afrikan people and the need for catharsis. Catharsis is defined as "3. A release of emotional tension, as after an overwhelming experience, that restores or refreshes the spirit." [7] With this definition the connection between the spiritual healing and the mental and physical healing of Afrikan people is very clear. We have a great deal of tension built up that must be released and expressed to refresh the Afrikan spirit. Additional insight on what catharsis is proves informative. "4. <u>Psychology</u>. a. A technique used to relieve tension and anxiety by bringing repressed feelings and fears to consciousness. b. The therapeutic result of this process; abreaction." [8] So clearly catharsis is necessary for the masses of Afrikan people. Haki Madhubuti has asserted that,

> The frustration that conscious black men and women undergo in this country is nothing less than extraordinary. The psychological stress and strain that the West puts on us (depending upon our consciousness) is vast, and for us to remain sane and politically active under such weight is a phenomenon of the mind and body. [9]

The Maafa with all of its destruction, murder, brutality, rape, kidnapping and psychological mutilation, as well as its continuing legacy, has had a lasting effect on Afrikan people and our pain has been repressed. It has been asserted in this work that CONSCIOUS RESISTANCE IN AN ENVIRONMENT OF HOSTILE OPPRESSION IS NEITHER MILI-TANT NOR RADICAL. IT IS SANE, NORMAL AND DESIRED BEHAVIOR. However, the repressed pain of the masses of Afrikan people has made conscious resistance something seen only in the relatively small number of Afrikan soldiers for liberation. In her book, *Killing Rage*, bell hooks makes observations about this problem. (We set aside bell hooks' misguided references to Ani's *Yurugu* in her book, *Killing Rage*, for the usefulness of the following insights hooks offers.)

> To perpetuate and maintain white supremacy, white folks have colonized black Americans, and a part of that colonizing process has been teaching us to repress our rage, to never make them the targets of any anger we feel about racism. Most black people internalize this message well. [10]

hooks goes further to explain that

> Even though black psychiatrists William Grier and Price
> Cobbs could write an entire book called *Black Rage*, they used their
> Freudian standpoint to convince readers that rage was merely a
> sign of powerlessness. They named it pathological, explained it
> away. They did not urge the larger culture to see black rage as
> something other than sickness, to see it as a potentially healthy,
> potentially healing response to oppression and exploitation. [11]

So we re-emphasize that *CONSCIOUS RESISTANCE IN AN
ENVIRONMENT OF HOSTILE OPPRESSION IS NEITHER MILITANT NOR RADICAL.
IT IS SANE, NORMAL AND DESIRED BEHAVIOR.* This is *nyansa nnsa da*, to be
able to make this judgement and position it as true, valid and a director
of our behavior. We haven't found our rage as a people; rage that is
justified, normal and has healing properties.

There has been success in waging war against Afrikan people
and eventually breaking down and stigmatizing resistance. We say
eventually because, as was discussed in *The Maafa & Beyond*,
Afrikans rocked the foundations of the Western Hemisphere with
resistance during The Maafa. Our lack of resistance today is a
relatively recent phenomenon. Over time our people, notwithstanding
the sister and brother soldiers amongst us, have had their resistance
broken and the war against us has continued. With this war raging,
there has been a large measure of success in not allowing Afrikans to
identify and "call out" those who have waged war against us for
hundreds and even thousands of years. We haven't been allowed to
call this European *asili*, and its proponents, the enemy. Thus
regardless of the pain, we have had to swallow the normal reaction to
it and have been told instead that this act of swallowing rage is normal.
Therefore, with the aggression against Afrikans, you have Europeans

and Afrikans who leap to reprimand and adversely label those who identify this pain, and refuse to swallow rage, as racist and full of hate themselves. What a paradox! We are still today, after all of the pain of the Afrikan existence, being told that to scream out in pain is pathological and unacceptable. In addition, we haven't mourned the loss, brutalization and rape of millions, nor has society defined our experience as worthy of mourning. This represents only one of many major areas we can identify to substantiate the Afrikan need for catharsis.

A second area in which the need for healing can be identified is found when we look at the possible ways in which The Maafa's chronic trauma and captivity impacted Afrikans during this destructive historical process and even until today. We can do this by looking at some conventional understandings of trauma, realizing that these understandings are not broad enough for The Maafa, but will suffice to make certain points. Afrikan people will have to use *nyansa nnsa da* to develop our own constructs to extend the present understanding of our trauma; to take the history of extreme trauma where it does not wish to go, The Maafa.

In a book entitled *Trauma and Recovery: The aftermath of violence—from domestic abuse to political terror,* we gain a basic understanding of trauma.

Traumatic events call into question basic human relationships. They breach the attachments of family, friendship, love, and
community. They shatter the construction of the self that is
formed and sustained in relation to others. They undermine belief
systems that give meaning to human experience. They violate the
victim's faith in a natural or divine order and cast the victim into a
state of existential crisis.

The damage to relational life is not a secondary effect of
trauma, as originally thought. Traumatic events have primary

effects not only on the psychological structures of the self but also on the systems of attachment and meaning that link individual and community. [12]

With our understanding of The Maafa, the existence of trauma in our historical experience of enslavement and beyond is without question. *The Maafa & Beyond*, as an Afrikan reconceptualization and redefinition of this unique experience, is a book that makes this clear. Our trauma continued after enslavement and continues at present. Specifically as relates to captivity, we find that

> Captivity, which brings the victim into prolonged contact with the perpetrator, creates a special type of relationship, one of coercive control...
>
> In situations of captivity, the perpetrator becomes the most powerful person in the life of the victim, and the psychology of the victim is shaped by the actions and beliefs of the perpetrator. Little is known about the mind of the perpetrator. Since he is contemptuous of those who seek to understand him, he does not volunteer to be studied. [13]

Our experience of enslavement in the Western Hemisphere, The Maafa, is the best example of the above observations of Dr. Herman. To this day Afrikan people, especially in the U.S. and Azania (South Afrika) but also throughout the world, remain in rather intimate contact with the perpetrators of our intense trauma. Fortunately, we have begun on a larger level to break through the paradigm that keeps us from critically analyzing and understanding the mind of the perpetrator. Two sisters, Dr. Francis Cress Welsing and Dr. Marimba Ani, have been amongst the foremost minds in analyzing European culture, thought and behavior; understanding the mind of the perpetrator. These sisters have taken many of us from the defensive victim posture, to the offensive posture of those taking control of our reality and destiny as a people. Dr. Welsing's seminal work was *The Isis Papers*. Dr. Ani's work, the most profound and systematic analysis available, is called *Yurugu*. We have broken down the mystery of the perpetrator's sick mind and begun to shed its corrupting influence. However, we still have much to do.

To get a little more precise in understanding the trauma of The Maafa and the totality of the Afrikan existence in connection with Yurugu, we must understand that the hundreds of years of this particular crime can only be understood as chronic trauma. Not only has the mental and physical hostility directed toward the Afrikans in this hemisphere been consistent and pervasive up until the present, but distorted realities caused by the chronic trauma of The Maafa have resulted in behavioral changes and distortions. These behavioral changes and distortions, which have gone without treatment or recovery since the initial traumatic inflictions, have become the learned behaviors of generation after generation. Therefore, we have a complex reality in which chronic trauma and distorted realities have been passed through generations as learned behavior, while increasing distortions are heaped upon the Afrikan existence by the continuous nature of chronic trauma. Additionally,

> People subjected to prolonged, repeated trauma develop an insidious, progressive form of post traumatic stress disorder that invades and erodes the personality. [14]

Post traumatic stress disorder was discussed to a degree in *The Maafa & Beyond*. Its possible connection to Afrikan experiences in this Western Hemisphere was illustrated, yet at the same time there is the realization that post traumatic stress disorder is informative but not completely sufficient to analyze The Maafa. New constructs must be set forth by Afrikan psychologists to adequately address The Maafa. (We make the distinction between Afrikan psychologists and Negro, as well as European, psychologists. Negro psychologists will always be ineffective and unable to help Afrikan people due to their use of Yurugu's norms and standards of behavior to analyze Afrikans.)

One additional reference to the nature of trauma may help our understanding of a necessary direction for healing.

> Prolonged captivity also produces profound alterations in the victim's identity. All the psychological structures of the self— the image of the body, the internalized images of others, and the values and ideals that lend a person a sense of coherence and purpose— have been invaded and systematically broken down. In many totalitarian systems this dehumanizing process is carried to the extent of taking away the victims name. Timerman calls himself a "prisoner without a name." In concentration camps the captive's name is replaced with a nonhuman designation, a number. In political or religious cults and in organized sexual exploitation, *the victim is often given a new name* {italics mine} to signify the total obliteration of her previous identity and her submission to the new order. [15]

With the systematic nature of the destruction of the psychological structures of Afrikan people, from identity to taking our names, the trauma of our experiences becomes all the more clear. Not only do we recognize the chronic nature of our trauma, but also the fact that the numerous areas of trauma identified to this point have not been addressed to date in order to facilitate the healing of the Afrikan masses. The necessary therapy, reconnection and return to psychological and spiritual health have been replaced by a societal encouragement of pathological adaptation of these pathological conditions as normal; hence, Amos Wilson's positing of "pathological normalcy" or what has been referred to by others as functional insanity. The European *asili* has had a major role and vested interest in naming and defining a reality of pathological normalcy.

So, in practicing *nyansa nnsa da* here we have been able to step outside of the boundaries of pathological normalcy and identify and name reality for ourselves. Of the trauma that we suffer as a people, we have identified:

1) Spiritual trauma in which The Maafa and the European *asili* continue to cause imbalance.

2) Repressed emotions, fears and consciousness, as dictated by European societal norms, definitions and conceptions of Afrikan experiences, having been imposed upon Afrikan people.

3) Physical and psychologically traumatic events throughout our stay in the Western Hemisphere.

4) Chronic trauma, added to traumatic events and resulting largely from the captivity of The Maafa.

****

Thus far we have shared some of the ways in which our conscious minds and our spirits must be transformed. *Nyansa nnsa da*, as a concept that allows Afrikan people to think on a larger level than current circumstances, aids in bringing these psychological, paradigmatic and spiritual shifts to fruition.

We have some healing to do; healing that will generate a new people who take action to change their existence. The discussion in this chapter and the previous chapter represents transformation not only on the social level, but on the level of consciousness. In the next chapter we take it a step further to more specific aspects of this healing process.

CHAPTER 5

OOOOOOOOO

HEALING AS A PROCESS: HEALTHY COPING MECHANISMS, EXPANDED CONCEPTIONS OF TREATMENT AND SOCIOTHERAPY FOR A PEOPLE

Having recognized the trauma of Afrikan people and the general theoretic basis for catharsis, we must be more specific about how Afrikan people can return to health as a prerequisite for and a part of our return to The Way. Healing is more than the recognition of the illness and its nature, it is a process. This is especially so when a people have endured systematic destruction to their psychological, cultural and spiritual being.

Having suffered through *at least* the four areas of trauma outlined in the previous chapter; spiritual disruption and trauma, repressed emotions and fears, physically and psychologically traumatic events, and chronic trauma over hundreds of years, we gain understanding into the areas in which healing must be facilitated and the type of thinking changes we must undergo. The question then becomes how to launch such a significant endeavor?

This is an especially cogent question since even most conscious Afrikan people have traditionally sought to recognize the reality of their existence, know themselves and then NAVIGATE the madness of the current world reality, instead of creating a new reality. Even those who have sought professional help from the fields of psychology and psychiatry have been treated within the framework of the flawed and abnormal nature of the present world reality.

We now realize that this strategy is just not good enough to achieve true liberation and psychological health as a part of that liberation. It must be taken many steps further to the degree that we must address all of the problematic areas of our existence, identify the trauma and proceed to create and *control* all of the life-giving and life-sustaining institutions that make the shaping of a new reality possible, while at the same time systematically developing the processes, theories and new conceptualizations that would make these institutions functional. Put more simply, our approach must be the systematic destruction of the pathologies, traumatic conditions and Yurugu within the Afrikan psyche and community. It must be the systematic destruction of these things; a destruction that comes about as a result of our systematic creation of a reality that replaces the present world reality dictated by Yurugu.

Understanding this, we recognize healing as a process to be developed by our creation of sane standards, concepts, definitions and the ability to effect these upon the masses of Afrikan people through institutions. We must develop coping mechanisms and, because the masses of Afrikan people cannot sit on the psychologist's or psychiatrist's couch, we must develop sociotherapeutic models as well. The need for sociotherapeutic models comes from the recognition that we have been placed in our condition as a collective and not for any individual reasons. The Maafa was not an event affecting millions of individuals, but a process impacting a people. Because of this, we have to understand that our trauma is a collective trauma and,

Sociopathology precedes psychopathology. Collective

pathology precedes individual pathology. That is, *diseased* social interactions *between* groups generate *diseased* social interactions *within* groups, and furthermore, *diseased* social interactions within groups generate *diseased* psychological interactions *within* individuals who are their constituents. The discontents of individuals reflect the discontents of groups; and these, the discontents of the societies and cultures they constitute. The Great Chain of Discontents inextricably binds together individual, group, society, and culture. [1]

Consequently, we recognize the need for healing a people through sociotherapy to be further examined later in this chapter. In addition, we must utilize those scholars we have and cultivate more individuals capable of bringing this healing process to fruition.

So, in terms of how to develop a healing process for Afrikan people, we must first acknowledge that European psychological constructs and standards, upon which the fields of psychology and psychiatry are currently based, are inadequate to facilitate the healing of Afrikan people. They are not only inadequate in terms of neither acknowledging nor being knowledgeable of the trauma we have identified, but they are fields grounded in the European *asili* which have actually been very detrimental to Afrikan people. We can identify any number of examples of this danger psychology and psychiatry have represented for Afrikan people.

In 1887, G. Stanley Hall, founder of the American Journal of Psychology and first president of the American Psychological Association, theorized that Africans, Indians and Chinese were members of "adolescent races" in a stage of "incomplete growth." As such, this justified psychiatry and psychology's intervention to save them from the 'liabilities and dangers' of freedom. [2]

Regarding the attitude toward our people and our children, we find that "Director of the Kaiser Wilhelm Institute of Anthropology, Human Heredity, and Eugenics in Berlin, psychiatrist Eugen Fischer urged the annihilation of 'negro children.' " [3] Even Margaret Sanger, the founder of Planned Parenthood of America, proposed the cessation of the growth of Afrikan babies in the U.S. As heinous as this is, a more ludicrous realization is found in diagnoses of Afrikan people's mental illness, erroneously concocted by Europeans.

As early as 1851, Samuel A. Cartwright, a prominent Louisiana physician, published an essay entitled "Report on the diseases and physical peculiarities of the Negro race" in the "New Orleans and Surgical Journal." Cartwright claimed to have discovered two mental diseases peculiar to blacks, which he believed justified their enslavement. These were called "drapeto-mania" and "dysaesthesia aethiopis."

The first term came from *drapetes*, a runaway slave, and mania, meaning mad or crazy. Cartwright claimed that this "disease" caused blacks to have an uncontrollable urge to run away from their "masters." The "treatment" for this "illness" was "whipping the devil out of them."

Dysaesthesia Aethiopis supposedly affected both mind and body. The diagnosable signs included disobedience, answering disrespectfully and refusing to work. The "cure" was to put the person to some kind of hard labor which apparently sent "vitalized blood to the brain to give liberty to the mind." [4]

The list of ridiculous pseudo-scientific abuses and atrocities is of course much longer, therefore, our mental health professionals must operate on the foundations of new conceptions of normal, sane and desired behavior which we establish; old/new Afrikan paradigms. They must operate on the knowledge of the Afrikan existence and the disruptive nature of Yurugu. And, Afrikan mental health professionals cannot possibly be effective without a knowledge of the Afrikan existence and a consequent knowledge of self. As one of our Afrikan psychologists who is and has been doing just what we have said is necessary, Dr. Na'im Akbar wrote regarding mental health that,

> The transposition of this concept would suggest that mental health is reflected in those behaviors which foster mental growth and awareness (i.e., mental life). Mental illness would then be the presence of ideas or forces within the mind that threaten awareness and mental growth. From an ontogenetic or extended concept of self or mind (Nobles, 1972) we could conclude that mental illness is seen in any behavior or ideas which threaten the survival of the collective self (or tribe). With such a definition, we could understand the classification of an entire society as mentally ill if that society were entrenched in a set of ideas geared toward the self-destruction of the people within that society. [5]

Also in the mode of defining and creating in the field of Afrikan Psychology, Dr. Wade Nobles affirms,

> Thus to be normal is to possess thought and command and to have the ability to produce that which one wills. Attitudinally and behaviorally normal or natural functioning is represented by (1) a sense of self which is collective or extended; (2) an attitude wherein one understands and respects the sameness in oneself and others; (3) a clear sense of one's spiritual connection to the universe; (4) the sense of mutual responsibility; and (5) a conscious understanding that human abnormality and/or deviancy is any act which is in opposition to oneself and kind which really means abnormality and/or deviancy is any act which is in opposition to the Ka of God. [6]

Na'im Akbar has further approached the systematic
redefinition of psychology by giving classifications of disorders amongst
Afrikan people in the U.S.   Akbar's classifications are the alien-self
disorder, the anti-self disorder, the self-destructive disorder and the
organic disorder.

Dr. Akbar defines the alien-self disorder as one in which
individuals behave contrary to their own survival.   They are
individuals who have essentially been socialized to act in ways that are
really not beneficial to their future or the future of their children.
Unfortunately, these are the types of behaviors that are considered
desired and normal in a society dominated by Europeans. Akbar writes,

> The socialization of these alien-self persons has been
> geared toward a denial of social realities particularly as they relate
> to issues of race and oppression. They are encouraged to ignore
> the blatant inequities of racism and to view their lives as if slavery,
> racism and oppression never existed. They are asked to pretend
> that there are not forces of injustice threatening their collective
> survival. [7]

In addition, Akbar relates that this disorder is "occurring with
alarming frequency in middle class and professional African
American communities." [8] These individuals are also "substantially
similar to that dominant society which fosters material acquisition rather
than natural human cultivation" [9] and such individuals may be
"unwilling to seek the acceptance of others like themselves, and   unable
to be accepted by those whose acceptance they passionately desire." [10]
Some of them may be confused and miserable because of this dilemma.

This particular redefinition of mental health is important in
that it calls into question the behaviors and psychological health of
many of those Afrikan people who are considered successful in this

society, even though many of them neither perceive of the need for an Afrikan liberation struggle nor identify with their Afrikanness. This makes it clear that a sister or brother is not psychologically healthy simply because they wear a suit, drive a nice car, have a "good" job, get "good grades" or live in a fancy house. In fact, Kobi Kambon says that,

> not only is it the criminal and homicidal Africans, the suicidal and drug/substance addicted-abuse Africans, and the ghetto dwelling, school dropout, and unskilled and unemployed Africans who suffer from this pervasive form of African personality disorder, but it is also the so-called Average Joe Africans (the hard-working, bills-paying, family-oriented, church-going, apple-pie-eating, etc.), or the "You-and-Me Africans" as well. This mental disorder affects the vast majority of our population. [11]

Such "Average Joe Africans" suffer from Kambon's Psychological/Cultural Misorientation or Akbar's alien-self disorder. The anti-self disorder is described as somewhat of an extension of the alien-self disorder in that the individual acts out direct and indirect hostility toward other Afrikan people and, consequently, toward themselves. "The dangerous aspect of this group is that unlike the alien-self disorder, they feel quite comfortable with their alien-self identification." [12] The aspects of Supreme Court Justice Clarence Thomas' public life that we have been exposed to seem to exhibit these characteristics. His hostility has been evident in his adverse rulings toward Afrikan people and he has claimed that it would be against God to write anything, in the way of a decision, against Europeans.

The self-destructive disorder is found in individuals who have suffered oppression directly, in terms of living conditions, economic circumstances, etc. and have resorted to measures for survival which are self-destructive, i.e. crime, drugs, prostitution, violence and other such behaviors often directed toward other Afrikan people.

Finally, organic disorders represent those with specific physiological, neurological and biochemical problems, while understanding that even these types of problems can result from oppression and its mental toll, as well as the physical environment and oppressive social circumstances.

As Afrikan psychology portends to deal with coping mechanisms for Afrikan people and recognize the disruption caused by Yurugu and The Maafa, Afrikans must have their rage validated and encouraged as a cathartic coping mechanism. Where Afrikan people are in denial and delusional, they must be systematically confronted with our reality. Where Afrikan people suffer the everyday stress of being in the presence of Yurugu, Afrikan health care professionals must aid in the alleviation of this stress and management of it through techniques they are equipped to use or will develop, understanding and acknowledging the presence and source of the "everyday stress" Afrikan people face. Psychology textbooks must be written specific to the Afrikan reality as we have defined it. Psychological institutions and organizations must be created and operate within an understanding of The Maafa and Yurugu. Wade Nobles shares that,

> As a reconstruction of the systematic and cumulative ideas, beliefs and knowledge of our people, the role of psychology is the mental liberation of our people. As such it must provide an analysis and understanding of our Beingness and Becoming which will filter, organize and transform our natural "sensations" into particular mental, impressions and behavioral dispositions and/or responses that affirm our Being and resist our oppression. [13]

The importance of all Afrikan health care professionals participating in this process is enormous. The way in which our healing must be wholistic and complete is expressed well in a book called *Healing and the Mind*, based on a PBS series by Bill Moyers. In a dialogue between Moyers and Candace Pert, a Ph.D. at the Center for Molecular and Behavioral Neuroscience, we can glean validation of our need for catharsis, as well as implications for our need to address Afrikan health in many other areas because of the types of trauma we have suffered.

> PERT: It's clear to me that emotions must play a key role, and thatrepressing emotions can only be causative of disease. A common ingredient in the healing practices of native cultures is catharsis, complete release of emotion. Positive thinking is interesting, but if it *denies the truth* {italics mine}, I can't believe that would be anything except bad.
>
> MOYERS: So a part of health is letting these true emotions of grief and sorrow and anger and fear worm their way through catharsis. Is there anything in your research that suggests that repressing emotions is bad for us?
>
> PERT: Not in my research, because that is on the molecular level, but there is a growing body of literature, much of it European, that suggests that emotional history is extremely important in things like the incidence of cancer. For example, it appears that suppression of grief, and suppression of anger, in particular, is associated with an increased incidence of breast cancer in women. This research is controversial, and there are always methodological issues to address—but its very interesting. [14]

Here we see that a part of the process of healing is the catharsis that we have discussed. The need for catharsis in healing is underscored by the understanding that it is possible that the failure to address Afrikan trauma will probably be not only psychologically harmful, but physically harmful as well. And, we see that denial of the truth is also unhealthy. Afrikan physicians then enter the picture as the proportions of our traumatic existence in the Western Hemisphere escalate and our need to cease to swallow rage, bolster and encourage resistance, deal with the truth, and identify our enemies takes on an enormous importance as relates to health. Afrikan physicians and health care professionals are therefore required to be conscious Afrikan soldiers for liberation in direct relationship to fulfilling their calling and oaths in health care.

In addition, we find that the dimensions of this healing can be very large if we look not only at cancer, depression and other illnesses, but also at some as common and seemingly clinical as heart disease and hypertension. Another of the physicians in Moyers' book, *The Mind and Healing*, points out that,

> The technology for assessing heart disease is so advanced that we can measure the effects of the mind on the heart with greater precision than we can measure the effects in other areas. For example, if you put people under emotional stress, even just having them do mental arithmetic, you can use PET scans to measure decreased blood flow to the heart. Because heart disease is still so prevalent—it kills more Americans than all other diseases combined—its a *good* model for looking at the effects of mind/body interventions not only on the heart, but by extension, on many other illnesses as well. [15]

Looking at this quote we can ask a question for which we already know the answer. Is the everyday stress and psychological abuse that Afrikan people endure, on subconscious levels with symbols and language, as well as overt manifestations of the European *asili*, more significant an emotional stress factor than doing "mental arithmetic?" The answer is of course YES! There are very likely direct or indirect corollaries between the stress of Afrikan life and the incidence of stroke, heart disease, hypertension, etc.

Nyansa nnsa da, or thought without boundaries, comes into play here in numerous ways also. With the implications of what has just been presented, we must understand that it is Afrikan people who must engage this knowledge for the healing process. This is an endeavor in which Afrikan people will have to soar above the thought boundaries of ideological and scientific dependency and European paradigm.

Even with the seemingly progressive nature of the European physicians who are doing this medical research, there are several limitations. First of all, they will not dedicate themselves to the application of their science in the development of a new reality and health for Afrikan people. Secondly, they cannot do this primarily because of the European *asili* not allowing them to even make the connections of their research to the conditions of Afrikan people that have been put forward here. Thirdly, these physicians are themselves considered to be researching in the area of "alternative" medicine and many of them are on the fringe or marginalized by their colleagues. Finally, as progressive as these physicians seem, in many of them we can still see the despiritualized European *asili* at work. For example, the dialogue that ensued between Moyers and Dr. Pert reveals that, much like Aristotle's belief in *demonstrable* science, there is an attempt by these progressive doctors and scientists to break mind, emotion and spirit down to demonstrable material science. Even with constant and countless examples of successful medicine in indigenous cultures and examples of true healing in the West on a non-material plane, if the material mechanism cannot be identified it is not considered valid by Western medicine. This is made clear in the introduction by Bill Moyers.

As usual with the exploration of complex subjects, there are more questions here than answers. And there are dangers, too. When I first proposed the series, one of my associates wrote an impassioned challenge to my intentions, for she feared that, "encouraged by the series, the desperately ill patient" might defy the physician, discard the medicine, stop the chemotherapy, and embrace an "alternative" treatment; or that the series might appear to support the kind of glib mind-over-matter thinking that makes people feel guilty about their illness. [16]

This is an ideological attachment to the material and demonstrable science manifested in a focus on drug therapy and sickness rather than health, chemotherapy, and other tangible ways of dealing with the body which do not seek to treat wholistically and maintain health, but often seek to mask the symptoms of larger problems. The challenges posed are real with regard to the dangers of patients going to individuals for "alternative" treatment and abandoning Western medicine. Some "alternative" practitioners may be genuine, but fail in their treatment because they and the patient try to understand and apply mind and healing within the context of the European *asili*. This is the true danger and not the validity or conceptual nature of spirit, emotion and healing, although the European *asili* dictates that its adherents believe that spirit and emotion are the problems. This is probably why Dr. Pert's work is on the molecular (material) level and she even mentions the controversial nature of the research around emotions and the "methodological problems" to be worked out. The European *asili* is obsessed with the material and therefore compulsive when it comes to method, regardless of results and absent of spiritual understanding. *Nyansa nnsa da* breaks us from this ideological matrix and frees us to make ourselves healthy again.

HEALING MODELS

Getting back to some of the mechanisms for psychological healing, the structure of healing models can include certain generically defined stages. It is generally understood that trauma causes a disconnection from a normal reality and the stripping of empower-ment from the victim. This systematic disconnection produces an environment that is unsafe psychologically, physically and spiritually. Therefore, one of the first stages of recovery from trauma in a general sense is **Safety**.

> Trauma robs the victim of a sense of power and control; the guiding principle of recovery is to restore power and control to the survivor. The first task of recovery is to establish the survivors safety. [17]

Safety for Afrikan people then may mean economic, intellectual, emotional, cultural and physical safety. Perhaps one of the best sociotherapeutic means of Afrikan health through safety involves removing individuals from the madness of this insane culture, in as much as we are successful in building and creating not only the concepts and definitions of a new, sane reality, but also the institutions which break Afrikan dependence on European educational institutions, acculturating influences, socializing influences, employment, housing, politics, etc. In short, we are speaking of self-determination and self-sufficiency as sociotherapy. We need to place Afrikan people in safe environments.

A very telling and applicable quote referring to this element of our struggle is found in *Trauma & Recovery* by Judith Herman.

> ... creating a safe environment required the patient to make major changes in her life. It entailed difficult choices and sacrifices. This patient discovered, as many others have done, that she could not recover until she took charge of the material circum-stances of her life. Without freedom, there can be no safety and no recovery, but freedom is often achieved at great cost. [18]

Hence, our constant and continuous movement toward true liberation is itself a part of recovery and healing. The very participation in this reality revolution is liberating *and* healing. Again, we realize that most who have written about trauma have left the Afrikan experience of The Maafa out of their writings. Consequently, we will have to be responsible as a people for developing this type of work. The information that is available directed specifically at trauma is simply being used in this book as a thought stimulator or stepping stone. With this in mind we can move forward.

Remembrance and mourning is often the second stage of recovery. *The Maafa & Beyond* was a contribution to remembrance and mourning in that it reconceptualized our traumatic experiences, redefined them and reclaimed them for us, the sufferers. Through this type of empowerment we transform our memory and make it functional for our survival, despite the trauma of the memory itself. We become the tellers of the story, therefore controlling the memory and thus the history of experiences that are ours to control. We transform the memory so that the pain can be felt and the horror seen, without shame. We can feel the emotions and rage that have for so long been choked down.

In this process the importance of language is just as crucial, because, amongst other reasons, "To name things is personal power." [19] Using the example of our experience of enslavement, we have already exercised a kind of power in ceasing to use an inadequate term like the "Afrikan Slave Trade" and using a term of our choosing, The Maafa, instead. This is an aspect of remembering our experiences more accurately and in a way that is functional for the rememberer. By using inadequate language we as Afrikan people have already vividly experienced how "what was felt deeply and never articulated, shared, or put into a context fades from conscious awareness." [20] There is probably not a better example of this than Afrikan people with The Maafa. We have traditionally failed to articulate or put The Maafa into an appropriate context because of the language describing the experience, which has played a large role in our inability to conceptualize the experience to our benefit. Consequently, not only have we not shared it, but many Afrikan people do not even have more than a pitiful knowledge of our enslavement.

The time is now that we remember and mourn, dispelling the conscious and subconscious myth that our denial and/or refusal to mourn denies victory to Yurugu. We begin to understand that it is the act of remembering that we were not supposed to achieve, therefore our lack of memory was and is victory for Yurugu. So we remember and mourn. In conjunction with this remembrance and mourning there is also the issue of accountability. We find that,

> An additional reason for confronting our abuser(s) and asking for their acknowledgment and apology is so that we can know we have tried everything to help heal the unfinished business of our abuse experience. Even though a survivor may express their experience to their abuser and co-abuser, it is common for them to deny the existence of the abuse and to try to invalidate their experience. They may also try to shame them about their recovery work, and as has happened frequently with many, even attack their methods of healing. [21]

This issue of accountability is also a part of healing; the ability to confront the perpetrator. True to form, our recovery work has been shamed and attacked, as Afrikans who seek to remember are accused of dwelling on the past and placing blame. And, surely, the recovery work of Afrikan people seeking to reclaim themselves has been invalidated. Conscious Afrikans seeking to return to themselves have been called fringe, militant, trouble-makers, etc. With great frequency we continue to see attempts to diffuse our ability to hold people accountable for our pain.

We should note that these very healing mechanisms that have been absent are not only necessary, but they are the very steps that allow Afrikan people to take control of their destinies and lift themselves up. This is the complete opposite of the sentiment that says this healing is placing blame and wonders why Afrikan people don't just clean up their act instead of blaming others.

One of the more common attempts at diffusing this process is to remind us that Afrikans helped facilitate The Maafa by selling other Afrikans. This is voiced by Afrikans and Europeans alike, as if the issue of accountability ends with this bit of information and all talk of the experience should cease. One way we counter this, of course, is in dealing with the accountability of the European *asili*. Another way we overcome this obstacle, short of complete historical analysis, can perhaps best be expressed through analogy. If we look at the European Jewish Holocaust, we must understand that there were Jewish people complicit in perpetuating that experience in several ways, including those who processed their fellow Jews into the concentration camps. This fact has not served as an impediment to European Jews holding Nazi Germany accountable and has not represented an obstacle to the mourning of those who died and suffered in those camps. Likewise, the feeble attempt to derail Afrikan remembrance and mourning by over-emphasizing that Afrikans participated in The Maafa is a ploy of the perpetrator; it is being used even by some of the victims to derail Afrikan healing, prevent accountability and avoid Afrikan liberation. So accountability is important and, as has been discussed, the analysis of the European *asili* allows us to hold its functionaries accountable.

Also useful to look at are the models for healing found in a book entitled *The Courage To Heal: A Guide For Women Survivors of Child Sexual Abuse*. Again, although the book is specific to the trauma of women who have endured child sexual abuse, the stages presented for the healing process are informative. The first three stages include making the decisions to heal, the emergency stage and remembering.

The fourth stage is believing that your abuse or trauma really happened. This involves trusting your perceptions and feelings of the experience, even in the face of often times sophisticated attempts to invalidate the experience. For example, Afrikan people who may consciously or subconsciously want to deal with the pain of The Maafa often find themselves being bombarded with opinions and perceptions of themselves as complainers, troublemakers, radicals, etc. This usually occurs in conjunction with the experience of enslavement being made generic and belittled so that the person seeking catharsis begins to doubt their very own feelings and the validity of their feelings. One may find oneself asking if it is really worth it to go through all the trouble of struggling and remembering, questioning which sometimes leads the individual to wonder if they really are making a big deal out of nothing. This fourth stage of the healing process, where the victim believes uncompromisingly that it really happened and is important, is essential to healing.

The fifth stage of Bass and Davis' healing process is breaking silence or telling others about what happened. The sixth stage is understanding that what has transpired in the way of trauma was not the fault of the victim. This point relates back to what was related earlier in this chapter regarding attempts to diffuse our ability to hold people accountable and the issue of Afrikans' participation in The Maafa. No matter who participated or what the circumstances, it does not change the fact that millions of Afrikans suffered, bled and died, not by any fault of their own. Consequently, millions of Afrikans suffer, bleed and die today. In the larger scheme of things it is not by any fault of their own that they are in America and living in this madness. It is also by no fault of the children of The Maafa that we have healing that must be done due to continuous assault by Yurugu.

The seventh stage in this healing model deals more specifically with women and child sexual abuse, so we move to the eighth stage which is trusting yourself or trusting your feelings, perceptions, etc. It is becoming confident enough to call the structure of American society a lie and being comfortable with the feeling that you have suffered and someone *is* responsible. The ninth stage is grieving and mourning, an aspect of healing that has already been expressed a great deal in this book and in *The Maafa & Beyond*.

The tenth stage of healing in this model is a very important one. It deals with anger and specifically is called "Anger—the Backbone of Healing." We usually hear that it is not good to be angry. We see and hear the label of the "angry Black man" with frequency and with a tone of ridicule, not a validation of this justifiable, normal anger. Bass and Davis write that

> Anger is a powerful and liberating force. Whether you need to get in touch with it or have always had plenty to spare, directing your rage squarely at your abuser, and at those who didn't protect you, is pivotal in healing. [22]

They go on to share that,

> One way survivors cut themselves off from their anger is to become so immersed in the perspective of the abuser that they lose connection with themselves and their own feelings. This approach is enthusiastically endorsed by most of society. Many people find it easier to sympathize with the abuser than to stand up as a staunch advocate for the victim. [23]

This perspective has some powerful parallels to the experience of Afrikan people. We are in the process of extricating ourselves from the perspective of the abuser. Additionally, the pushing of the European *asili's* perspectives on its victims is certainly endorsed in a vigorous manner. It is also easier for many Europeans and Afrikans alike to sympathize with a powerful society which has its glorified images erected in memorials and monuments, lifted up in song and written in texts; it is perceived easier to sympathize with this powerful and overwhelming structure than to sympathize with Afrikans fighting this country, its cultural *asili* and calling out its ills. This is a testament to why it is important to also erect and display our images, in addition to our critical writings, etc., an issue addressed later in this work.

Some of the final stages in this healing process model are disclosures and confrontations, forgiveness, spirituality, and resolution and moving on. Forgiveness is a stage that has a question mark after it in *The Courage to Heal*, because they say that forgiveness of the abuser is not a necessary part of healing. This is a stage referring most importantly to forgiving oneself.

We have already dealt with spirituality and the final stage of this Bass and Davis model, resolution and moving on, also leads us into the final stage of our general model; the general model having already covered safety, as well as remembrance and mourning.

We come full circle in this general model for healing and involve ourselves in the final stage, the **Reconnection** that is our reality revolution and return to The Way. Similarly Bass and Davis' resolution and moving on says that,

> While you won't erase your history, you will make lasting changes in your life. Having gained awareness, compassion, and power through healing, you will have the opportunity to work toward a better world. [24]

We are moving toward making a better world by redefining our reality. So this is where we find ourselves, at the threshold of a reality revolution. We are re-educating ourselves by re-creating ourselves. We are able to identify our pathology because we know we are not pathological. This is critical.

For so long, Europeans have told us that we are a pathological

146

people. They continue to do so, as the *Bell Curve* shows us. The European focus on Afrikan pathology has caused us to adopt a philosophy of resiliency that is good and necessary, but in which we have failed to heal because we have refused to acknowledge the pain and destructive success of Yurugu. The good news is that because we are naming and defining our reality, we can lovingly and truthfully identify pathology, knowing full well that we are not pathological as a people; and despite the existence of pathology we are still resilient and wonderfully strong because we should not have survived had it not been divine natural order.

SOCIOTHERAPY

With the knowledge of some of the possible stages of healing, the work of Afrikan psychologists, and the understanding of stress and mental imbalance as a contributor to dis-ease, perhaps it is possible to begin to conceive of sociotherapeutic models that go beyond the theory of healing stages examined thus far. As was mentioned previously, one of the best sociotherapeutic situations may be removing individuals from the madness of this insane cultural existence by building and creating institutions, acculturating influences, etc., to go along with theoretical work. To this end, Kobi Kambon tells us, in *The African Personality in America*, that,

The Great Challenge, then, for preventative-intervention in African mental health (especially under the abnormal and unnatural conditions of European cultural oppression/white supremacy domination here in American society) is to create cultural conditions, African cultural-centered conditions, that will develop and foster African self-consciousness (a Pan-African nationalist consciousness) in African people 'from the cradle to the grave.' In other words, Africans must create the cultural infrastructural conditions that will foster African Nation-building/maintenance, i.e., the ultimate creation of an African World Order. [25]

In dealing with sociotherapy, what Kambon calls preventative-intervention, it is possible to create what I will call a Rites of Return program that is designed specially as therapy to facilitate healing. The effectiveness of such a program as sociotherapy for the masses will to a degree be contingent upon our ability to nationbuild. In other words, our ability to create what Kwame Agyei Akoto has called "liberated space;" space that may be physical, psychological or spiritual. Liberated space is our own institutions, our own land and our own conceptual constructs.

However, such a program could immediately impact communities with consciousness transformation amongst grassroots sisters and brothers that comes as a result of healing psychological and spiritual ruptures. The program would generally represent a **safe** environment of liberated psychological and spiritual space; employ a means of **remembrance and mourning**; allow for **reconnection** in the form of separation from Yurugu, participation in Afrikan ritual, and nation building activity.

Such a model or program might look like the following proposal and could begin as a single session of one-half day or a full day. (It should be noted that much of what follows is borrowed from Kobi Kambon, in his book *The African Personality in America*, on pages 188-194.)

RITES OF RETURN

I. Opening Libation

II. Naming Ceremony

III. Afrikan Identity Reclamation Ritual

IV. Historical Consciousness and Memory

V. Cathartic Expressions

VI. Consciousness Transformation Commitment

VII. Ujima and Ujamaa

VIII. Closing Reconnection Ritual

I. OPENING LIBATION

The opening libation is something that can be fashioned into a variety of acceptable forms. Some of the more generic (generic not being used in a condescending or negative way) forms are such as the general framework prescribed by Maulana Karenga, the originator of Kwanzaa. It is what Karenga calls the Tamshi La Tambiko or the libation statement. His example is as follows, from his book *The African American Holiday of Kwanzaa*:

> Our fathers and mothers came here, lived, loved, struggled and built here. At this place, their love and labor rose like the sun and gave strength and meaning to the day. For them, then, who gave so much we give in return. On this same soil we will sow our seeds, and build and move in unity and strength. Here too, we will continue their struggle for liberation and a higher level of human life. May our eyes be the eagle, our strength be the elephant, and the boldness of our life be like the lion. And may we remember and honor our ancestors and the legacy they left for as long as the sun shines and the waters flow.
>
> For our people everywhere then:
>
> For Shaka, Samory and Nzingha and all the others known and unknown who defended our ancestral land, history and humanity from alien invaders;
>
> For Garvey, Muhammad, Malcolm and King; Harriet, Fannie Lou, Sojourner, Bethune and Nat Turner and all the others who dared to define, defend and develop our interests as a people;
>
> For our children and the fuller and freer lives they will live because we struggle;
>
> For Kawaida and the Nguzo Saba, the new system of views and values which gives identity, purpose and direction to our lives;

For the new world we struggle to build;

And for the continuing struggle thru which we will inevitably rescue and reconstruct our history and humanity in our own image and according to our own needs. [26]

This again is a general libation that can itself be altered in terms of the names called in the libation, the libation form or structure, etc. Kobi Kambon also offers a general libation which is as follows:

We call upon our Ancestors far and near,

Fathers of our fathers, mothers of our mothers

To bear witness to what we have done,

And by their example, to continue to inspire us

toward, Reclaiming our African minds, regenerating our African spirit,

Liberating our home land, and reclaiming our greatness as a people.

We pour libation to bring into our midst their venerable African spirit, radiating their great wisdom, courage, dedication, and unyielding commitment to victory by any means necessary.

It is in the honor of our Creator, our Ancestors, our Children and their children, and all Africans to come after us that we pour libation.

For the Creator, Amon, and the various manifestations of the Creative Spirit;

We pour libation. (The audience responds "Aṣe")

For our esteemed Ancestors, who laid the foundation for human civilization, who provided the wisdom by which we live, and the models by which our lives are guided;

We pour libation. (Audience respond "Aṣe")

For our esteemed Ancestors who suffered the atrocities and horrors of our Maafa of the "middle passage" and the slave plantations, for those who perished, and for those who suffered unimaginable indignation, brutality and pain, and yet demonstrated the victorious power of the African spirit against any

adversity, by maintaining their human dignity no matter the cost;
We pour libation. (Audience respond "Aṣe")
And for those Ancestors who survived and made it
possible for us to be here today to continue on their valiant struggle
for African liberation, vindication and redemption, so that our
Goddest Maat may one day return to her eternal seat of harmony
within the African Universe;
We pour libation. (Audience respond "Aṣe")
For these our esteemed Ancestors surely represented the
very best that Africa could give to the world, And who's courage
and indomitable African spirit will live eternally in our hearts and
souls, For them, in their honor;
We pour libation. (Audience respond "Aṣe")
And finally, for our Children and their children and future
generations of Africans to come, that they too in their time will
vindicate our glorious race from all adversaries and continue to
imprint upon the world the great genius of African humanity,
We pour libation. (Audience respond "Aṣe")
May their venerable African spirit engulf this occasion to
reaffirm our Africanity.
It is done.
Amon Hotep. [27]

These libations are good general frameworks to be utilized or
modified according to preference. As Kambon mentions in his book,
it is good to use Afrikan language forms in libation as well. This is
seen in Kambon's use of "Aṣe" for example. "Aṣe" is a Yoruba term
and is a reference or affirmation of spiritual power being present in the
performance of the libation. The "A" in "Aṣe" is pronounced "ah," the
"ṣ" is pronounced like an "sh" and the "e" like a hard "a," so that the
word sounds like "ashay," as Kambon points out.

To add further impact to the power of calling the Creator and
the Ancestors during libation, it is good to call them by their Afrikan
names. This could be as simple as using an Afrikan language in place

of words like "Ancestors." For example, the Twi language term for Ancestors is "Nsamanfo ɔ ," or "Nana Nom Nsamanfoɔ ," which means "revered ancestral elders."

In addition, I can personally speak to the profound difference that there is when specific Afrikan names for God are used, as well as specific names for Afrikan deities or manifestations of the Supreme Creator. As an extension, when one is able to pour libation in an Afrikan language completely, the spirit and impact is enhanced that much more.

The following is an example of how Afrikan names and terms can enhance the spiritual presence and power in the praise and the invocation of ancestral and divine presence in the pouring of libations. This suggested framework for libation employs an amalgam of Afrikan language and culture, which is partly because most individual Afrikans have been severed, to a large degree, from knowledge of a single tradition that was theirs. This mixture of Afrikan language and culture is also appropriate since we Afrikans throughout the Diaspora are a mixture of Afrikan traditions and most of us cannot trace our lines genetically, culturally or geographically back to one place or another because of the destructive rupture caused by The Maafa. But, as is the divine nature of time and cycles, perhaps it is our task to draw strength from our bringing together of the best in Afrikan tradition, genetics and culture.

Terms (A difficulty that often arises with Afrikan terms is the fact that many Afrikan languages have characters that we do not have in the English alphabet. Therefore, the spellings of the following terms are both spellings using Afrikan language characters and using English phonetic spelling in place of Afrikan language characters. One should not attempt to assess true Afrikan written language using this example, nor should one look for consistency in the use of either Afrikan language characters or phonetic spelling. To reiterate, the Twi character," ɔ ," has a sound like "ore.")

ASHE (Yoruba) = the response that all gathered will say aloud after each pouring occurs during libation.

ME DAA ASE (Twi) = Thank you very much.

ABOSOM (Twi) = divine manifestations of the Creator / deities

ORISHA (Yoruba) = divine manifestations of the Creator / deities

NETCHERU (Kemet) = divine manifestations of the Creator / deities

NSAMANFOɔ (Twi) = ancestors

NSA (Twi) = drink or have a drink (libation poured after this (nsa) is said by person offering libation and "Ase" is echoed by those gathered after water is   poured)

ASAASE YAA (Twi) = Mother Earth/ counterpart to Onyame (God)

ONYAME (Twi) = God

OLUDUMARRE (Yoruba) = God

AMMA (Dogon) = God

NGALA (Bambara) = God

MUNGU (KiSwahili) = God

ASUO TAN ɔ (Twi) = Akan, river abosom, associated with fertility

ASUO GYEBI (Twi) = Akan, river abosom

BOSOMTWE (Twi) = Akan, sacred lake abosom

OBATALA (Yoruba) = orisha of peace, purity, serenity, calm, clarity

SHANGO (Yoruba) = orisha of power, control of enemies, fire, thunder and lightening

ESHU (Yoruba) = orisha messenger between divine and mortal

YEMANJA (Yoruba) = orisha of maternity, womanhood, the ocean

OGUN (Yoruba) = orisha of war, iron, steel

OSHUN (Yoruba) = orisha of love, marriage, beauty/rivers
AUSAR (Kemet) = the Father in the "Holy Trinity" of Father,
Mother and Child. Father of Heru.

AUSET (Kemet) = the Mother in the "Holy Trinity" of Father,
Mother and Child. Mother of Heru.

HERU (Kemet) = Child of Ausar and Auset. Bears such titles
as Lord of the World, Prince of Peace, Counselor, Re-
deemer, Son of God, etc.

DJEHUTI (Kemet) = Divine Scribe, Divine Scientist and
Mathmetician, Messenger between Netcheru and humans.

HAPI (Kemet) = Nile river netcher, associated with fertility

MAAT (KEMET) = Netcher of truth, order, balance, reciprocity,
harmony, compassion and justice. She is the path of
righteousness.

Libation

AS WE GATHER IN THIS PLACE LET US RECOGNIZE THAT AFRIKAN
PEOPLE EXIST IN SACRED TIME, WHERE WE SEE NO DISTINCTION BETWEEN
PAST, PRESENT AND FUTURE. INSTEAD, THE PAST, PRESENT AND FUTURE ARE
ALL INTERTWINED AND DEPENDENT UPON ONE ANOTHER. THIS IS WHY WE
ACKNOWLEDGE THE ANCESTORS, THE LIVING AND THE YET UNBORN IN THE
POURING OF LIBATIONS; BECAUSE WE CAN ALL COME TOGETHER AT ONCE IN
SACRED TIME AND SPACE.

SO, WE HAVE GATHERED HERE AND WE HAVE MADE THIS SPACE
SACRED AND WE EXIST IN SACRED TIME. LET US WELCOME THE PRESENCE OF
AFRIKAN SPIRIT HERE WITH US.

ONYAME, OLUDUMARRE, NGALA, MUNGU, AMMA, AMEN RA, NSA
AND ALL THE MANY GREAT NAMES THAT AFRIKAN PEOPLE HAVE
CALLED THE ONE GOD, TO HIM WE GIVE HONOR AND ASK HIS PRESENCE. TO
THIS WE SAY... (LIBATION POURED, ALL PARTICIPANTS SAY "ASHE.")

ASAASE YAA, NSA,
SHE WHO NURTURES LIFE AND CRADLES HUMANKIND, OUR

MOTHER AND COMPANION OF THE ONE GOD, TO HER WE SAY... (LIBATION POURED, ALL PARTICIPANTS SAY "ASHE.")

WE INVOKE THE PRESENCE OF THE ABOSOM, THE ORISHA, THE NETCHERU TO GIVE US GUIDANCE AND POWER IN OUR STRUGGLE; TO GIVE US CLARITY OF PURPOSE IN OUR LIFEWORK OF DESTROYING DESTRUCTION AND RETURNING NATURAL ORDER WHERE THERE IS CHAOS.

BOSOMTWE NSA

ASUO TANƆ NSA

ASUO GYEBI NSA

OBATALA NSA

SHANGO NSA

ESHU/LEGBA NSA

YEMANJA NSA

OGUN NSA

OSHUN NSA

AUSAR NSA

AUSET NSA

HERU NSA

DJEHUTI NSA

HAPI NSA

MAAT NSA

FOR ALL THOSE WE MAY NOT HAVE CALLED OR MAY NOT KNOW AS THEY WORK IN OUR LIVES, WE POUR LIBATION (AUDIENCE RESPOND "ASHE").

NANA NOM NSAMANFOƆ NSA

TO ALL THOSE WHO COULD NOT BE HERE WITH US IN BODY, BUT HAVE LEFT A LEGACY OF STRUGGLE, RESISTANCE, LOVE AND CARING. TO THESE NSAMANFOƆ WE POUR LIBATION (AUDIENCE RESPOND "ASHE")

AT THIS TIME WE CALL OUT THE NAMES OF THOSE ANCESTORS WE APPRECIATE AND GIVE HONOR TO AND WHOSE PRESENCE WE INVOKE. (AUDIENCE NOW CALLS OUT THE NAMES OF SPECIFIC ANCESTORS, I.E., NAT TURNER, MALCOLM X, QUEEN NZINGA, ETC. AFTER EACH NAME IS CALLED THE POURER OF THE LIBATION SAYS "NSA" AND THEN POURS THE LIBATION TO

WHICH THOSE GATHERED RESPOND "ASHE.")

WE ALSO CALL THE NAMES OF THOSE NSAMANFOƆ WE HAVE KNOWN, WHO HAVE BEEN CLOSE TO US, OR ARE FAMILY MEMBERS. (NAMES CALLED IN THE SAME FASHION AS WITH THE GENERAL HISTORICAL FIGURES.)

WE HAVE GIVEN PRAISE AND HONOR TO THE CREATOR, THE ABOSOM, ORISHA, NETCHERU AND THE NSAMANFOƆ. LET THEM BE PLEASED AND FEEL OUR DEEP GRATITUDE. WE HAVE CALLED THEM AND THEY HAVE COME. LET THEIR PRESENCE MOVE OUR GATHERING TO ANOTHER LEVEL OF PURPOSE. LET US BE SERIOUS ABOUT THE LIBERATION OF AFRIKAN PEOPLE AND DO HONOR TO THESE WE HAVE INVOKED TO BE IN OUR PRESENCE.

AS THE MOON REFLECTS THE SUN, SO TO SHALL OUR STRUGGLE BE UNENDING. AS NIGHT FOLLOWS DAY AND DAY FOLLOWS NIGHT, WE UNDER- STAND DIVINE CYCLES AND THE CERTAINTY THAT AFRIKAN PEOPLE SHALL RISE AGAIN. SO IT IS SAID, SO IT SHALL BE DONE. ME DAA ASE, ME DAA ASE!

****

This is a general structure for a libation that, like the others, can be altered to meet the specific needs of the gathering or praise.

II. NAMING CEREMONY

As a part of the cleansing process, participants of Rites of Return who do not yet have Afrikan names, will be given time to select one for the purpose of leaving old ways behind and taking a step back toward the Afrikan way. A single name, i.e., Kwesi, Chike, Akosua, Abena, etc., is sufficient for Rites of Return purposes. Participants should be given the explanation for adopting an Afrikan name and made aware that they are to be referred to by Afrikan names and Afrikan names only during Rites of Return. Participants should also be allowed time to choose from a list of names with their meanings. Name tags should be filled out and worn, after which each person should then stand a recite the following individually.

Naming Ceremony

In the spirit of Afrikan resurrection, redemption and a victorious return to The Way, I take the name _____ . I wear
it proudly and shall respond to nothing else during Rites of Return. I
am _____, I am _____, I am_____, Ashe!

III. AFRIKAN IDENTITY RECLAMATION RITUAL

This third aspect of the sociotherapeutic Rites of Return
model is taken directly from Kambon's model in *The African Personality in America* with modifications in wording and some of the
substance. In the Rites of Return session, the ritual is to be led by
one or more of the facilitators of the program, with Rites of Return
participants following their lead and repeating their words.

Afrikan Identity Reclamation Ritual [28]

I stand before the Creator, the Abosom and the Nsamanfoɔ to
declare that from this day forth I divest from the European *asili*. I
claim True liberation, which is self-knowledge, self-definition,
psychological health, self-determination and self-sufficiency.

1. In this act of Afrikan True liberation, on the blood of the Nana Nom
Nsamanfo ɔ who suffered, bled and died during The Maafa and its
continuous legacy for hundreds of years, I renounce my conscious and
unconscious fulfillment of the European *asili*.

2. In this act of Afrikan True liberation, under the watchful eyes of the
Creator, the Abosom, the Nsamanfoɔ and in the presence of the
Afrikan Global Community, I wash my hands as a symbolic act of
purging, from my liberated psychological and spiritual space, the
European *asili* and washing away the blood and muck of any
complicitness, conscious or unconscious, that I may have practiced in
supporting brutalizers and murderers of our Nsamanfo ɔ . (Ceremo-

nial washing of the hands should now take place.)

3. In this act of Afrikan True liberation, I dedicate/rededicate myself to the vindication of the Nsamanfoɔ who suffered through The Maafa and atrocities that have come at the hands of people, from enemies in all corners of the world. I dedicate/rededicate myself to nationbuilding and establishing an Afrikan reality more glorious than any in time. My lifework is the restoration of confidence in the Afrikan Way. It is the destruction of the lack of confidence that has Afrikan people clinging to European cultural, ideological and philosophical systems as though there was nothing valid in Afrikan tradition prior to the rape and pillage of Afrikan life, accompanied by the imposition of the European *asili*. In this restoration I strive to return the sanctity to Afrikan life and culture, and dismiss the distortions and devaluation of Afrikan life, culture and existence.

4. In this act of Afrikan True liberation, I declare with all of my heart that I will never allow Afrikan children to be miseducated, abused, psychologically devastated and turned against their own people as the waste product of insane processes of socialization and acculturation alien to them. It is my duty to maximally educate my Afrikan children, any children that I will have in the future and/or any Afrikan children who fall within the sphere of my influence.

5. In this act of Afrikan True liberation, I vow to never again swallow the rage that is my natural reaction to oppression. I vow to never allow injustices to be committed against Afrikan people without speaking out strongly against them, whether on the job, in the community, or in my presence wherever I am. I will channel my justified and natural anger and rage into productive action toward the building of a new Afrikan nation and reality.

6. In this act of Afrikan True liberation, I will strive to maintain the stability of my Afrikan mind and that of my family by engaging daily in Systematic Enemy Analysis. I know that this is the type of dedication that any people who want to be free must have.

7. To this oath I dedicate my total committment as I make True liberation my lifework.

May the Creator, the Abosom, the Nsamanfoɔ and the Afrikan Global Community take pride and be revitalized by my commitment to fulfill the destiny of Afrikan liberation. So it is said, so it shall be done. Ashe!

****

The oath and this ritual are to be performed with the utmost seriousness and symbolic nature. As with the entire Rites of Return program, there should be no icons and symbols of European culture within the liberated space of the program. To this end a Rites of Return space should be chosen that has neither secular nor religious European icons and symbols, or one in which such symbols can be covered up for the length of the program. In conjunction with this aspect of seriousness and liberated physical, spiritual and psychological space, Rites of Return participants should wear clothing with no symbols or icons of the European cultural reality. This includes clothing and apparel with sports logos, professional or business logos, etc. This is necessary to insure the purity and maximal effectiveness of the psychological and spiritual changes to take place within the program. This also makes it easier to take one's mind off of the world dominated by the European *asili*, which is outside of the Rites of Return program. It goes along with the assumption of an Afrikan name specifically for the program for those who do not have Afrikan names already.

IV. HISTORICAL CONSCIOUSNESS AND MEMORY SESSION

A prescribed amount of time should be taken to share The Maafa concept, tell The Maafa story and show pictures of the brutal lynchings, beatings, etc. The types of trauma Afrikan people have suffered should be shared, as well as the long lasting nature of this trauma, and the role of therapy.

V. CATHARTIC EXPRESSIONS

In this portion of the program, participants are encouraged to express themselves fully. It is a no holds barred expression of rage, sadness, joy and whatever emotions people feel. It is a chance to say those things that are often thought, but seldom shared in the day to day stresses and frustrations of Afrikan people. It is a chance to openly express disgust in our condition, identify enemies, share joy in our movement, etc.

Participants may also share stories of fears, hurt, frustration and anything that is on their minds. It must be made clear that respect is a major component of this portion of Rites of Return. Judgements are not to be passed on anyone for what is shared openly amongst this family gathering. Everything is also shared in confidence and the following oath is to be taken.

Oath of Silence

Liberation is serious and healing is a part of liberation. Therefore, I vow to hold all that is shared in Cathartic Expressions in confidence. I do this so that we are all free to heal and so that I will not violate the trust we will establish here today. My sisters and brothers have my word that my silence is out of respect and their protection. I do this in the presence of the Creator, the Abosom, the Nsamanfoɔ and the Rites of Return family. Ashe!

VI. CONSCIOUSNESS TRANSFORMATION COMMITMENT

At this point, Rites of Return are nearing their end. Participants once again must reaffirm their commitment to transforming their consciousness and being a different person upon leaving Rites of Return than they were when they entered.

Consciousness Transformation Commitment

I declare that I will walk in the path of Maat and actively seek to change my life once I leave this place. My commitment to my people is real; my commitment to my family is real; my commitment to the children is real; my commitment to myself is real. It is a new day, Ashe!

VI. UJIMA AND UJAMAA SESSION

Participants have the opportunity to mingle with one another sharing business, institutional and community contacts, while establishing grounds for possible collective work and cooperative economics. If there are skills and resources that are needed by participants and can be found within other participants sphere of influence, this is the time to establish contacts.

VII. CLOSING RECONNECTION RITUAL

The day is closed allowing for final comments and questions. Final business is taken care of, such as giving participants the Rites of Return T-Shirt and making sure everyone has reading lists, etc. Rites of Return is ended with the Closing Reconnection Ritual.

Closing Reconnection Ritual

All that I have pledged today, I will uphold. I have reconnected and reaffirmed my connection with the Afrikan Way. I recognize that my return to The Way is a lifelong process that I must work at from day to day. I must pass the knowledge and the process to the children. If I should fall in the line of this duty, as the odds are stacked high against Afrikan people, I know that I will rise stronger than I was before my fall and will be harder to knock down the next time. My strength is Spirit.

On my side is truth and natural order. The cycles of life have brought us to the time of our rising once again. It is our time, let us fulfill our calling.

The Creator, the Abosom and the Nsamanfoɔ have blessed this gathering, let their return to their places of rest be peaceful and full of our thanks. So it is said, liberation! So it shall be done, Ashe!

****

As with everything we do, such a sociotherapeutic model as Rites of Return will be enhanced and refined by those who are serious and concerned with the mental health of Afrikan people. And of course, there are the little things that must be done around such a program, such as the development of materials for participants, the securing of Afrikan symbols and icons to fill the liberated space of Rites of Return programs, the training of Rites of Return facilitators, the set up of registration mechanisms, development of promotional materials (i.e., t-shirts, hats, etc.), and the list goes on.

This is simply one model that might be used to specifically address Afrikan mental health and a return to stability and sanity. It does not replace programs such as Rites of Passage, but complements them. It differs in that it is specifically dedicated to addressing the psychological needs of Afrikan people concerning pathology, The Maafa and existence within the confines of a world dominated by the European *asili*.

So as we look at healing as a process, the discussion in this chapter represents only a portion of the coping mechanisms and socio-therapeutic concerns that we will need to address as a people. It is another of the many areas in which we as a people have much work to do.

CHAPTER 6

ooooooooo

LET US MOVE ON

Without a doubt, our old/new conceptual framework, or Afrikan consciousness, will be supported by and necessitates action. It is much more than concept and ideology. The Afrikan *asili* represents the germinating principles of an Afrikan reality revolution; principles that have always been in place, but that we have strayed away from. This revolution is a revolution that demands a return to these principles and much more than transformed consciousness. In return, it offers healing and true liberation. There are two concepts which serve as components of an old/new Afrikan consciousness to guide our action: *nkoso⊃* and *daakye abra b⊃* . In this chapter we will examine these conceptual levels of struggle.

As we have examined our trauma and prescribed remedies, we understand that Afrikan people must not only be master scholars and theorists, but also doers and nationbuilders. And, this must extend to all Afrikans at one level or another in order for there to be a process of healing and the mechanisms to put it in place.

Nkoso⊃ (movement)

Nkoso⊃ is a Twi word that means "progress going on," with our conceptual equivalent of "movement." *Nkoso⊃* , or movement, is a level of struggle that might be correlated to short-term action. It involves the concrete actions that we must participate in day to day, from survival and sustaining family to reading, studying, building and creating. *Nkoso⊃* represents what must be done to meet the immediate needs of the individual and the collective Afrikan global community. Theories and concepts are generally far removed from *nkoso⊃* in a sense. *Nkoso⊃* is movement; it is Afrikan people taking an active role in the everyday advancement of struggle and movement toward liberation.

Recognizing that for many Afrikan people day to day survival is an overriding concern, *nkoso⊃* must involve mechanisms for the mental and physical improvement of the standard of living. For example, the ability to have healthy and nutritious meals each day is a must. A hungry child cannot learn to his or her maximum potential; concentration suffers, reflexes are slow and mental functioning is hampered. Studies bear this out. A hungry adult is consumed with figuring out how to eat, not understanding Cheikh Anta Diop for example.

Free breakfast programs, in conjunction with free adult education and our children's education in independent institutions, are examples of *nkoso⊃* which meet immediate survival needs. Yes, our children's education is an immediate survival need. Another example is the ability of Afrikans returning to The Way to provide employment as well as liberation activities for our people. Coming together to develop organizations that provide physical and mental protection and nurturing is another example of *nkoso⊃* .

On yet another level, many Afrikan people are in a quandary, where they are struggling to make a better life for themselves, but lack true vision as to what that means. If an Afrikan sister or brother is working for a Fortune 500 company for example, it must be with definitive *nkoso ⊃* or short-term goals in mind. It must be with an eye toward accumulating capital, skills or knowledge to be used toward true liberation. For instance, while you are working you must set specific time frames for your existence within such a money driven environment. Within that time frame you must move to acquire whatever skills and resources necessary, not simply to boost your own standard of living, but to save money and plan for your departure into something meaningful and fruitful for yourself and Afrikan people; things such as preparing to be an entrepreneur within the Afrikan community, accumulating capital to build institutions in the Afrikan community, developing skills to be utilized within Afrikan organizations and institutions, etc. The bottom line is that we can ill afford to waste time busting our butts in corporations with no other plans, except being promoted, keeping our jobs, making more money, hoping that status quo doesn't change and being satisfied with dependency and the madness of the world.

If our energies are to be used "in the system," which many must do for survival in a monetary society, we must be using twice as much brain energy figuring how we will use our time and resources to benefit Afrikan people and free ourselves. In other words, *those Afrikan people who are not self-sufficient, entrepreneurs, institution builders or working within Afrikan institutions must be infiltrators in "mainstream" America and not assimilators.*

Our talented sisters and brothers are too valuable to be wasted simply working for an abnormal society and nothing else. If our jobs don't allow time or energy for us to devote to the liberation of Afrikan people, we need to make time. If we cannot make time, we need to make plans to leave and become self-sufficient through entrepreneurship or get a different job if it happens to be the only viable short-term option. If one obtains a different job, it should preferably be with Afrikan people moving in a positive direction. If this fails and one gets a job meaningless to Afrikan liberation beyond paying one's bills, one must become an infiltrator, using their time, resources, and money to move toward a definite short-term plan that allows them to function in the service of Afrikan liberation.

If one chooses to maintain employment within institutions of the European *asili*, then this employment has to allow for direct, clear and substantial benefit to the Afrikan community. If you "buy the company line" and engage in enthusiastic pursuit of the so called "American Dream," you are lost. And, you'll be hurting your people in the process.

Our lives must have a purpose beyond the material. *Nkoso⊃* must drive our activities, not the pursuit of material possessions and green colored paper. A life spent in fulfillment of the European *asili* is empty, if not for us then for our children who will end up fighting the same battles that we had to fight, or that we labored through while refusing to fight. Our children might also end up being casualties, because of our inactivity and lack of preparation, at the hands of an insane world. Working for someone else all of our life with no plan and no contribution toward Afrikan liberation is not only a betrayal of ourselves and our people, but of our young children and those yet unborn. What will we have to pass on but the madness and insanity that we failed to challenge? The ultimate goal, regardless of our current employment or circumstances, is true liberation. True liberation is self-knowledge, self-definition, psychological health, self-determination and self-sufficiency; a return to The Way.

If liberation is not the ultimate goal, everything else is hollow and meaningless. If liberation is not the objective, then our lives and pursuit of material success are an exercise in comfortable captivity. Comfortable captivity is ignoring our oppression, dysfunctionality and dependency, and instead seeking material comfort and *false* financial security within a captive existence.

Many Afrikan people who say, regarding working for liberation, 'why bother, everything is fine?,' need to be smacked into reality. Also, such statements often come from disenchanted Afrikans who are wondering why those who have 'made it' would bother with liberation. Aside from the multitude of obvious reasons that such a statement is false, which need not be reiterated here, there is another very significant reason such a statement is flawed.

We can approach such attitudes from a perspective other than one which states that injustice anywhere is a threat to justice everywhere. This is not always real or meaningful to people. It must be realized that most Afrikans who think everything is fine do not know what fine is. Even those who are a little better off financially than others have had encounters with "racism" and have dealt with the day to day strain and stress of being Afrikan in America. Some will deny it, but denial is also part of our pathology, so that's not surprising. Day to day stress and strain can be something as simple as seeing a crime on the news and praying that it wasn't committed by an Afrikan for fear that it would make you look bad. This stress and strain may be the extra work and constant worry over appearance and performance that Afrikan people must endure in corporate America. It may be the fact that Afrikans in certain environments cannot "be themselves." It may be the twinge of discomfort when you are the only Afrikan in a room and a joke is told about Afrikan people. It may be the dissatisfaction with your hair texture or wide nose because the current dominant standard says you are ugly as your natural self. It may be that those with the most material wealth still find the need to surgically or chemically alter their appearance. (Yes, Europeans do this also, but the European *asili* is unhealthy for Europeans as well.) All of these are things that even Afrikans who have so called "made it" must deal with and such circumstances are not okay. And, these only represent the small inconveniences within a reality of destruction and oppression.

Most Afrikan people do not realize that these stresses, worries and strains, are not normal nor do they have to be lived with, despite the fact that we have endured them so long we see them as part of life or as necessary evils. We are often ignorant of what it means for everything to be okay, because our existence has been so troubled and our minds so manipulated that this current reality is all we know. Many have no idea what it is like to live a life free of the additional stresses and strains that come simply because we are Afrikan people in this world. We have no idea how drastically different it might be not to worry many of our worries and enjoy harmonious development with only the insignificant trifles of life occasionally disrupting our peace. That would be normal; that would be a life where everything is fine. That is a life that is possible if we are all willing to fight for liberation. If we are not struggling and resisting, as we should be simply because as those like us suffer for who and what they are, we will suffer sooner or later; or because it is right to do what we can to alleviate the pain of the Afrikan existence for the masses; or for the realization of our trauma and pathology; then even the most selfish amongst us can find reason to move toward liberation when they realize that their privileged and materially wealthy or psychologically disturbed comfortable existence is still plagued with things that do not have to be.

There is a world that Afrikan people have not known for ages that is better than this madness and abnormality that we are currently living. There is a world of comfort, pleasure, mental peace, balance and harmonious being that has been cast aside for the insane, abnormal and flawed reality we are living in.

So, whatever our reasons, we all do have reasons for returning to The Way. We all do have reasons for seeking true liberation. We all do have reasons for engaging in *nkosoɔ* and *daakye abra bɔ*.

Nkosoɔ and Education

For our children independent education is a must **right now**! Independent education is *nkosoɔ*, or movement. We currently have the independent institutions and the ability to build more, so it is short-term action that must be taken. Parents must begin to recognize the necessity of proper education for their children. We have examined the European *asili* and the general madness of the current world reality and now must realize that public education serves as a socializer into the madness and a perpetuator of the *asili*. The function of today's public education is to generate and strengthen the *asili*, as students learn about Plato and his cohorts, obtain material values, view life's purpose as securing a good paying job, learn negative perceptions of themselves as the cultural other, adopt the norms of the present world reality, etc. With the masses of Afrikan children and young adults continuing to go through 12, 16 and 18+ years of this indoctrination, we will find that true liberation, a return to The Way, is virtually impossible. We will see Afrikans incapable of understanding how or why to move toward liberation; as is the case with those countless millions who suffer without treatment from the destructiveness and trauma of our existence in the Western Hemisphere. And we will probably see the continued rise in Afrikans who fulfill and are guided by the European *asili*, becoming not only useless, but destructive to the rest of us who represent the cultural other.

As we continue to build independent schools, those we have should grow exponentially in terms of student population.

We must educate, at the very least, 70% of our children. This is to mean that we must control the content, values and administration of their education. Our children must be viewed as our valued and cherished promise for a new tomorrow. [1]

Not only must the numbers of students in our independent institutions grow, along with the building of more institutions, but these schools must also rise to the occasion. They must be constantly growing physically and in the substance of the education offered. Education cannot be the narrow framework that passes for education in America. Parents who bring their children to our institutions must be made aware that the children are not there to learn how to better "fit in" with the present society and get a "good job." Our definitions of education must change so that we are not mimicking European education in Afrikan clothing.

When we continue to allow an abnormal and insane society to educate or indoctrinate our children, we have already lost the war of true liberation. We are foolish to then ask why our children behave the way they do and why the masses of children are failing in school. For us this failure should include those who leave with no knowledge of how they will participate in the liberation of Afrikan people, as well as those who have no knowledge of self and who fulfill the European *asili*, regardless of their "academic achievements."

Without participating in our children's maximal development, we are foolish to ask why our masses are lost to the knowledge of themselves and why our suffering seems to be overwhelming and never ending. We cannot even justifiably ask these questions if we are not engaging in the fundamental *nkoso ɔ* of taking care of what reality and consciousness our children, tomorrow's adults, will be taught and nurtured in.

To date there has been a failure to reach our children and many Afrikan adults have performed the disgraceful act of "writing off" a generation of young people. They have thrown their hands up and claimed that they cannot reach our troubled youth. They have abdicated their responsibility as adults and Afrikan people. The problem is many fold.

One of the reasons that Afrikan adults cannot reach the youth is because we consistently lie to them. Afrikan adults have been guilty of not acknowledging that this country, America, and this world are both diametrically opposed to the survival and maximal development of our young people. Instead, they have held out the insistence that going to school and getting a "good education" is the answer. All the while the youth know, while they may not be able to articulate what they intuitively observe, that the world is crazy, they are being miseducated and they are not cared for. As a consequence many of our wayward young people do not even wish to listen to adults who come offering what they think is help. Young people, being the astute observers that they are, can see madness when it is present all around them. They also see the contradiction in materialistic, money hungry adults trying to tell them not to deal drugs. The young people know that through dealing drugs they can achieve the same material things that the majority of the country aspires to. They also see "white collar" crime re-enforcing their belief that quick ways to this material acquisition are not only possible, but viable.

Perhaps we should rethink our approach and be honest with our young people. If we are to fail at any aspect of their salvation, let us fail to write them off and fail to look down on them in condescension. Let us fail to refuse to hear their points of view and their problems. Our children are our responsibility and our future. We must educate them and build the institutions to do so.

Also, when we develop our own institutions, but they produce an Afrikan imitation of the European *asili*, our *nkosoɔ* ceases to be and we stagnate. We place ourselves on the road to return to The Way by having our own institutions, but we are still walking in the wrong direction and continue to move further from The Way when we model them after the European *asili*. Although we have control of the institution, we operate within the same conceptual framework, using the same definitions of reality and epistemological principles we have determined to be flawed.

For example, an independent educational institution run by Afrikan people, which openly embraces Mother Afrika, but teaches aspiration toward financial gain as an end of the educational process; recognizes the "American Dream" as valid; envisions as a goal ways to fit into a European dominated society; such an institution represents a contradiction. While there may be some success within the parameters of a reality whose success is defined by the European *asili*, the ultimate Afrikan success of true liberation, a return to The Way, cannot be achieved in this manner.

The task then is to shape the old/new Afrikan consciousness that frames our new reality. We then extrapolate from this old/new Afrikan consciousness and define an educational reality. The shaping of an old/new Afrikan consciousness will be a task undertaken by many sane Afrikan people who utilize *nyansa nnsa da*, or thought without boundaries. Thus, *nkoso ɔ* as relates to education, and *nkoso ɔ* in general, must always be moving toward the fulfillment of the Afrikan *asili*.

A partial list of independent Afrikan schools follows (provided in part by the Council of Independent Black Institutions, with philosophies and mission statements provided by the schools themselves). The purpose of the list in this publication is so that we can begin to take control of the education of our young people, by enrolling them in independent schools. The philosophies and mission statements of many of the schools are listed so that parents can make informed decisions. It should be realized that there are many schools that may not be included in this list. This list is to assist the placement of our young people in the proper environments and is being placed right in the middle of this text, not in an appendix, because of its importance.

A-T SEBAN MESUT (Washington, D.C.)
5924 Georgia Avenue, NW

A-T Seban Mesut (School for the Children of Ausar [God]) is an independent parochial school founded by the Ausar Auset Society, Washington, D.C. Branch. Since 1983, the school has been committed to "African Centered Education with a Spiritual Foundation."

PHILOSOPHY: Our children are a priceless asset. Their years of growth and development are a valuable means of establishing a stable future for all African people.

A-T Seban Mesut exists in order to provide means through

which African children can be nurtured with the fundamental African principle of One God who expresses itself as the Creator. This view of reality serves as the unifying principle in the African world which includes the Neteru (Angels, Archangels), and Shepsu (Enlightened Ancestors).

Our philosophy is that the "spirit" serves as a vehicle for all facets of education. Therefore, we stress the cultivation of spiritual faculties as a means for creating a balance amongst the factors that play a role in learning and living.

Academy of the Way (Philadelphia, PA)

African-American Academy for Excellence (Columbus Ohio)

African Caribbean Self-Help Organization (Birmingham, UK)

Afrikan Children Advance Learning Center (Oakland, CA)

AFRIKAN PEOPLE'S ACTION SCHOOL (Trenton, NJ)

27 East Paul Avenue

PHILOSOPHY: The Afrikan People's Action School was founded to provide what Dr. Woodson described as "real education." Dr. Woodson defined real education as inspiring people to live more abundantly, to learn to begin with life as they find it, and make it better. Following Dr. Woodson, our program rests on three basic beliefs. The first is that education transmits knowledge and wisdom from one generation to the next to prepare young people to be future leaders. The second is to perpetuate a cultural perspective. Third is motivation comes from parents, school and the child.

Aisha Shule & Dubois Preparatory Academy (Detroit, MI)

Atlanta Progress Academy (Atlanta, GA)

Children's Village at Harrity (Philadelphia, PA)
Community Development Institute (East Palo Alto, CA)

_____

CUSH CAMPUS (Brooklyn, NY)
221 Kingston Avenue

The operation of the Cush Campus Schools is based on the philosophy that children are natural learners and that educators should seek to draw forth from them instead of trying to put something into them. This process must entail a recognition of the impact of historic as well as present circumstances.

MISSION STATEMENT: Cush Campus, a dedicated nonsectarian community-based school, prepares children to compete in a culturally diverse, technological society. Students are prepared for college level study and equipped with the critical thinking and analytical skills that will allow them to succeed in a global community.

_____

Delaney Learning Center (Seattle, WA)
Each One Teach One (Columbus, Ohio)

_____

FLORENCE JACKSON ACADEMY (Atlanta, GA)
1581 Fairburn Road, SW

PURPOSE: Florence Jackson Academy is dedicated to preserving the heritage of African people by reflecting, protecting, and sustaining values consistent with the cultural worldview of African people. Bradley's motto, "Education for Liberation," expresses the school's pledge to liberate the minds of the students for their continued social, cultural, moral, political and economic advancement, thus preparing them to make positive contributions to their communities and to the larger society as well. Specifically, the academy seeks to provide its students with:

1. An educational environment that fosters maximum intellectual stimulation, a sense of social responsibility, and sound cultural identity;

2. An atmosphere that promotes the creative and dynamic exchange of ideas whereby the student can deal critically with reality for the transformation of themselves and society;

3. Preparation and grounding in the cultural tradition and values that will foster cultural transmission to subsequent generations;

4. Preparation in the scholarly tradition that will support academic pursuits;

5. Experiences that will promote an awareness of, and sensitivity to, societal structures which persistently provoke the climate and substance of social change;

6. An understanding of and respect for others rooted in the moral and spiritual values of African people.

7. Competent teachers who serve as easily identifiable role models who along with the institution will provide opportunities for research and innovation, respect for individual differences among students and ways of providing for these differences.

FREDERICK DOUGLASS INSTITUTE (St. Louis, MO)
Office: 1724 N. Taylor

MISSION STATEMENT: To promote the (inter)national sovereignty of African people as: 1) the God-ordained, and therefore best, condition under which African people should live; and, 2) as the key to our challenges, cure for our problems and the only workable definition of liberation.

To promote universal, systematic, comprehensive, and lifelong (womb to tomb) God-based African education as the natural and only means by which we can develop perpetual generations of African people who "possess the moral direction, intellectual fervor, cultural/political intelligence, desire and personality" necessary to bring about and maintain that sovereign and rebuilt nation.

To promote and expand the international African education system - including insistence on the critical mass (minimum 80%) of African people attending full time African schools through the "critical period" of our lives - as a prerequisite to the implementation of African education, behavior, sovereignty and the rebuilt nation.

To coordinate, maintain, promote and expand that system specifically in the Missouri/Southern Illinois region through the building and maintaining of a system in each community, including the St. Louis Metropolitan area where the system's enrollment goal is 40,000 African youth (ages 4-18) by 2030.

To maintain and expand liberation zones, outposts and communities as working scale models of the spiritual, social and physical character of self-determination, and thus, to demonstrate the workability, advantages and positive results of African education, behavior, and eventual sovereignty.

Copyright 1981 by F. Douglass Institute, revised January 1990.

Harambee Educational Foundation (Riviera Beach, FL)
Harambee Home School (Hampton, VA)
Holloway College (London, UK)
H.O.M.E. - Helping Our Minds Expand (Atlanta, GA)

THE IAMBIEN INSTITUTE (Wilmington, DE)
1022 West 6th Street

MISSION: To yield confident, caring students (and families) who can empower and nurture self, sustain their families and advance / contribute to their community (Nation).

EDUCATIONAL AIM:
(1) To educate students (and their families) for personal, family, community and economic development, greatness and empowerment. (2) To enhance, affirm and utilize the knowledge, skills and abilities of students and their families (Villagers) as producers, developers and contributors to self, family and community building and empowerment. (3) To utilize the community in the development and education of the student.

ILE OMODE SCHOOL (Oakland, CA)

PHILOSOPHY: The Wo'se Community School Program, as embodied in Ile Omode, is grounded in academics and cultural principles which provide a foundation for the development of self-determined scholarship and leadership. Our goal is to create a learning environment which encourages creative problem solving, teamwork, and confidence. Through learning experiences that are both challenging and fun, we are preparing our children to compete in a technologically advanced society. We emphasize African values and community as a framework for the utilization of this technology. Our vision is that our students become highly motivated and creative leaders who are both capable and committed to the betterment of our nation.

We stress the development of our students' bodies, minds, souls, and consciousness. We develop our bodies by eating a proper diet and exercising daily. We develop our minds by acquiring knowledge and skills that are useful to our advancement. We develop our souls by developing our relationship with the Creator and with our people based on Maat-Truth, Justice, and Right Order-and reciprocity. We develop our consciousness by attaining self-awareness, identity, self-control, and discipline.

Our children, today's children, represent our tomorrow; what they are gives us an indication of our future as a people. Ile Omode joins parents in the task of nurturing the development of superior children.

Knowledge is like a garden;
If it is not cultivated,
It cannot be harvested.
-Guinea

IMHOTEP CENTER OF EDUCATION (Atlanta, GA)
541 Harwell Road, NW

PHILOSOPHY: Imhotep Center of Education is building its educational program around the concept currently known as "Afrocentric" or African-Centered education. Our wholistic approach to education is based upon the premise that our children will only excel academically and intellectually when the curriculum, teaching methodology, and environment reflect who we are as well as where we are going as African-Americans.

It is vital that we begin this approach with our children at the earliest possible age. For this reason, we feel that exposing our children to take pride in their own history and heritage is the kind of first impression that will begin them on the road to self confidence and self esteem.

We teach our children to understand and respect other ethnic groups, but our main focus is to teach them to truly love themselves, their history, and their heritage. They will be able to love others and to appreciate the contribution other ethnic groups have made to this society, because they will begin with a familiarity and an affinity for their own unique and rich culture.

African-Centered or Wholistic education is much more than just familiarizing children with our culture; it is also devising teaching methods to motivate our students and put them firmly on the path of true academic excellence. We at the Imhotep Center of Education have realized that many of our brightest children have been mis-educated or stigmatized as "slow", simply because they were taught with invalid, ineffective techniques. In addition, some of our best students are often trapped in school environments that fail to motivate them or to build self-confidence.

The Imhotep Center of Education makes the creation of an inspiring, enriching school environment one of its primary objectives.

Imhotep Independent School (London, UK)
Johnson Preparatory School (Brooklyn, NY)
The Lotus Academy (Philadelphia, PA)
Martin Luther King Jr. Academy for Youth (Vineland, NJ)
Maarifa Children's Center (Baltimore, MD)
Mali Yetu (Cleveland, OH)
Mandelas Educational Institute (Compton, CA)
Marcus Garvey (Los Angeles, CA)
Marcus Garvey Shule (Philadelphia, PA)
Marcus Malcolm Shule (St. Louis, MO)
Meadows-Livingstone School (San Francisco, CA)
NationHouse Watoto School & Sankofa Institute (Washington, DC)

New Concept Development Center (Chicago, IL)
7825 South Ellis Ave.

Philosophy of Education: Like Kwame Nkruma, NCDC believes that "Knowledge without purpose is blind." Our goal is to develop young people who see themselves as fundamentally linked to their families, communities and Black people in the broadest geographical sense. We believe that even the youngest of children construct their conceptual understandings by drawing upon what they already know and by applying those understandings to meaningful problems. The NCDC curriculum stresses critical thinking, problem solving and application of knowledge in everyday experiences which are couched in terms of the cultural, historical, social and political experiences as well as the needs of the African American community. NCDC is a place where children love to be and where children love to learn. We believe the school should be a place of both self-discipline and joy, a place of personal happiness as well as community commitment.

Nile Valley Shule (Buffalo, NY)

Nsoroma Institute (Highland Park, MI)
13220 Woodward Avenue

Philosophy: Nsoroma Institute is an Afrikan-Centered Institution. We are guided by a philosophy which seeks to: develop within our children insight into their individual gifts, talents and missions, connect our children with the rich and diverse historical and cultural legacies of Afrikan peoples, and seek to restore a world view which reflects an understanding of the inter dependence of humans, plants, animals, the air, water, soil and natural elements which create the delicate balance which sustains life on the planet earth.

Inherent in this world view is the understanding that oppression is wrong. Any system or set of circumstances which limits a people from realizing the fullest expression of their human potential must be replaced with ways of relating spiritually, socially, politically and economically which facilitate peace, prosperity, health, happiness, and maximum human development.

Our Afrikan-Centered perspective provides us with a window through which we can look inward at ourselves, and simultaneously look out at the various expressions of human culture. An Afrikan-Centered perspective does not mean that we study only about Afrika and Afrikan people. It means that we view the study of our own experience as being of primary importance, but, that we study the world, its history, peoples and cultures from our own unique vantage point. At Nsoroma Institute there is no contradiction between Afrikan-Centered and Multi-Cultural education.

Our approach to education is holistic because we structure our program to: stimulate the intellect of our students with a vigorous academic schedule, provide daily opportunities for physical development, and encourage spiritual awareness and development through the teaching of meditation techniques. Nutrition is stressed as a tool for contributing to a balance between mind, body and spirit.

Our instruction is multi-modal because we present lessons in a variety of ways to address the learning styles of all of our students. Most students have one of the following as their dominant mode of learning: visual, auditory or tactile. Students who are visual need lots of color, respond well to writing on the board, photographs and videos.

Students who are auditory learners like music, can absorb information from lectures and respond well to poetry and rhyme as instructional tools. Students who are tactile learners must have artifacts, manipulatives and plenty of hands on experiences. These students are physically oriented and learn by doing. In reality most students learn through a blend of these learning modes.

Finally our educational philosophy is consistent with the ancients who believed that education is the process of drawing out that which is already inside of the student. Education is primarily a process of self-discovery. It is a journey of self-realization. The "teacher" is actually a guide who provides nurturing, love, information and experiences which aid in growing into knowledge of the individual and collective self.

Nyerere Education Institute (New Brunswick, NJ)
Omowale Ujamaa Shule (Pasadena, CA)
Operation Get Down (Detroit, MI)
Phase: Piggy Back, Inc. (Harlem, NY)

ROOTS ACTIVITY LEARNING CTR. (Washington, DC)

PHILOSOPHY: Our philosophy is that exposure is the key to intelligence. Our students are exposed to academic knowledge on a high level and thought provoking questions that enhance their building of keen analytical and problem solving skills. Our students are exposed to technology through many types of teaching equipment.

Our school is designed to facilitate organized activities using open spaces which are strategically divided. Students are grouped in a multi-grade fashion so as they can grow and develop naturally as siblings in a family do—the younger learning skills faster and older acquiring a sense of responsibility and maturity along with advanced academic skills.

The curriculum is strong and includes numerous performance objectives in art, music, physical education, social studies, and especially language arts, mathematics, and science. These areas are taught creatively through a black experience approach using trips, songs, games, books, and various teaching technology.

S.R. Martin College Preparatory School (San Francisco, CA)
Sankofa (Cincinnati, OH)
School Tech Services (Chicago, IL)
Shule Mandela Academy (East Palo Alto, CA)

TIMBUKTU ACADEMY (Trenton, NJ)
712 Stuyvesant Avenue

PHILOSOPHY: The society in which we live has shown how separating arcas of a child's development (such as health/nutrition, education, recreation and the family) may be greatly enhanced by a more wholistic approach to child-rearing. Part of our mission is to encourage parents to see the importance of integrating the parts into a whole for a more balanced life for the child. We seek parents support for our philosophy and methods of education by encouraging them to include these ideas in their child rearing so that the education experience will be truly consistent and wholistic.

Toussaint Institute (Brooklyn, NY)
Tuwohofo-Holly International School (Ghana, West Afrika)
Ujamaa Shule (Washington, DC)
Winnie Mandela Supplementary School (London, UK)

UMOJA NYUMBA (Baltimore, MD)
2300 Garrison Boulevard

MISSION STATEMENT: Umoja Nyumba intends to be a community based Afrikan centered educational institution serving the childcare needs of the greater Baltimore Metropolitan area. Umoja Nyumba will endeavor to optimally educate by providing quality, yet economically affordable childcare services in an enriched Afrikan cultural setting. The learning experiences at Umoja Nyumba are uniquely designed to address the educational and developmental needs of the Afrikan child. To this end we are absolutely committed without reservation or apology. Umoja Nyumba will be dedicated to cultivating positive self images which we presume will lay the necessary foundation for the psychological, emotional, social, and academic well being of our children. We intend to provide each child with the skills necessary to not only survive, but actually prosper in a society that consciously fears their collective development and in many ways has been and is today hostile to their very presence. Our ideology is simple **"Nation First"**! Our perspective without question is **Pan Afrikan**. The foundation of this paradigm springs forth from the teachings and beliefs of our wise and noble ancestors and elders and as such all children will be immersed in tradition from **"MAAT"** to **"N'GUZO SABA."** Our goal is to serve as many families as there are in the village regardless of economic ability. Umoja Nyumba will serve best those parents who are consciously seeking a secure, well structured, and creative educational alternative experience for their watoto.

Possessed with the spirits of the Honorable Marcus Garvey, Honorable Elijah Muhammad, Hatshepsut, Queen Tiye and Nzinga. We will never settle for our present oppression. **Freedom Is Our Right and We Demand That**.

One can also use the Institute of Independent Education as a resource in the quest to find a sane environment for a child's maximal development. The information for this organization is as follows:

Institute of Independent Education
1313 North Capitol Street, NE, Suite 200
Washington, DC 20002
(202)745-0500

The Council of Independent Black Institutions' information is as follows:

Council of Independent Black Institutions
National Executive Office
P.O. Box 1327
Buffalo, NY 14215-1327

While the above mentioned institutions must be held to standards, such as those mentioned earlier, and the personal standards of the parents, these institutions must also be weighed against the present public educational environment. Is the particular independent school a better educational environment than the public school, even if it does not meet the high standards of true liberatory education? If the independent school is at least a better environment for learning and acculturation, it can be a short term vehicle or given true liberatory direction by involved parents. The bottom line is that we move on this issue now. It cannot wait.

If the jump to an independent institution is too much financially at first, then one can begin by enrolling the child in a Saturday independent program, an after school program or a summer program dedicated to putting them on the road to maximal development. There must be *some* action or movement once the inadequacy of the present world reality is recognized; even if it means parents spending as much extra time as possible with their children's re-education and proper socialization.

In this scenario of parents giving conscious supplementary education and socialization to children, this supplementary education and socialization is usually opposed to what the children are getting in the public school experience. Children, being the intelligent observers they are, recognize opposing forces that work in their lives. Generally, school and society pack a socialization punch difficult to match by a few hours in the home, so conscious parents in this situation must be honest with children and tell them what is happening. They must let them know that what they, as parents, are trying to convey is opposed to what is being purveyed in school, why and how to deal with the contradictions.

It is incumbent upon us to find a way or make a way to rescue and nurture our children. They are our future and cannot be sacrificed. If it means the family has to budget and stop going to the movies, concerts and watching videos in order to save money, it seems well worth it to do so. Liberation requires discipline and sacrifice and these types of things are small prices to pay. One can even make the healthy and cost saving sacrifices of giving up smoking and drinking, as well as other expensive and unhealthy habits, so that a child or children might be saved.

Not only are these types of *nkosoɔ* small concessions for a serious and sane Afrikan, but they serve as an example of strength, dedication, love, pride and sacrifice for the children. It is a sad statement if we can find ways to pay the cover every Friday night at the club, buy liquor, cigarettes, concert tickets, new clothes and unnecessary trinkets, yet we cannot find a way to protect and nurture our children.

Even though these types of sacrifice may be small in the whole scheme of Afrikan liberation, they aren't necessarily easy. Some planning and discipline may be required. If anyone needs to be reminded of why they are doing what they are doing, look back to chapter 2 and recognize the madness. This should keep one vigilant and focused enough to do the necessary things, such as budgeting the money saved from sacrifice and the cessation of bad or unnecessary habits. This money can then be allocated toward making the Afrikan child's life positive and sane instead of being lost to other trifles of consumption.

In addition, Afrikan parents must put themselves in a position to impart as much knowledge, consciousness and sanity to their children as possible. If one has a child, ignorance and lack of self-knowledge is something that needs to be overcome. The parent must embark upon the quest for knowledge simply for the child's sake if for no other reason. Study groups, books, audio tapes, lectures and dialogue with conscious people are all modes for this type of necessary growth.

Pathological behaviors that result from the insanity of the European *asili* and the psychological devastation of The Maafa can be passed from one generation to the next. Learned behaviors are acquired by children from their parents. For this reason, if parents still suffer from the damage of The Maafa and the European *asili*, then this same damage will be passed on to the children. This has been the case for generations of Afrikans in the Western hemisphere and if it is not remedied the attempt to rescue our children is severely impaired.

Therefore, *nkoso* ꙅ must not only include attempts to change the environment and consciousness of the child, but the parent or adult must also undergo consciousness transformation.

Nkoso⊃ and Ujamaa

The Afrikan collective must engage in *nkoso* ⊃ where Ujamaa, or cooperative economics, is concerned. As Afrikan people constantly speak of the 400 billion dollar spending power of Afrikans in America, we must realize by now that this is a useless asset without the ability to discern what is to be done with so much money. We have a habit of spending outside of the Afrikan community, not supporting entrepreneurs and failing to build institutions with this collective capital. Consequently, it is obvious that economics without conscious-ness is fruitless for the liberation of Afrikan people. Economics within the European framework of consumption, greed, competitive individualism and the illusionary American Dream is of no use to Afrikan people. This is a reality even if it hurts the feelings or upsets the sensibilities of negroes who have obtained some degree of financial status and contribute in no way to the return of Afrikan people to The Way.

Conscious Afrikan people can begin to exercise Ujamaa on any number of levels. As Maulana Karenga has defined Ujamaa, it means building and maintaining our own stores and other businesses, while profiting together. On the level of simply purchasing as much as possible from Afrikan businesses who give back to the Afrikan global community, this is a simple way of profiting together. It is *nkoso* ⊃ that can benefit us today and tomorrow with no waiting and little planning.

Afrikan people should be building stores, businesses and institutions that serve our struggle. In doing this, we have involved ourselves in cooperative economics, Ujamaa, by sharing our expertise with Afrikans moving along the same path toward true liberation. Entrepreneurship is a must, because it is a way for us to reap the benefits of our work and become self-sufficient, instead of working for a salary all our lives and helping to make someone else wealthy. We can also build institutions together, pooling our monies or we may simply aid in supporting an individual or organization who is doing what we may be unable to do at the present time.

This is the nature of *nkoso ɔ*. It is a level of struggle that can be very simple and in which the masses of Afrikan people can participate. *Nkoso ɔ* on the level of economics, like all *nkoso ɔ*, must be conscious and moving toward liberation for Afrikan people.

Nkoso ɔ and politics

Political activity is *nkoso ɔ*, short-term action. Political activity is not a *solution* to any of the problems facing Afrikan people. There must be an understanding that contrary to what has been espoused and believed, political activity is not a viable form of *daakye abra bɔ* nor is it *nyansa nnsa da*, limitless thought, by any means. It is acknowledged that civil rights and political activity have allowed Afrikan people in America to arrive at an important place in our history. The struggles of our sisters and brothers for voting rights and civil rights have been invaluable. However, it is time to recognize that politics is simply a tactic and not a strategy.

> There must be no confusion between tactics and objectives/strategy. A tactic is defined as "An expedient for achieving a goal: a maneuver." [9] The fact that a tactic is an "expedient" and the strategy is the goal itself and means of achieving it, allows a distinction to be made. What has often happened to us is we have been tricked into believing that our tactics are our strategy. In other words, in the heat of battle we believed that the tactics of sit-ins and integration legislation were our strategy, when actually these were tactics that were part of the strategy to secure freedom, justice and equality. [2]

Our movement in the arena of legislation must be sustained, but with far less weight and priority assigned to it. Politics must not be viewed as the way to solve the problems facing Afrikan people, but instead must be viewed as a necessary activity, a tactic, to be maintained as we embark on the more important activities of liberation; self-knowledge, self-definition, psychological health, self-determination and self-sufficiency.

Amos Wilson shared that,

> There are so many of us who believe that fair housing laws, anti-discrimination laws, civil rights laws, voting rights laws and so forth guarantee our freedom. That is an illusion. What a flight in fantasy! [3]

Civil rights legislation and political action are futile activities if viewed as long-term "fixes," which is the stance that many Afrikan people tend to take. The first and most obvious indications as to the long range futility of such activities as civil rights legislation can be seen by simply taking a look at history and the contemporary landscape. Whatever legislation Afrikan people in America have been able to win to alleviate some of the criminal treatment received in America, it has been temporary and easily reversed.

Law and legislation also played a role in making freedom an illusion. After the Emancipation, certain legal fixtures were set in place to protect the rights of African people and all people. The Fourteenth Amendment, ratified in 1868, basically protected African people from discrimination. Along with the Civil Rights Bill of 1875, the legal protection provided by the Fourteenth Amendment gave African people rights on paper, but even this emancipation was quickly revoked.

An 1883 Supreme Court ruling on the Fourteenth Amendment declared that while the Amendment forbade the **state** from discriminating, it does not refer to discriminatory practices of **individuals**. So the Supreme Court took it upon itself to insure the legality of discrimination by distorting the meaning of an existing legal document. The 1896 *Plessy vs. Ferguson* decision made it legal to discriminate against African people in a "separate but equal" ruling. This ruling upheld a state statute requiring segregated railway coaches. [4]

In addition, we were to see an era of so called Jim Crow that returned Afrikans to enslavement in a new form. Civil rights laws were reversed, etc. We are currently seeing reversals of civil rights laws, attacks on affirmative action and numerous other political slaps in the face.

The second indication of the long-range futility of civil rights legislation and the reason the conditions just mentioned are allowed to happen, has to do with the fact that legislation deals with the law and the law was developed by and is operated by the flawed ideological matrix and conceptual system that we have been speaking of in this text. *Legislation is therefore law, not justice. There is a difference.*

So, a legal system based on a flawed, abnormal and insane European *asili,* and run by individuals who fulfill this *asili, is* doomed to be flawed, abnormal and insane itself. The legal system run by the fulfillers of the European *asili,* like the *asili* itself, is diametrically opposed to the "cultural other" or anyone who threatens the status quo that law maintains. The European *asili* dictates norms, values, terms, standards and definitions that are designed to perpetuate, defend and extend it. Given this, Afrikan people struggling against oppression and legal injustice, while scoring short-term legal victories, are doomed to failure if they utilize the reality and ideological matrix of the system we struggle against. The legal system was not built by people foolish enough to *willfully* allow their own destruction (Although the system will be destroyed regardless of the will of those who support it.). So, in the long-term, the European fulfillers of the European *asili* are not concerned with the contradictions of striking down affirmative action in an obviously racist country or incarceration rates for Afrikan people in America higher than Afrikans in Azania (South Afrika.) It practices hypocrisy as a way of life. While we may gain small legal victories with legislation and mistakenly have believed we remedied the situation, the fulfillers of the European *asili* will rationalize their eventual dismantling. They will do this without remorse because it is an *asili* of the "rhetorical ethic" and accepted hypocrisy. Ani tells us that,

> Within the nature of European culture there exists a
> statement of value or of "moral" behavior that has no meaning for
> the members of that culture. I call this the "rhetorical ethic." [5]

With all of this said, we must understand that operating within the flawed and abnormal framework of Western society can only be for short-term survival at best. We must be actively engaging in *nkoso ɔ* toward true liberation. Despite the fact that we have conceded that politics still has some utility, *nkosoɔ* in the realm of politics for Afrikan people must be very different from our current activities. Independent parties, voting power in blocks and grass roots, politically conscious, lobbying organizations must be a part of *nkosoɔ*, if politics is to even remain a recognizable tactic.

If we are to vote, it must mean something and it means relatively little if we remain attached to the pants legs of the existing political parties. We can exercise strength in the numbers of conscious Afrikans who recognize a specific purpose for their political involvement and vote accordingly. Afrikan political involvement cannot be clouded by "party politics" and concerns over issues peripheral to the Afrikan community. We must have an agenda and direct policy according to it. Although people use the diversity of the Afrikan community as an excuse not to move in a singular direction, there is one ideology that we can all agree on. That ideology is the survival and sanity of Afrikan people. And, even if we cannot agree on what our sanity is, we can agree that our survival is a must.

The Umoja Party, an independent political party that has arisen in Washington D.C., and is spreading to other places, is a good example of independence with an Afrikan agenda. The preamble of the Umoja Party is an indicator of the potential of this party.

BELIEVING IN THE ULTIMATE POWER OF THE CREATOR AS MANIFESTED IN EVERYTHING, EVERYWHERE ALL AT ONCE, AND BELIEVING IN THE STRUGGLE OF OUR ANCESTORS TO ESTABLISH AND MAINTAIN CIVILIZATION BUILDING UPON ORIGINAL MORAL-CONSTITUTIONAL LAWS. WE OF AFRIKAN ANCESTRY HEREBY EXPRESS AND EXERCISE OUR HUMAN RIGHT TO CORRECT THE POLITICAL CONSCIOUSNESS AND RELATIONSHIPS WHICH HAVE BEEN IMPOSED UPON OUR PEOPLE BY THE VERY PERPETRATORS OF SLAVERY, COLONIZATION AND GENOCIDE. BELIEVING IN THE TRADITIONAL AFRIKAN PRINCIPLES OF MA'AT AS EXPRESSED THROUGH TRUTH, JUSTICE, RIGHTEOUSNESS, HARMONY, BALANCE, RECIPROCITY AND ORDER, AND IN THE NGUZO SABA PRINCIPLES OF UMOJA (UNITY), KUJICHAGULIA (SELF-DETERMINATION), UJIMA (COLLECTIVE WORK AND RESPONSIBILITY), UJAMAA (COOPERATIVE ECONOMICS), NIA (PURPOSE), KUUMBA (CREATIVITY), IMANI (FAITH), WE EQUALLY COMMIT OURSELVES TO THE RESPONSIBILITY OF JOINING TOGETHER WITH SOLIDARITY, OBLIGATION, RIGHT-DOING, A SENSE OF COMMUNITY, PURITY (MORALS, ETHICS, VIRTUES AND VALUES) AND SPIRITUAL LAW AND SOCIAL ORDER.

If we cannot viably run candidates on the national level, which we may not want to do anyway, then we influence the vote with a huge voting block ready to move in concert. In local arenas, especially major cities, Afrikans can run and win, with no worry of compromising the vision expressed in the preamble of the Umoja Party.

Another qualifier to any political activity is that those Afrikans who involve themselves in the political system must not be politicians, but instead operate as activists for Afrikan people. Re-election politics, popularity, nepotism, immoral behavior, pedophilia, thievery and all of the other madness that comes with politics must be avoided by Afrikan activists. No deals need be made and underhanded associations formed for political clout because we understand that our aims while operating within this system are very different. In return for this type of political activism, the conscious Afrikan people of parties like the Umoja Party would make sure that their representative is supported. *If we are unable to separate ourselves from the process in this way, then electoral political activity is not viable and needs to be abandoned.* We would have to relegate ourselves to a position as one of the largest and strongest lobbying groups in the country, one with a 400 billion dollar budget. The bottom line is that there can be no compromise or departure from our objective of a return to The Way. There can be no slipping and forgetting the nature of the European *asili.*

NKOSOƆ AND RESISTANCE

A key to the existence of Afrikan people, especially since The Maafa, has been resistance. The numerous brothers and sisters who shook the foundations of the Western Hemisphere represent a spirit, without which we would not have survived and if absent today will mean our destruction. "CONSCIOUS RESISTANCE IN A HOSTILE ENVIRONMENT OF OPPRESSION CANNOT BE VIEWED AS RADICAL!" [6] The substance of this statement should be examined in its contemporary context. In *The Maafa & Beyond* there was a chapter entitled "Resistance That Allowed Us To Exist." It basically dealt with our Afrikan historical paradigm of resistance. Here we need to deal with what resistance means and is for us today.

To start at the most basic level, what do we mean when we say that conscious resistance is not radical? First at the physiological level, we find a response called "fight or flight."

Epinephrine and norepinephrine cause a wide variety of dramatic changes in the body when an emergency arises. Their release, usually a reaction to danger, fright or anger, brings on what is called the "fight or flight" response. The two hormones affect circulation by accelerating heart rate, thus increasing cardiac output, and by shunting blood into skeletal muscles and away from other organs such as those of digestion and reproduction. [7]

Hence, at the physiological level, the body has a natural response of resistance in which the body's natural mechanisms prepare one physically for resistance to whatever danger is present. Blood is shunted to the skeletal muscles which means the body is preparing to fight a glorious fight or run like the wind. Natural body processes are preparing for resistance. This preparation can begin at the threat or perception of danger. It does not wait until the body is beaten or harmed to kick in.

At the instinctive level self-preservation is the first law of nature. An organism's first instinct and obligation is to preserve and sustain its own life; to survive. Perhaps the only instinct that is comparable is that of an animal mother to protect her children. At the common sense level it seems natural for a sane person to recognize that when their life, the lives of family members and the lives of people like that person are threatened, they must defend themselves. When God-given, natural, human rights are compromised, why wouldn't a sane person resist such an intrusion? The answer is, a sane person would resist and only one who's judgment and psychology have been impaired would not resist. Why have the masses of Afrikan people ceased to resist? Our answers can be found in some of the discussion in the earlier chapters regarding pathology. Resistance is normal behavior for the oppressed.

Nkoso⊃ and Fear

As we have shared, *nkoso⊃* means movement and is similar to what we might call short-term action. Whether we are speaking about politics, Ujamaa, education or resistance plain and simple, the Afrikan community in the United States at present has a problem with *nkoso⊃* . We talk a good game, but the masses have been inactive for a long time. Of course we recognize that there are many sisters and brothers making positive strides, but the burden of the masses is placed on too few Afrikan soldiers. Unfortunately, even many of the Afrikans that have any level of consciousness are also rather ineffective, showing a great lack of creativity and insight in moving our people forward.

Amos Wilson posed the question, "Why are we in a new day saying the same thing that someone said 100 years ago?" [8] He was expressing frustration at the fact that we're still clinging to politics and legislation, among other things, despite the fact that we had numerous Afrikan legislators in government and even mayors during reconstruction in the late 1800's. Despite the proven historical ineffectiveness of this, many Afrikans still pursue the political agenda as an end. And, as we mentioned earlier regarding politics, the European *asili* controls the law and will rationalize it away when it feels this is necessary. Thus we experienced the so called Jim Crow era after reconstruction.

So, why the lack of creativity and new direction on the part of so many of our sisters and brothers, even those who are supposed to be leaders? Why the repetition of the same strategies which have failed time and time again? One explanation might be historical ignorance. If one is not aware of the cyclical historical failure of the same types of activities, then they might repeat these activities with every belief that they represent a legitimate *strategy*. However, this explanation ceases to be sufficient when we realize that many Afrikan people are at a time where our access to knowledge and historical consciousness is growing. The so called leaders certainly cannot be excused with a plea of historical ignorance. So why the stagnation? Perhaps another explanation is the fear factor that was mentioned in chapter 3. This seems like a more viable explanation since a very large part of our criminal internment in the Western Hemisphere has been dominated by the use of fear to physically and psychologically twist and break Afrikan people. Our fear is sometimes conscious and articulated, while other times it is subconscious fright. We are afraid of what people will think of us as we are advocates for liberation; afraid of what will be said about us; and afraid of what will be done to us, whether it is job loss, being ostracized, or suffering physical abuse. The fear is pervasive, and could be useful if and when it stops at healthy caution and fails to progress to paralyzed stagnation which is where our community often finds itself consciously and subconsciously.

Any Afrikan with a clear understanding of European thought and behavior might naturally have a level of fear of Europeans and their tendency toward remorseless and destructive assaults on Afrikan people. The conscious Afrikan uses that healthy suspicion and fear as a catalyst for critical analysis and productive counter measures to European destruction.

****

So, we understand that there is something for every Afrikan to do as we move toward liberation. *Nkoso ɔ* is a grassroots concept in which all of us must be engaging in struggle at one level or another. There is no shortage of work to be done.

DAAKYE ABRA Bɔ (DISTANT PLANS)

Daakye abra bɔ is a Twi term which means "life that includes struggle, the future" or "how you make your life, plans." It might be correlated with what is sometimes called long-term planning or distant plans. Afrikan people must begin making a practice of planning for what we intend our individual and collective lives and circumstances to be in the future. This is what we call *daakye abra bɔ* , or distant plans. We must be able to affect our future by envisioning and conceiving of what should happen 10, 15, 25 and more years down the road, making sure that *nkosoɔ* is in line and on course with these *daakye abra bɔ* , or distant plans. And, of course, *nyansa nnsa da* expands the boundaries of what *daakye abra bɔ* might be.

DAAKYE ABRA BƆ AND EDUCATION

If our *nkosoɔ* includes our own independent educational institutions, it must be because *daakye abra b ɔ* are directed toward Afrikan school <u>systems.</u> We can envision these systems as being the safe havens for the maximal development of the masses of Afrikan children. Therefore, *daakye abra bɔ* provide for these Afrikan school systems that will also serve to validate and institutionalize the ways that we as a people utilize *nyansa nnsa da* to create an old/new Afrikan consciousness. Again, recognizing the flawed nature of the European *asili* that dominates the world, the obligation falls upon us to make *daakye abra bɔ* that provide sufficient *means* for validating, standardizing and institutionalizing all of our levels of struggle as we return to The Way.

As a natural extension of Afrikan school systems, real higher educational institutions must also be a part of *daakye abra bɔ* . As the masses of Afrikan children matriculate through Afrikan school systems, they must have some place to go. We are not serious if we are satisfied with continuing indefinitely to place our Afrikan youth in universities and colleges which are microcosms of the larger insane society and perpetuators of the European *asili.* Afrikan universities (knowledge systems or some more appropriate description) must be a conceivable vision that is planned for within a specified period of time. Our talented young people who go to Harvard, Howard, receive their education in the street, or at home via the works of John Henrik Clarke, Diop, Marimba Ani, Haki Madhubuti, etc., should be able to be maximally developed by Afrikan people in *our* institutions. They will then maintain their sanity and contribute to our return to The Way, instead of being socialized to participate in the madness of society or rebelling against society in self-destructive ways.

So, as an alternative to matriculation in the world's colleges and universities, our young people need to enter our own Afrikan independent institutions of higher learning to be nurtured with higher learning of the profound Afrikan spiritual and intellectual type. The youth need to be groomed in the value of self-determination, the necessity of self-knowledge and the power of self-definition. Young people in Afrikan institutions would also be nurtured in a sane and normal environment, while being prepared to shape these same new realities for our people. They would be in the process of becoming better human beings capable of moving the world forward.

The endeavors of our students of liberation would still be in the many disciplines such as mathematics, science, engineering, agriculture, language, medicine, cosmogony, etc. To this end, an essential part of our *daakye abra bɔ* should be the development and grooming of Afrikan young people in all of these essential areas or disciplines to perpetuate or build Afrikan institutions of higher education. It would almost be a corps of young people prepared to build, administer and teach in new institutions without the need for outside training or intervention. As a consequence, Afrikan people will be more able to seek self-determination, realizing that the only way to truly be self-determined is to control all aspects of our existence and be able to sustain ourselves independent of anyone. This would allow us to then choose who we will do business with, share resources with and trade technology with. We must eventually be capable of not only selling our own underwear, shoe laces, toilet paper and other essentials, but also manufacturing these things. Perhaps the most important extension of this, however, is to not only manufacture, but to control the raw materials from the time they leave mother earth to the time they are being made into shoes, toilet paper, combs, etc.

Our ability to achieve this type of independence is contingent on many things, not the least of which is the emergence of thousands, and eventually millions, of Afrikan young people who possess the skills to truly build a nation. The role of our independent educational institutions in making these kinds of nation building preparations is crucial. Our independent educational systems must produce the conscious, sane Afrikans to go on to learn the skills to build and manage our independent institutions of higher learning. These institutions will then produce people willing and able to continue the creation of businesses and institutions which will accept new generations of Afrikans into a liberation work force. It is then and only then that we will reach the true point of self-determination and self-sufficiency.

Additionally, our *daakye abra b ɔ* should include our Afrikan independent institutions of higher learning claiming and supporting those of our scholars who struggle for our minds. Whether we are speaking of John Henrik Clarke, Haki Madhubuti, Marimba Ani, Ivan Van Sertima or any number of our Afrikan scholars whose expertise is currently being used in institutions we as a people do not control; it is the responsibility of Afrikan people, especially the generation from 18 to 39, to build and create a place for these sisters and brothers to go. They have benefited us so greatly that we are obligated to begin this work of building Afrikan independent institutions of higher learning to harvest their knowledge and expand their own minds, instead of having them exist in institutions where they often struggle against policy, culture and insanity. How powerful it is to understand that the work of our sisters and brothers who are developing conceptual frameworks and mentally liberating ideologies is being done under conditions conducive more to arrested development than productive output. If our scholars can produce the brilliant works they are producing under such conditions, imagine what they could do in an Afrikan independent institution of higher learning built on sanity, culture, spirituality and so much more. And, these are the same institutions that will nurture and cultivate more young Afrikans to follow the scholarly examples of the sisters and brothers who have elevated us through serious knowledge.

DAAKYE ABRA BƆ AND A "PROTECTION SOCIETY"

Daakye abra bɔ should include visions for national and international watchdog organizations founded by Afrikan people, run by Afrikan people, in direct contact with the masses of Afrikan people and operating for the sole purpose of Afrikan safety and liberation. Such a protection society should be ready to check Yurugu wherever it manifests its destructive ways against Afrikans. This type of organization could be tied into educational networks, financial networks and political networks to direct the masses in decisive action against those whose deeds show them to be enemies of Afrikan liberation. This type of organization could be the conduit of information being funneled from Afrikan people around the world alerting us to threats to our liberation; mobilizing us financially, politically and defensively against those threats as a unified, conscious community. This is being included as a part of our *daakye abra bɔ* because it is our Afrikan school systems, higher learning institutions and other institutions that will make the unity and conscious mobilization of our masses, in this manner, possible.

A protection society would act and react to all of the madness taking place wherever Afrikan people exist. It would not simply cry out in protest to Afrikan people being killed, brutalized and harassed. This organization would react with power and affect serious repercussions on individuals, organizations and institutions which disrespect Afrikan life. This is a long term objective. This is *daakye abra b⊃ .*

DAAKYE ABRA B⊃ AND UJAMAA

As a part of our entire process of liberation, the ability to manage and take care of the *billions* of dollars that Afrikan people are losing to more prudent money managing communities and the United States culture of consumption is of extreme importance. Despite the fact that we place our money in some banks, we cannot get loans from them. *Daakye abra b⊃* would seem to necessitate the mass building of our own banking institutions. The beneficial aspect of the larger nationbuilding picture as it relates to Ujamaa is that Afrikan people's consciousness will be undergoing transformation, thus many of the bad habits and irresponsible tendencies, that make lending money to anyone very risky and difficult, will be eliminated.

Daakye abra b⊃ for Ujamaa should also include Afrikan businesses reaching a level of consciousness and maturity in which the pure profit motive is substantially reduced and the pooling of resources to engage in the large scale building of new businesses is encouraged. For example, if several Afrikan businesses exist in different markets and identify a community need for a new business, they could come together to support one of their sisters or brothers in building such a business. Particulars could be worked out ahead of time to make sure that the agreement is cooperative for all parties, as is the nature of Ujamaa. All of this is of course dependent upon Afrikan consumers, not spending more money, but spending less money in general while supporting Afrikan businesses to a much greater degree than is done at present.

If we support one another, undergo consciousness transformation and engage in cooperative economics, the Afrikan community is capable of servicing all of our own needs. From publishing companies to book bindery and manufacturing companies; financial management companies to banking systems; agricultural producers to Afrikan markets; private practice physicians to hospitals and HMO's; independent schools to universities and colleges; whatever our needs, we spend enough money frivolously and outside of our communities at present to support all of these endeavors if we practice Ujamaa.

****

DAAKYE ABRA BƆ : A VISION

Thirty years from now in the year 2026, perhaps we will see the emergence of "Little Afrikas," "New Afrikas" or Alkebu-lan communities throughout the United States. You enter these communities, which are actually like cities unto themselves, and the first thing you see is the Alkebu-lan University Campus of Baltimore, for example. Students pour in and out of the modest building that was built with precise architectural alignment to the heavens, taking advantage of the rays of the sun and position of the stars. The streets are remarkably clean in front of the building and no one passes another individual without warm greetings. Strong hand shakes accompany embraces; left cheek to left cheek, right cheek to right cheek and back to the left again.

Across the street from the university, students lounge on the benches that surround The Baltimore Maafa Memorial. Some of the students rise to accompany the elementary children across the street, who are walking to Delaney Elementary School a couple of blocks over. Reading and study groups are plopped on the lush and plentiful grass in various spots around the university and the memorial. As is a frequent occurrence, Afrikan tourists from around the world mill about the street snapping pictures and speaking to the students, residents and business owners of Alkebu-lan/Baltimore.

As you move further down the main street, it is lined with light poles from which the images of great Afrikan liberators hang. There are various stores, institutes and other buildings lining the street just past the university, including fresh produce markets, health food stores, a large Afrikan bookstore, a few doctor's offices, a large law office, The Afrikan Liberation Library, The Maafa Museum and Institute, The Yurugu Research Consortium, the Sankofa Cultural Center and various other buildings leading to Resistance Circle which has a large symbolic monument in the middle of it.

As you round Resistance Circle, the first right turn leads you to the Garvey Hotel, the Nzinga Hotel, and the Alkebu-lan/Baltimore Convention Center and Meeting Facility. The next road, which leads straight ahead, leads to Sojourner Truth Elementary School, Queen Tiye High School and begins the large residential area of Alkebu-lan/ Baltimore. The standard of living is high and everyone is fairly comfortable, none lacking the necessities of life. There is no extreme poverty and no gross excess. The idea and implementation of the Ujamaa principle has served the community well.

Nondescript guard houses blend in with the surroundings as children play under the protective eyes of the Alkebu-lan Security Force. They are there to protect the community from the destruction outside of it. There is never really a need to "police" the residents of Alkebu-lan. No one enters Alkebu-lan/Baltimore and disrespects or harms its women and children. The men are also well protected from what was once a concerted slaughter and incarceration in America. Self-destruction is an abnormal manifestation of past realities when it occurs at all.

Native American families and communities also thrive in Alkebu-lan communities. Alkebu-lan represents a safe haven that respects and encourages the Native American return to their way. Although the destruction of these original inhabitants of the Americas has for all intents and purposes been complete, one can see Native American children speaking in their ancestral languages to one another and many of the Afrikan residents. The Native American languages, some of which have undergone a revival, intermingle with Akan languages, Wolof, Yoruba and any number of Afrikan languages being spoken by Afrikans born in America, as well as Afrikans from the continent. English is also spoken, but the Afrikan and Native American languages are also encouraged in schools.

The third turn off of Resistance Circle leads to the Alkebu-lan Security Force Building, Yaa Asentewaa Park, The Afrikan Sacred Burial Grounds, Umoja Party Headquarters, Technology and Industry Circle, Alkebu-lan Bank, The Auset Farm Lands, Malcolm X High School and various other institutions. The entire community is peaceful, but in a constant state of vigilance and preparedness due to the hostile and decaying nature of the surrounding society.

****

Afrikan people must plan for the future. We must think way ahead of our present circumstances. We must develop *daakye abra bɔ*. The *daakye abra bɔ* we develop must also be aided in development by *nyansa nnsa da*. There should be no limit to what our plans for the future will be. We have to be people of great vision.

The levels of struggle dealt with in this chapter are meant to be operational for Afrikan people on a day to day basis. They should represent a validation of activity we are already engaged in or a direction for future activity to impact our people. We have to begin changing ourselves and transforming our own consciousnesses, before we are able to impact anyone else. Certainly we want to be able to take care of our families at the maximum level of efficiency and security. It is time to move.

CHAPTER 7

OOOOOOOOO

GRASSROOTS AND PRACTICALITY: FUSING CONCEPT AND REALITY

Having addressed conceptual levels of struggle, it is important to acknowledge that we often see that there is a divergence and separation between concept and reality, especially as concerns Afrikan liberation. For this reason, now that we have taken a look at the concepts of *nyansa nnsa da, nkoso ɔ* and *daakye abra bɔ*, what follows are some of the everyday practical circumstances in which these concepts apply. In this chapter there are numerous quotations and situations which represent the "present world reality." These are followed by comments on the relationships of the concepts in this book to this present world reality and the quotations presented that manifest the present world reality. This can also be seen as a part of the Systematic Enemy Analysis addressed in chapter 2.

Therefore, there are numbered scenarios, each of which consists of the present world reality and practical responses to this reality based on *nyansa nnsa da, nkoso ɔ* and *daakye abra bɔ*. This can serve as somewhat of a mini-workbook for life. It addresses many of the questions and obstacles this world presents daily and establishes a model for how additional obstacles might be dealt with. One should keep in mind that in this context the present world reality represents a distorted and flawed reality.

REALITY

1) PRESENT WORLD REALITY
"My kids are in the public school system and they're doing fine."
NYANSA NNSA DA
Can any Afrikan existing within a distorted and abnormal reality be doing fine? What is "fine"? Is the child in a school environment free of the psychological stress of being in an anti-Afrikan culture? Is the child learning and acquiring self-knowledge? Is the Afrikan worldview anywhere in the child's educational process? Is the child being taught consciously that resistance to oppression is sane and desired, or is the implicit message that there is no *real* oppression; this message with the assumption that Malcolm, Nat Turner, Boukman, Black Panther types represent deviant, trouble-making, radical behavior? Is the child being taught to simply buy into the conceptual system or *asili* which facilitated and perpetuated The Maafa, Tuskegee Syphilis Experiment, COINTELPRO, the myriad forms of present day insanity and a rotten, inept, despiritualized, material, abnormal worldview?

These are some of the questions that one should think of or ask. Once the questions are asked and answered, the concept of *nyansa nnsa da* leaves the abstract intellectual realm. It allows the individual to think outside of the present world reality. It allows people to think outside of the definitions and norms that are accepted now. It allows one to conclude whether or not the child is really doing fine and why.

An Afrikan child who is not being taught about the normal and sane manifestation of resistance in this openly hostile, anti-Afrikan society is not fine. An Afrikan child who is being taught to buy into this European culture's *asili* is not fine. Even if they are getting good grades in school, that only represents a fraction of the educational experience. Yes, we like to see our children achieve in this way, but not at the cost of assimilation and socialization into an *asili* which is psychologically, and immanently physically, damaging to the child as she or he navigates a world hostile to the Afrikan existence without the skills and knowledge to recognize the enemy.

An Afrikan child who is not learning a knowledge of self and a cultural consciousness is not receiving an education at all. An Afrikan child who is seeing the world through someone else's eyes is not fine. An Afrikan child who has not received therapy for the psychological devastation of The Maafa is not fine.

However, there are steps to be taken towards changing the present reality, the present conditions and circumstances. An Afrikan child who knows resistance, is protected, nurtured, healed, acquiring knowledge of self, utilizing ancestral memory and cultural consciousness is a healthy Afrikan child who is doing alright. So, what can be done for our children?

NKOSƆƆ

There are several things that can be done to change what *nyansa nnsa da* has allowed us to recognize as necessary to be changed and changeable. We have realized that "fine" is a relative term. In order for your Afrikan child to really be doing fine, remove that child from the current school environment and enroll them in an independent institution that practices the values we have determined as "fine" in the previous chapter.

DAAKYE ABRA BƆ

Your child's protection and proper education should also be part of your *daakye abra bɔ*, or distant plans. If your child is not already enrolled in a full-time independent institution for reasons beyond your immediate control, *daakye abra bɔ* should make this goal a future reality. The "how" of doing this was discussed in the previous chapter.

One should also participate in the building of new schools if possible. This can be either through initiating *daakye abra bɔ* for one's own school or helping another sister or brother already on such a path.

Activities along this line are also not limited to sisters and brothers who already have children. First of all, every Afrikan has a responsibility to Afrikan children. Secondly, those who intend to have children one day need to formulate *daakye abra bɔ* for the yet unborn Afrikans' nurture and protection. If you intend to bring children into this world, start your preparation now, whether it is building institutions or attaining your own knowledge of self.

So, in looking at the initial statement, "My kids are in the public school system and they're doing fine," we can at least begin to understand how the concepts of *nyansa nnsa da, nkosoɔ* and *daakye abra bɔ* apply to this as well as similar statements and mind sets.

2) PRESENT DISTORTED REALITY
"Slavery is over. Besides, there's always been slavery."

NYANSA NNSA DA
Slavery has existed throughout the recorded history of the world in many different forms, however, The Maafa has only happened once! The Maafa is a unique Afrikan experience of enslavement that is **not** over because it is a historical process with contemporary manifestations. (The reader should refer to my previous book, *The Maafa & Beyond*) In much the same way, human suffering and genocide is not new and has happened throughout history, but the European Jewish Holocaust happened once. The above statement about "slavery" being over is a result of a distorted reality when it often comes from Afrikan people; ironically due in large part to The Maafa itself.

The Maafa was and is more devastating and intense than anything the world has ever seen. Its effects, psychological mutilation and physical debilitation, last even until present times and Afrikan people must go through a healing process that as of yet has been absent.

Nyansa nnsa da allows us to look at our current existence and its relationship to The Maafa, thus coming to the understanding that the mind states of Afrikan people are immensely affected by it. Consequently, recognizing The Maafa and Yurugu, we can see ways in which to change ourselves, our people and the world.

Just as those Afrikans who issue statements about enslavement like the one that began this section are victims of a distorted reality, so to are many of our Afrikans who hold positions as scholars and fail to function as perpetuators of liberation. For example, Thomas Sowell, an Afrikan scholar with "mainstream" credentials, has written about enslavement. He puts forward and spends much time on the predictable position that "slavery" has always existed in various different cultures. He spends a lot of time outlining and examining the different manifestations of enslavement around the world and throughout time. His lack of focus on the reality of the Afrikan existence in enslavement, and at present, can be seen in a passage from his book.

> For slavery to be understood as a global phenomenon, it must be analyzed beyond any particular national background—and yet in the light of numerous real national and historical settings, rather than as an abstract model. To explain slavery as being a consequence of certain European ideas leading to bondage for Africans is to ignore the glaring fact that slavery extended in time and space far beyond Europeans and Africans, and far beyond those who shared particular European ideas. [1]

This position of Sowell's is problematic for a number of reasons. First, he has chosen to view "slavery" as a global phenomenon, thus extricating himself and Afrikan people from their own unique experience with the enslavement of The Maafa. He has chosen not to allow Afrikan people to view The Maafa for what it was; the enslavement, brutalization, physical and psychological rape of Afrikan people, with Europeans as the primary perpetrators and bene-factors in the Western Hemisphere. It is unnatural for him not to address the "phenomenon" of enslavement from a perspective that deals with the particular European root that has allowed for himself and millions of other Afrikans to currently be in the Western Hemisphere.

Sowell's analysis represents a dilution of the Afrikan experience. Even though his chapter is called "Race and Slavery," he makes a point to lump the "race" based Afrikan experience of The Maafa with other people's experiences of enslavement having nothing to do with "race" and representing a completely different dynamic. One might posit that Sowell is simply being an objective academician, but there are two major problems even with this. Number one, objectivity and scholarship void of values is a myth and impossibility. An individual cannot leave their values and judgements out of the work they perform, no matter how hard they try to be "objective." A person cannot be separated from the work they do. One person may have less bias than another, but there is always some bias and value influence. This occurs even in the most "scientific" of investigations because results will have to be interpreted and ways of knowing and interpret-ing reality can differ from culture to culture, individual to individual.

Given this fact, Afrikans who have bought into the myth of objectivity, as it has been viewed by European *utamawazo*, are attempting to leave their own Afrikan values out of their scholarship for so called objectivity. The problem is that since there can be no scholarship absent of the values and influence of the scholar, Afrikans are often bringing European values to the table. These values, of course, operate in the best interest of European people. The way in which this happens time and time again is that [1] Europeans have projected themselves and their culture as universal, standard and objective; [2] as a consequence, in numerous instances Afrikans who are vigorously trying to be "objective" leave their Afrikan interests by the wayside and promote European interests, positioned as objective; [3] Europeans promote their own interests with obvious bias because their *utamawazo* says that their interests and cultural viewpoint are not only objective, but superior as well.

Additionally, and as a consequence of the aforementioned points, an Afrikan in the Western Hemisphere cannot claim to work for an objective scholarly view that fails to address the trauma of the Afrikan existence. The only objectivity is a fair dealing with and representation of Afrikan interests. The failure of Afrikans to address their own interests is akin to an individual who is a prisoner of war wishing or claiming to do research on war crimes that in no way relates to his own imprisonment or contributes to his freedom. About this so called objectivity, Chancellor Williams says,

> Our own "ivory tower" was smashed long since. We are, therefore, "unscholarly," for we take stands. We render "value judgments." We are not always "objective," either. And we are *biased*. We are biased in favor of equal opportunity for every human creature, and we are *prejudiced* towards all social, political, and economic arrangements everywhere that oppose this in actual practice. [2]

Williams is unapologetic about his stance, because he understands that his values and dedication to liberation cannot be separated from his scholarship. Sane Afrikan scholars must dedicate all of their studies to liberation in one way or another. As intense as it may sound, as long as one is enslaved, scholarship for its own sake is useless. It is simply falling prey to the European *asili's* myth of objectivity.

As a another point buttressing off of Sowell's lack of focus on

The Maafa as a unique historical process, it is not surprising that he does not apply the same principles of broadness and generality to the European Jewish Holocaust. If he were to be consistent, he would need to remove the European Jewish Holocaust from its unique historical position and place it in the global context of human suffering and genocide that has existed and been executed in many other instances throughout history. He, of course, does not do this.

Finally, Sowell's immersion in the ideological matrix of the European *asili* comes through as he fails to understand the machinations of history, the concept and facts of historical continuums, and the specific implications of The Maafa that can be traced even until today. He shows this flaw when he says,

> Another distortion of history is to assume a priori that social problems afflicting contemporary blacks in the United States are a "legacy of slavery." Broken families, lower rates of marriage, and lower rates of labor force participation have been included among the social phenomena explained and excused on grounds of a "legacy of slavery." In reality, most black children were raised in two-parent homes even during the era of slavery and for generations thereafter, blacks had higher rates of marriage than whites in the early twentieth century, and higher rates of labor force participation in every census from 1890 to 1950. Whatever may be the real causes of the very different patterns among blacks in the world of today must be sought in the twentieth century, not in the era before emancipation. [3]

Sowell is correct in that we should not assume things "a priori," so we analyze critically and discover that his contentions that contemporary problems should not be addressed by looking "before emancipation" is a faulty contention. It is really nothing short of ludicrous to dismiss a historical process such as The Maafa, which lasted hundreds of years and continues to dish out intense psychological mutilation, as the wrong place to look for the source of contemporary realities. Critical analyzers of history can easily explain present day declines in life sustaining areas and understand the context within which Sowell attempts to show that we were better off after emancipation than we are now; an attempt to dismiss the present impact of The Maafa. Much of what is taking place with Afrikan people is largely resultant from a continuum of Psychological/Cultural Misorientation and the destructiveness of the European *asili*. Much of our existence in the Western Hemisphere up until now has been spent trying to join or gain access to a European reality we failed to see as pathological. We fled our own schools, stores and other institutions to be able to sit, learn and do business next to Europeans (I realize our reasons were more complex and meaningful than this, but it was a good portion of the motivation.) So, having gradually integrated ourselves more and more into pathological European conceptual and ideological systems since our so called emancipation, it is no wonder our condition has become worse. The point is still that the trauma of The Maafa was in large part responsible for our imposed adoption of the belief that we desire the European worldview (that of the inflictor of our trauma) as the highest manifestation of civilization and value.

The presence of the dysfunctional European *asili* in Sowell's work is witnessed in the fact that he is an obviously intelligent man who is often unable to apply the same logical thinking, that he so values, to his own people and our overall predicament. The figures he quotes in the above excerpt are overly simplistic for the purpose of analysis. They show that Sowell is overlooking the historical processes extending from The Maafa that have worked even until today directly against Afrikan people's mental and physical welfare. There are also the indirect complexities of the gradual and more pervasive Afrikan adaptation of the European *asili*. Such adaptation leads to further degradation of the Afrikan existence and is largely a result of what

Sowell dismisses as being excuses based on what took place "before emancipation."

The Maafa is not over, but we can end it. Slavery has always existed, but The Maafa has not. Sowell and other Afrikans like him also illustrate the point that it is not the ambiguous concept of "race" that represents the problem, but the European *asili* that is dominating the world's people. Sowell is an Afrikan whose "race" does not define the nature of his distorted reality. He operates on the terms and definitions of the European *asili*.

NKOSOƆ

In order to fight the predominate urge to dismiss the Afrikan experience of enslavement as relevant to today, begin to exercise the power of language, inherent in naming and defining our own experience, by using the term Maafa. (Refer to pages 17 and 18) Learn more about The Maafa and remember our ancestors, which begins the healing process and leads to an understanding that comments like, "Slavery is over. Besides there's always been slavery," coming from an Afrikan, represent a distorted view of reality. Use and explanation of the term Maafa at all times in communicating with others helps to do away with the distorted perceptions currently surrounding and insulting our collective experience of enslavement, kidnapping, rape, brutality, psychological destruction and murder.

DAAKYE ABRA BƆ

Participate in efforts to build memorials and/or standardize the use of the Maafa concept by all people. A good example of standardization is the way in which European Jews have standardized their Holocaust. There are efforts currently being initiated to begin building museums and memorials to The Maafa. Participate in such efforts.

3) PRESENT REALITY

"Go to school and get a good education so you can get a good job. Education is the key."

NYANSA NNSA DA

While this type of philosophy allowed us to survive in this abnormal European-dominated world, seasons change. Mere survival is not good enough anymore. We must now ask what exactly is a good education? What is a good job? Where should we be going to get an education and for what purposes?

Nyansa nnsa da allows us to formulate answers to these questions which are outside of the accepted standard European *asili*. As was mentioned, survival is not good enough anymore. Afrikan people need to be proactive now and working toward true liberation. Going through elementary and secondary education and getting good grades is not adequate because that is simply a beginning, a survival measure that allows one to function a little more efficiently within a crazy society.

Consequently, it is now necessary to go through elementary and secondary institutions that we hope will be dedicated to providing mental and physical skills not designed to get a job and survive, but to create a new reality and thrive. Our children and adults should have in mind that a good education teaches an oppressed people what is necessary to be truly liberated. It teaches that true liberation is a return to The Way, which is achieved through self-knowledge, self-definition, psychological health, self-determination and self-sufficiency. A good education teaches us to consciously resist an abnormal, insane world reality in the most clever, productive and liberating ways.

A good job is one that contributes to liberation. It may be entrepreneurship that leads to Ujamaa or cooperative economics. It may be working a regular job and using the skills and resources gained to the benefit of the Afrikan liberation struggle. As expressed in chapter 6, those Afrikans working in "mainstream" America must become infiltrators instead of assimilators. That is when a "mainstream" job becomes a good job.

When we are clear about Afrikan liberation and our return to The Way, we then can say go to school and get a good education. We should be able to provide the school, the education and the liberation that comes as a result.

NKOSOƆ AND DAAKYE ABRA BƆ

Education has been previously discussed as to its importance and the necessity of independent institutions. Therefore, we will examine a grassroots and practical scenario that makes a good education possible for more Afrikans. This is a scenario that can be adopted to different people and different sized groups. It represents one of a multitude of possibilities for *nkoso ɔ* and *daakye abra bɔ*.

ONE COMMUNITY BUILDS AN INDEPENDENT AFRIKAN SCHOOL

Nkosoɔ

1) 40 people in a given Afrikan community

2) Each individual gives $10 a week to a centrally managed fund or account. That weekly $10 dollars can come from any number of sacrifices and does not have to represent an increase in income. For example, the sacrifice of not buying that extra bottle of liquor represents $10 dollars. The sacrifice of skipping a music concert represents $10 a few times over. The sacrifice of cutting back a carton of cigarettes a week represents money for the fund. The point is that there are many easy things to sacrifice when you understand that it is for our children and liberation.

Daakye abra bɔ

3) The group has established *daakye abra bɔ*, or distant plans, for what is to be done with the money. The plan is a 5 year plan.

4) Curriculums are being developed, ideologies shaped and the mission of the educational institution articulated.

5) In one year those 40 people have saved $20,800
6) In 5 years those 40 people, each saving $10 dollars a week, have collectively saved $104,000.
7) The $104,000 saved is put toward the opening of an independent community-based educational institution, for which the curriculum, ideology and mission have been in formation over the past 5 years.
8) **Afrikan children now have a place to go and receive a "good education."**

There is, of course, flexibility with the parameters of such a plan. It could include greater or fewer numbers of people, greater or smaller contributions per person, different choices of institutions to build, etc.

4) PRESENT WORLD REALITY
There tends to be a belief that capitalism and communism are the only two viable alternatives for economic development; and given the collapse of the U.S.S.R., American-style capitalism is assumed to be the only way. Consequently, Afrikan people, especially in America, look no further than American capitalism and do not realize that it runs counter to liberation.

NYANSA NNSA DA

Nyansa nnsa da stops us from panicking at the disparagement of capitalism, because we realize that capitalism is *a* conceptual system and not *the* only conceptual system of economics that can provide for life. Ujamaa, cooperative economics, is a value that is in conceptual conflict with American capitalism, a fact which should limit the anxiety of this discussion. In fact, as we will see, capitalism has not served the masses very well and many love it for the promise of potential prosperity that it offers, not the actual productivity of it. Capitalism has sufficient problems to prompt a search for an alternative or supplementary economic reality.

For example, American capitalism stems from a cultural ideology that manifests in the marketplace as profit at any cost, including moral bankruptcy and human suffering; a minimum functional percentage of citizens unemployed or working poor; consumption of unnecessary and hazardous goods and services; exploitation of both consumers and employees; misplaced priorities where time spent working away from the family far outweighs quality family time; rape, destruction and a lack of harmony with nature, which is seen as a vehicle for profit; and these are only a few of the problems with American capitalism.

> ... economic arrangements in America support vast inequality, extensive poverty, as well as racial, ethnic, and sexual discrimination. Moreover, general unemployment at a 5 percent level, jumping to 9 percent and perhaps even higher during deep recessions, appears endemic to American capitalism. Monopoly, high prices, and exploitative profits are also common in the American capitalist system, as are considerable waste and pollution. But on the more positive side, American capitalism is capable of enormous productivity which translates into a notably high standard of living for the majority of its citizens. [4]

From this quote we not only find a "mainstream" analysis of capitalism and its problems, but also the rationalization of its problems by "productivity" and "a notably high standard of living." This is a rationalization that supports American capitalism regardless of its "racial, ethnic, and sexual discrimination." Two major problems with the standard of living argument are that standard of living in an insane society is not very important compared to what a sane society could offer; and the standard of living is only high compared to societies that have been underdeveloped by the aggressive, exploitative nature of capitalism within the European *asili*.

Most Afrikans who have any level of material comfort wouldn't complain about it and their relative material comfort prevents many of them from resisting the European *asili*. Many Afrikans even attach comfort and living standard to the European *asili*. The ironic part of this is that people look around the world and think that America is as good as it gets, even with its insanity. However, without the benefit of seeing civilization absent of the disruption of the aggressive, destructive European *asili* manifested in capitalism, we really do not know how Afrikan or other societies could have thrived in harmony with nature and themselves. Ancient Afrikan, Native American and other civilizations give us good indication that a harmonious, productive, happy existence is attainable without destruction, greed, exploitation, mass poverty, etc.

Chancellor Williams places capitalism into a historical context in his book, *The Rebirth of African Civilization*.

> Capitalism gained its great strength through its alliance with the newly rising nation-state. Each was the making of the other through mutual support, and the explorations and discoveries of new lands that characterized the expansion of Europe over the whole world set the pace of the mad race for wealth that became the foundation of the nation-state with its new spirit of nationalism on the one hand, and the new economic system of capitalism with its spirit of conquest and enslavement on the other. The political support of the national state tended to obscure the true nature of its "economic arm," and so much so that colonialism is not always seen as capitalism in disguise. [5]

It is clear that Chancellor Williams saw capitalism as an extension of colonialism, which would make it inseparable from the European *asili*. Additionally, with regard to the European nation-state as a system of governance, Oba T'Shaka shares his observations in his book, *Return to the African Mother Principle of Male and Female Equality.*

> Just African governance operated in a fashion directly opposite to European nation states. As we have seen, the European nation state, starting with Greece, originated out of societies where males suppressed females, and the masculine principle was worshipped as the representative of reason with the feminine principle being degraded to the level of irrational, confusing, disorderly emotions. Western nation states, whether Marxist, republican, or other forms of authoritarianism, all operate on the principle of the "will to power," because they have suppressed the female and the feminine principle. [6]

T'shaka makes the connection between the European nation-state and the masculine feminine imbalance of its *asili*, just as Williams makes the connection between the nation-state, capitalism and enslavement. If we are speaking about a return to The Afrikan Way then we must necessarily entertain alternatives to capitalism, not within the narrow range of the European *asili* (i.e. communism), but using *nyansa nnsa da*, or thought without boundaries, to conceive of old/new alternatives. As a chilling and forthright reminder of our need to depart from this economic aspect of the European *asili*, Williams goes further to say that

> It will be a colossal joke of history if Africans wholeheartedly reject political domination and at the same time wholeheartedly embrace the very economic system that enshackled them in the first place.
>
> This, it seems to us, would be reason enough for not embracing capitalism as their principle way of life. Yet there are

other reasons far more important than the fact that colonialism is capitalism in disguise. One is that the very nature of capitalism is incompatible with the developmental needs of underdeveloped peoples. For capitalism very definitely is not concerned with social and economic advancement of *all* people. [7]

Whether we want to acknowledge it or not, the masses of Afrikan people in America are an underdeveloped people. In fact, the masses of <u>all</u> people in America are underdeveloped under the current economic realities. We have also seen that even though we have Afrikan millionaires and corporate C.E.O.'s, very few of them are contributing to the building of Afrikan institutions and the creation of a new reality. This is precisely because their economic consciousness is intricately woven into the European *asili*, an expected circumstance given the analysis of Williams and T'Shaka.

Nkosoᴐ

New economic realities will have to be shaped within the context of an old/new Afrikan consciousness. Therefore, a move by individuals to break with Yurugu, ideologically, philosophically and culturally, is a must. Within the capitalist realm that we all are living in, Afrikan people must utilize Ujamaa to empower one another. We must make cooperative use of our skills and resources, essentially operating as an Afrikan communal cooperative within a capitalist system.

This may occur in many forms such as business consortiums where Afrikans may buy food, material resources, business products, real estate and other Afrikan global community needs collectively. At the same time, we must be involved in the collective building of the necessary institutions for our liberation, financial included.

We gave the example earlier of a community plan to build a school. This could be adapted to financial and other institutions also.

Perhaps the most immediate and obvious example of beginning this process is to come to an understanding with the many conscious Afrikan people who are in business, that you will use their services and they will use yours. All of us have needs and so there is built in business for Afrikan people if we are operating in a mode of consciousness, liberation and sanity. Working within even a small group to begin with is enough to build a cooperative economic power base that will allow its members to pool resources and build institutions.

DAAKYE ABRA Bɔ

Our distant plans should include, among other things, the formulation of systems of communal land ownership; communal profit sharing; cooperative building of the infrastructure of an Afrikan nation or self-sufficient Afrikan global community; cooperative ventures to supply education, housing and preventative health care for our masses, etc.

As an elaboration and extension of some of the community work that can be done to effect a new economic reality, the guidance of Chancellor Williams is helpful.

All of these proposed projects would have come out of the first stage community discussions of needs and possibilities. They are all tentative. But they have aroused the community to a new sense of its own worth and new possibilities for a brighter future. So the second stage, the preparatory, is crucial because the following decisions have to be made:

(a) What project or projects can be started first, and on what scale?

(b) How to proceed with extended family organization as the basic unit and how to develop the inter-family system of cooperation?

(c) How much capital is needed, and ways and means of raising it?

(d) What technical and managerial skills are required and how many such persons are there in the community?

(e) How many persons must go into training at once for the work ahead?

(f) What are the target dates for the beginning of various projects?

(g) How much employment will the various activities provide?

(h) What will be the plan of local consumption, distribution and services?

(i) What will be the plan of inter-community sales and services?

(j) What will be the rules of profit distribution among the members?

(k) What are to be the safeguards of finance and responsible financial management?

(l) Can the community itself raise the initial capital required, and if not, why not?

(m) What cooperative activities can be carried on to improve the beauty and life of the community that require little or no money?

(n) How to coordinate local planning with national planning? [8]

The principle of Ujamaa, if practiced, could be expanded into an Afrikan economic system. This is work that will take *daakye abra bɔ* by dedicated Afrikan people.

5) PRESENT WORLD REALITY

"White world supremacy is largely responsible for the conditions of Afrikan people, but let's realize that the situation is unalterable. Racism is not going away."

"Complaining about racism is like complaining about the weather."

NYANSA NNSA DA

This type of thinking has been expressed by many Afrikan people, including many of those who are either supposed to be leaders or educated. In fairness, many people who feel this way and say these things are doing so to get Afrikans to move beyond problem recognition to problem resolution. However, *nyansa nnsa da* lets us realize that there is another way. When our thought is limitless, racism and white world supremacy, as they currently exist in their stifling and development arresting forms, are not unalterable situations.

Amos Wilson says that,

> The oppressive configuration the White man has assumed in relationship to the Black man is in good part the result of the fact that we have permitted ourselves to remain in a complementary subordinate configuration conducive to his oppressive designs. *The White man cannot be what he is unless we are what we are as a people.* And one way of transforming the White man is through *self-transformation.* [9]

Marimba Ani has also provided us with an analysis of Yurugu, therefore we can follow Amos Wilson's advice and destroy Yurugu within us as Afrikan people. The destroyer, Yurugu, must be destroyed. The destructive ideological matrix upon which white world supremacy rests must be destroyed within the minds of Afrikan people first and foremost. This destruction in and of itself changes the reality of the world. We are ceasing to be what we are, taking away the ability for Europeans to be what they are. Afrikans and other people of color make up over 90% of the world's population and Europeans make up under 10%. *Nyansa nnsa da* leads us to conclude that white world supremacy and racism are certainly not unalterable nor should they be forgotten. If 90%, 50% or even 10% of the world's people cease to be what they are, the 10% that dominate and destroy can neither dominate nor destroy any longer. We cannot ignore racism. We must understand it to rid ourselves of it. Yurugu should not be forgotten, it should be destroyed.

NKOSOᴐ

Read, study and become aware of self, as well as the nature of what has put us in our current predicament. Move toward self-transformation. Recognize Yurugu and how to get rid of it in one's self.

DAAKYE ABRA Bᴐ

Plan, create and build the means of destroying Yurugu within the masses of Afrikan people. In other words, participate in institution building. Employ *daakye abra bᴐ* to alter the course of education, socialization, acculturation and attempted assimilation into the European *asili*. Participate in changing yourself first and then changing others by shaping and accepting an old/new Afrikan consciousness, along with the institutions to perpetuate it.

6) PRESENT WORLD REALITY

Is Europe really the root of all evil? The crimes of Europe against *lesser breeds {italics* mine} without law (not to mention even *worse {italics* mine} crimes-Hitlarism and Stalinism-against other Europeans) are famous. But these crimes do not alter other facts of history: that Europe was the birthplace of the United States of America, that European ideas and culture formed the republic, that the United States is an extension of European civilization, and that nearly 80 percent of Americans are of European descent. [10]

The above comments come from a book written by a man

named Aurthur Schlesinger. Schlesinger has won two Pulitzer prizes, written several books, contributed to the Wall Street Journal, taught at Harvard and City University of New York, advised President Kennedy from 1961-1964, been in the vanguard of attacks on multicultural and Afrikan-centered education, and participated in the formulation of curriculum guidelines for the state of New York.

NYANSA NNSA DA

Before even utilizing *nyansa nnsa da* to look at Schlesinger's thoughts, simple common sense will suffice. One has to wonder how a man of such stature and acceptance in "mainstream" America has been able to write a book, as recent as 1992, that talks about "lesser breeds" and crimes against Europeans being worse than crimes against these "lesser breeds." This should be insulting and distorted to even the least conscious of Afrikan people confined by the European *asili*.

Nyansa nnsa da allows us to think outside of the present abnormal world reality, understanding that Schlesinger represents a flawed conceptual system despite his credentials. He is insane. We should ask what "lesser breeds" are and why this has been espoused by a man who advised a President and taught at one of the most prestigious European universities?

We get, in the beliefs of Schlesinger, a very clear example of Yurugu and the justification of aggression toward the "cultural other" that we have examined earlier in this work. Schlesinger justifies crimes against "lesser breeds," which represent the "cultural other" to him. This "cultural other" applies to people who are not European. Additionally, to Schlesinger, crimes committed against other Europeans are far worse than crimes committed against "lesser breeds," another clear manifestation of Marimba Ani's analysis in *Yurugu*.

It is European cultural nationalism that provides the distinction between the European's behavior toward "others" and his behavior toward other Europeans. [11]

NKOSOƆ AND DAAKYE ABRA ƁƆ

Work to be able to understand these sorts of manifestations of the European *asili* and reject the *asili* itself; an act which is the beginning of engaging in reality revolution. It will require study, transformation (of consciousness) and subsequent changes in actions and behavior. Since this is a process that we will be referring to again, we will call it **S.T.A.B.** for study, transformation, actions and behavior.

7) PRESENT WORLD REALITY

> The sins of the West are no worse than the sins of Asia or of the Middle East or Africa.
>
> There remains, however, a crucial difference between the Western tradition and others. The crimes of the West have produced their own antidotes. They have provoked great monuments to end slavery, to raise the status of women, to abolish torture, to combat racism, to defend freedom of inquiry and expression, to advance personal liberty and human rights.
>
> Whatever the particular crimes of Europe, that continent is also the source—the *unique* source—of those liberating ideas of individual liberty, political democracy, the rule of law, human rights and cultural freedom that constitute our most precious legacy and to which most of the world today aspires. These are *European* ideas, not Asian, nor African, nor Middle Eastern ideas, except by adoption. [12]

This quote also comes from Aurthur Schlesinger who's background is mentioned in the previous example, present world reality #6.

NYANSA NNSA DA

Aurthur Schlesinger offers a good example of the European *asili* once again. We are perhaps fortunate to get such an unapologetic and straight forward example of European *utamawazo* from a contemporary, respected European. There is the justification of the historical behaviors of Europeans, Yurugu, based upon Europe being the so called "unique source" of liberating ideas, and Schlesinger's remarkably unenlightened historical understanding. This is a distorted reality steeped in supremacist ideas, historical ignorance, an abnormal conceptual system, and a justification of insanity based on a rationale of so called progress and superiority. Ironically and expectedly, each of the excuses made for the crimes of the "West" is also an indication of the chaos the West has caused. The West did not end "slavery," but brutally and relentlessly enslaved millions of people whose resistance made the West modify their means of control. The West has modestly raised the status of women whom the West itself devalues and demeans. The West has not abolished torture, but perfected it, used it less conspicuously and with a greater degree of moderation. The West has not combated racism, but modified its appearance, because the inherently racist European *asili* remains a dominant world power.

It is also important to look at the excuse of "the sins of the West are no worse than the sins of Asia or of the Middle East or Africa." This is an excuse and justification of European behavior that occurs frequently. For example, European mass media will compare the Skinheads and the Ku Klux Klan to Minister Louis Farrakhan in an attempt to misinform people about Minister Farrakhan and excuse European behavior. This misinformation, or expression of their own ignorance, effectually serves the purpose of justifying European aggression by making it equal to things being done by Afrikan people. However, the informed and critically thinking person sees that there can be no meaningful comparison made between Skinheads, the Klan and Minister Farrakhan. Skinheads, the Klan and myriad other European groups have not only advocated and articulated hatred, but they have murdered, raped and brutalized people, carrying through on their words. Despite the fact that neither Minister Farrakhan nor the Nation of Islam has ever been involved in the organized terrorizing and brutalization of European people, the comparison is made, emphasized repeatedly and accepted. Likewise, there is no other culture who can quite match the historical destructiveness of "the sins of the West."

This is a pattern of justification for Yurugu's actions and behavior. As another example, a "racially" motivated despicable murder of an Afrikan couple occurs, in which the three European male perpetrators had Nazi flags, pamphlets, etc., and is compared with an incident in which an Afrikan commits a heinous crime against Europeans. You have two horrible occurrences with completely different dynamics and implications.

On the one hand you have a systematic continuation of a pattern of unprovoked, pathological European aggression and murder committed against Afrikans. This is a dynamic that has been at work for hundreds, maybe thousands, of years and has been accepted social and government policy in America and other European dominated countries. On the other hand, Afrikan unprovoked aggression against European people is a true anomaly of the kind Europeans try to characterize their actions as. The influence of the chaotic Afrikan existence in America is also a real factor in Afrikan criminal behavior.

Even considering Afrikan criminals, there are no Afrikan organizations that seek out and brutalize other cultural groups; no dogma of Afrikan murderous aggression; no efforts to make Europeans accept Afrikan ways, etc. It is simply a steady and intense propaganda game that serves to justify the European *asili* and its *utamawazo*, thus clearing Europeans of accountability.

Nkoso‚ and Daakye abra b‚

S.T.A.B. In addition, the importance of controlling our means of information dissemination and weaning ourselves off of an addiction to European television are important, among other things.

8) PRESENT WORLD REALITY

"Black people need to get off of this conspiracy kick. It is ridiculous to believe that all white people get on a conference call every morning to decide what they are going to do."

NYANSA NNSA DA

It is only the brilliant "rhetorical ethic" and proactive propaganda of Yurugu that fools Afrikans into thinking that constant conspiracy in America and the world dominated by the European *asili* is not possible. It is a reinforced delusion, because evidence of such a reality, in which conspiracy and aggression are the order of the day against Afrikans, is voluminous and even obvious in the historical record as well as modern developments such as the "Good Ol' Boys Roundup."

The ability to break free of the European *asili* to be able to see its conspiratorial necessity occurs with *nyansa nnsa da*. We must cultivate the ability to depart from the sarcasm of a *literal* conference-call between all Europeans each morning and understand that the *asili* itself serves the ideological and behavioral function of a conference call by insuring thought and behavior are in line amongst the masses, especially subconsciously. In addition, there are indeed Europeans who conference with one another on a conspiratorial level. A rudimentary examination of secret societies and American government reveal conspiracies on a regular basis.

Our long-term health and departure from delusion are dependent upon proper historical understanding so that we are not deceived by the contemporary propaganda and craftiness of Yurugu.

NKOSOƆ AND DAAKYE ABRA BƆ

S.T.A.B.

9) PRESENT WORLD REALITY
"Some white masters treated their slaves well."

NYANSA NNSA DA
One must ask the question of how someone who has been enslaved can be treated well by someone who enslaves them. The condition of enslavement itself is severe mistreatment. As a matter of principle, the first step toward an enslaver approaching humanity is to not only free their captive, but atone and apologize for their barbaric actions, as well as pay financial, cultural and psychological reparations to their victims; by willfully paying them, returning to them confiscated and hidden knowledge, and providing them the technology and means to reassert themselves.

This is the kind of action that the Europeans in the United States, Brazil, Britain and other Maafa criminal nations would have to initiate to sincerely seek the favor, or return to a neutral status in the eyes of sane and conscious Afrikan people. It is simply absurd to classify any enslaver of Afrikan people as having treated them well.

A case in point is the absurd situation in Azania (South Afrika) in which the Afrikans are now expected to share their country today with those who practiced barbaric apartheid yesterday. Apartheid criminals are participating in government with the Afrikan people of that country, while still maintaining their stolen riches in diamonds, gold, labor, land, etc. The contemporary nature of apartheid really gives us the opportunity to recognize that true justice would have been the European forfeiture and repayment of stolen riches and land, and short of banishment from the country, at least a ban on government participation for all European apartheid criminals.

10) PRESENT WORLD REALITY
American blacks, no less than whites, belong to and are

shaped by American culture, to which they have so immensely
contributed and into which their own imaginations and deeds are
inextricably wound: All they have in common with African blacks
is their genes and, in the case of African states that were once
English colonies, the English language. [13]

NYANSA NNSA DA

First of all, while we acknowledge the abnormality and
insanity of the dominant world culture, or European *asili*, we also
acknowledge the reality that we are currently deep in this culture. We
are profoundly affected by it.

However, our connection to abnormality and insanity is not
irretractable when we have *nkoso ɔ*, *daakye abra bɔ*, *nyansa nnsa da*
and an understanding of Yurugu. We thus reject the premise of the
above quotation. At the same time, our castigation and rejection of
the European *asili* does not mean that every aspect of European culture
represents madness, but the *asili* is abnormal, flawed and insane. In
other words, the major constructs, institutions, historical processes and
conceptual frameworks are abnormal and insane.

A good corollary is that although there were Europeans who
consciously fought The Maafa, the experience still happened for
hundreds of years and encompassed millions of lives. The cultural
values that allowed The Maafa to happen and engulf the entire
Western Hemisphere are thus the dominant forces in the culture,
otherwise the "good" Europeans and the sane nature of the culture
would have been sufficient to overcome a few extremists or an episode
that didn't reflect the true culture. However, it was the true nature of
the culture that manifested oppression, rape and murder. The Maafa
wasn't an anomaly, but a manifestation of the insanity of a culture.

So, it is the European *asili* and its adherents which are insane,
thus recognition of the *asili* allows for strategies of extrication from it.
Reality revolution and the creation of an old/new Afrikan conscious-

ness is precisely for the purpose of removing ourselves from Yurugu or Yurugu from us. It was imposed systematically and its removal must be systematic. In addition, honest Europeans will see this as an opportunity for self-examination.

The other issue in the above quote by Robert Hughes, an admirer of Aurthur Schlesinger, as to our lack of commonalities with our Afrikan sisters and brothers around the world is a source of Yurugu conceptions and intentional fragmentation of the Afrikan existence. The author of the quote is a European who completely misunderstands Afrikan history and Afrikan spirituality. Our connection to Afrikan people around the world is one that is solidly based on history and cultural unity, as well as the spiritual dimensions of the Afrikan reality that one entrenched in the European *asili* is unable to understand.

Although The Maafa has caused a rupture in the history and minds of Afrikan people, only the ill-informed fail to see the worldwide prevalence of profound examples of Afrikan ancestral connections that exist today. *The Maafa & Beyond* dealt with some examples of the ways in which Afrikan people are in fact a global community, so we won't get further into that here. Additionally, in this work the spirituality of Afrikan people is dealt with in the chapter entitled "Spiritual Dimensions of Nyansa Nnsa Da and Afrikan Catharsis."

Therefore, our *nyansa nnsa da* places the quote beginning this section within the context of distorted reality and an extension of the intent of the falsification and destruction of Afrikan consciousness during The Maafa. The Maafa was in large part based on the disconnection and destruction of Afrikan cultural continuity and identity. The words of Robert Hughes contribute to and manifest the intentional thrust of The Maafa to disconnect, destroy and recreate Afrikans in the form of negroes.

11) PRESENT WORLD REALITY

A sister or brother may listen to a lecture on Afrikan liberation and upon leaving the lecture fail to engage in the action outlined as necessary for liberation.

Nyansa nnsa da

It is acknowledged that often times our lecturers do not give the practicality or program that must accompany theory, as Manu Ampim points out in his book, *Towards Black Community Development: Moving Beyond the Limitations of the Lecture Model.* But, more often than not our brothers and sisters are not approaching liberation seriously. If one listens to a lecture on liberation, *nyansa nnsa da* must allow the individual to match what is being said with the possibilities of making it happen. There must be the internalization of concepts and information that leads to personal transformation and action. Failure to do this is what Minister Khallid Muhammad calls "culture without commitment."

In a time when Yurugu has attempted to destroy The Afrikan Way, we cannot afford to have brothers and sisters attending liberation lectures simply for the entertainment value of a good orator. The goal should be to gain something of practical personal use for an individual contribution to our return to The Way. If it can be spoken of in a lecture by a conscious and sane Afrikan, it can be done.

*Nkoso‹ ₐₙD *Daakye abra b‹**

If it is necessary for the listener to move from passive listening to action, it is a good idea for such a person to always have a notepad with them when they attend lectures. You should identify specific points, concepts and activities that you can transfer from the spoken word to action. If you cannot discern these things from the lecture, ask that it be made more clear to you. Once this is done, what has been identified should serve as a checklist for future activities to be engaged within a specified period of time.

You might seek help in developing a book list and assign a certain amount of time a day or week for reading, as well as a time line for your completion of the book list. Or, you might join an Afrikan-centered study group which will structure your reading for you and provide discussion for better understanding the concepts and topics of the books you read.

The bottom line is that we become a nation of doers and act upon the knowledge we gain. To do this we might also heed the advice of Manu Ampim and move away from the lecture model into more of a workshop or community development model, which provides for more interaction and the development of processes and programs to move us forward.

12) PRESENT WORLD REALITY

I think the racial struggle in America has always been primarily a struggle for innocence. White racism from the beginning has been a claim of white innocence and therefore of white entitlement to subjugate blacks. And in the sixties, as went innocence so went power. Blacks used the innocence that grew out of their long subjugation to seize more power, while whites lost more of their innocence and so lost a degree of power over blacks. [14]

NYANSA NNSA DA

What an overly simplistic analysis we are given by Shelby Steele. It is also an apologetic, naive analysis that equates Afrikan motivations and actions with those of Europeans. Perhaps Steele has forgotten that the "racial struggle in America" has been one in which Afrikan people have attempted to alleviate the pain, brutality, murder and psychological mutilation of The Maafa and all of its consequences. It has been a struggle to end the lynchings, Tuskegee Syphilis Experiments, enslavement, rape, brutality, KKK activity, governmental COINTELPRO type activity, racism, degrading media images, mis-education and on and on. The motivations of Europeans who have operated as the aggressive psychologically disturbed fulfillers of the European *asili* cannot be compared to the motivations of Afrikans trying to survive the European *asili*. Perhaps the only comparisons of this type that can be made is between Europeans and Afrikans who have accepted, internalized and are aspiring to the standards of the European *asili*.

Nyansa nnsa da allows us to see that, as one who is bound by and aspires to the framework of the European *asili*, Steele is inevitably going to make analyses of such an inadequate nature as not to bring about solutions to Afrikan problems. In his book he states his position.

> There will be no end to despair and no lasting solution to any of our problems until we rely on individual effort within the American mainstream—rather than collective effort against the mainstream—as our means of advancement. [15]

It is almost as if Steele has a need to believe that Yurugu does not exist. He seems to be in a state of denial that leads to over simplification and delusion; and is unfortunately blessed with the ability to rationalize his Yurugu philosophy. Amos Wilson defined delusion as "false beliefs held by an individual which are stubbornly retained and defended despite their logical inconsistencies with objective reality and valid evidence to the contrary." [16]

If there is a struggle for innocence, of the type Steele mentions, this seems to be Steele's struggle to see the innocence of Europeans. This is a manifestation of the distorted world reality we are able to see when *nyansa nnsa da* allows us to think outside of this reality. It places this kind of thought in the realm of inadequate and abnormal.

The fulfillment, perpetuation and aggression of the European *asili* has been systematic. It takes a systematic approach to both understand Yurugu and solve the problems it has created.

Nkoso⊃ and Daakye abra b⊃

This type of abnormal thinking needs to be recognized, deciphered and avoided by conscious Afrikans. **S.T.A.B.**

****

As the title indicates, this chapter's intention has been to address grassroots and practical ideas and circumstances that arise in the lives of people everyday. In addition it is meant to provide "ammunition" for the reality revolution. It is one of the many areas of Systematic Enemy Analysis. Some of the scenarios dealt with addressed Afrikan writers and other so called scholars who identify with and fulfill the European *asili*. These types of Afrikans, or perhaps negroes is a better term since negroes are a creation of Yurugu, are often difficult for grassroots sisters and brothers to deal with. Although they are exhibiting delusional, insane and abnormal behavior, it is validated by the "mainstream" and their insanity is of a nature Amos Wilson referred to as "pathological normalcy."

> To be oppressed is by definition to have one's thought processes disturbed; emotions impaired; motives and values inverted; and one's body functions imbalanced. There can be no "normality" of consciousness and conduct for Blacks as long as they remain dominated by Whites—merely socially acceptable or

unacceptable adjustments to the ever changing demand characteristics of White supremacy. The normality of Blacks under White domination is by that circumstance, above all, a "pathological normalcy" —disturbances in Black consciousness and behavior which are deemed serviceable and beneficial to the needs of their White oppressors. [17]

This pathological normalcy, which for all intents and purposes is the functional insanity of the masses of Afrikan people, can be difficult to "'call out" in a society that deems it to be simply normal, sane, desired and acceptable behavior. In addition, those schooled in madness by European *utamawazo* have been so well schooled that they believe they are not mad at all, but are normal, rational human beings and they can make others who know no better believe it as well. Therefore, this chapter has sought to make the reality revolution more real to grassroots sisters and brothers, while aiding in the identification of the reality revolution at work.

The practical application of liberation concepts is very important. Sisters and brothers who are simply living their lives from day to day, must be able to apply these concepts as well as scholars and conscious Afrikans. The transformation in consciousness must be so broad because as the masses of Afrikans live or die, so will the individuals whether they are conscious soldiers or not. Also, as has been discussed, the spiritual and psychological ruptures that Afrikan people have experienced have touched so many of us. We need mass healing and concepts that will impact the masses of Afrikan people, if not directly, then through their influence in galvanizing new ways of thinking and nation building. Our ill health is pervasive to the degree that Kobi Kambon posits, regarding Psychological/Cultural Misorientation, that,

the vast majority (70 to 80%) of the African population in

America are hypothesized to be afflicted at the moderate level or range of this disorder, while as many as 10% (if not more) are probably severely afflicted, and at least some 10% may only be minimally afflicted. What this distribution suggests, then, is that most African people living under White supremacy domination may indeed be suffering from moderate to severe forms of Psychological/Cultural Misorientation. [18]

Those who are the least affected by the European *asili* and its destructive psychological effects need to be able to give something practical to their less healthy sisters and brothers. It is hoped that this chapter has addressed some of the general questions and answers regarding issues of pathological normalcy, cultural imposition, propaganda, and nation building processes that affect the masses day to day.

If we wait for our official experts, who knows when, if ever, they will dare feel free, or find it profitable, to talk candidly and intelligibly with us? For there are three sorts of experts--those for our liberation; those against our liberation; and those who contrive to appear to be on our side while they are indeed subtly working against our liberation. Advice from an expert who is not on your side, or from one who is against you, can be far worse than no expert advice at all... For there are some experts, some Africans included, who deeply cherish the privileges that go with defending or furthering the interests of the imperialists... Because of these kinds of experts, and because even those experts genuinely on the clients side are as capable of honest error as anyone, the client ought always to exercise vigilance and common sense in taking advice from experts. For eternal vigilance, in all matters, especially over the minutest details, is still the price of liberty.

Chinweizu, The West and the Rest of Us

PART 3

RETURN TO THE
WAY

CHAPTER 8

○○○○○○○○○

RETURN TO THE WAY:
THE NATURE OF AN OLD/NEW
AFRIKAN CONSCIOUSNESS

> We do not refuse the call of love, but let it be love growing
> along the way, and if the paths to the way are all now the hard
> paths of constant fighting against triumphant destruction, we crave
> no other procreation than that possible along these paths. The
> children we aspire to bring here, we should not be for them merely
> a horrid warning. How beautiful if, growing up, they saw us
> always fighting death, and by their natural learning grew also
> along our way, and saw the way as the natural aim of life!

Ayi Kwei Armah, Two Thousand Seasons

Our return to The Way as an Afrikan people will require a systematic creation of concepts and study of our predicament, as well as employing *nyansa nnsa da* and our spiritual essence to create an old/new Afrikan consciousness. Having been disconnected from the Afrikan Way because of the aggressive, destructive European *asili* and its fulfillment in The Maafa, we find ourselves needing to create again. Our creation of a new Afrikan consciousness given these circumstances requires that we use the concept of Sankofa, but also adjust for a contemporary world much different from that which was our Way before our disconnection. Thus, we are dealing with an "old/new" creation that takes the glory of the Afrikan past and compensates for the present madness.

In this chapter, suggested premises of an old/new Afrikan consciousness will be presented as a part of our systematic recreation. These premises are only a beginning, a rough draft to be revised, edited and added to by many other conscious, sane Afrikan people. They are as follows:

* MASCULINE AND FEMININE INTERNAL SYNTHESIS AND EQUALITY

* MASCULINE AND FEMININE EXTERNAL SYNTHESIS AND EQUALITY

* *NYANSA NNSA DA*

* A RETURN TO THE WAY MUST AVOID *NYANSA YEREKETSE*

* TRUE LIBERATION IS SELF-KNOWLEDGE, SELF-DEFINITION, PSYCHOLOGICAL HEALTH, SELF-DETERMINATION AND SELF-SUFFICIENCY

* AFRIKAN PEOPLE MUST MAKE THEIR LIFE WORK TRUE LIBERATION WHENEVER AND WHEREVER WE ARE OPPRESSED. COMFORTABLE CAPTIVITY IS UNACCEPTABLE

* THE HUMAN BEING CAN ONLY BE UNDERSTOOD IN RELATION TO THE COSMOS

* THE SPIRITUAL IS AN INSEPARABLE COMPLEMENT AND UNSEEN DRIVING FORCE TO THE MATERIAL

* WE ACKNOWLEDGE AND RESPECT THE *ABOSOM* (MANIFESTATIONS OF THE SUPREME CREATOR), THE *NSAMANFO* (ANCESTRAL SPIRITS) AND THE SUPREME

CREATOR, WHETHER CALLED *ONYAME* (AKAN), *OLUDUMARRE* (YORUBA), *AMMA* (DOGON), *NGALA* (BAMBARA), *MUNGU* (KISWAHILI) OR ANY OTHER NAME BY WHICH AFRIKAN PEOPLE CALL THE CREATOR

* BALANCE, ORDER, TRUTH, JUSTICE, RECIPROCITY, COMPASSION AND HARMONY ARE THE VIRTUES OF LIFE AND THE MOST NATURAL, DESIRED STATE OF HUMAN BEINGS, NATIONAL AFFAIRS AND WORLD RELATIONS

* THE PURPOSE OF EDUCATION IS "THE RITUALIZED REAFFIRMATION OF THE NATIONAL IDENTITY. IT IS ANCHORED IN THE REAL AND IDEALIZED HISTORY OF A PEOPLE. THE NATION'S EDUCATION IS SHAPED AND GIVEN IMPETUS BY THE CULTURAL AND IDEOLOGICAL ASSUMPTIONS, DYNAMICS, ESSENTIAL VALUES, PRIORITIES AND GOALS OF THE NATION." AGYEI AKOTO

* AFRIKANS MUST BEAR THE FULL RESPONSIBILITY FOR THE NURTURING, PROTECTION AND EDUCATION OF AFRIKAN CHILDREN.

* CONSCIOUS RESISTANCE IN A HOSTILE ENVIRONMENT OF OPPRESSION IS NEITHER MILITANT NOR RADICAL. IT IS SANE, NORMAL AND DESIRED BEHAVIOR

* WE ARE A COMMUNAL PEOPLE AND "I EXIST BECAUSE AND ONLY IF WE EXIST"

* INTERNAL AND EXTERNAL ENEMIES OF AFRIKAN PEOPLE MUST BE IDENTIFIED AND HELD ACCOUNTABLE

These are the premises to be expounded upon in this chapter. They represent, in many ways, a concise articulation of the principles and beliefs outlined in this work. There is necessarily some overlap in the premises, as we understand the interconnection of all aspects of Afrikan existence. Again, they are only a beginning. Our entire reality is subject to redefinition and new direction.

As we begin this endeavor we can revisit the madness of the present reality the world is immersed in. Oba T'Shaka, in his work *Return to the African Mother Principle of Male and Female Equality*, correctly observes that,

> On the eve of the 21st century, a century that promises by all indications, to be a century of profound change, a mature African vision of the just society comes to the United States and to the western world. Our vision of the just society comes at a time when the West and the United States are suffering a spiritual and a political crisis that threatens their future existence. Many Americans feel disoriented and off balance in a world that values the material... [1]

This disorientation and lack of balance is confirmed in a *Time* magazine article from the August 28, 1995 edition of the magazine. The article was entitled "The Evolution of Despair" and addressed the current problems people are having in contemporary American society, as well as a new field of study that examines how these problems could be tied to the fact that humans did not develop in the extreme environments they are currently forced to deal with everyday. It references a man called the unabomber, who has for years been a serial mail bomber.

> There's a little bit of the unabomber in most of us. We may not share his approach to airing a grievance, but the grievance itself feels familiar. In the recently released excerpts of his still unpublished 35,000 word essay, the serial bomber complains that the modern world, for all its technological marvels, can be an uncomfortable, "unfulfilling" place to live. It makes us behave in ways "remote from the natural pattern of human behavior." [2]

This represents, more or less, an admission of the current world madness and that of the European *asili*. The article agrees with the unabomber's observations to a degree and notes that,

> Rates of depression have been doubling in industrial countries roughly every 10 years. Suicide is the third most common cause of death among young adults in North America, after car wrecks and homicides. Fifteen percent of Americans have had a clinical anxiety disorder. And, pathological, even murderous alienation is a hallmark of our time. [3]

All this does is articulate what we already know regarding the European *asili*, but from the perspective of "mainstream" media which accepts the European *asili* and its *utamawazo*. The so called new science of evolutionary psychology that the article speaks about "suggests that a larger threat to mental health may be the way civilization thwarts civility. There is a kinder, gentler side of human nature, and it seems increasingly to be a victim of repression." The trouble with Europeans being able to address the problems, even with a "new field of science," lies in the European *asili*. It affects all aspects of the culture, even those intended to be therapeutic and heal the people within the culture. We were able to glimpse this corruption of psychiatry and psychology in an earlier chapter.

So, our "mature African vision of the just society," the creation of an Afrikan consciousness which fulfills our *asili*, comes not only at a time when Afrikan people need to return to The Way, but also when Europeans are getting indications that their way is flawed. We have no choice but to create an old/new Afrikan consciousness, because the present world reality is collapsing and even those who embrace it are questioning it.

On our return to The Way, we have guidance from numerous

sources. Marimba Ani who has provided us with so much of our understanding of Yurugu, the European *asili* and the concept of *asili* itself, shares that,

> Now that we have broken the power of their ideology, we must leave them and direct our energies toward the recreation of cultural alternatives informed by ancestral visions of a future that celebrates our Africanness and encourages the best of the human spirit. Each of the cultures historically victimized by Europe must reclaim its own image. As for those of us who are African, our salvation (redemption) lies in our ancientness and connectedness; not in a romanticized glorification of the past, but in a return to the center in which all contradictions are resolved and from which the spiral of development can continue with clarity. From the center, ikons can be retrieved in our image that will allow us to tap the energy of the collective conscious will of our people. [4]

In seeking clarity and direction, we can also look to the profound work of Ayi Kwei Armah in his book, *Two Thousand Seasons*.

> In us has been the need to spend life against the present killing arrangements, destruction's established system; to spend life cutting through deceiving superficies to reach again the essential truths the destroyers must hide from spirits if their white road is to prevail; to spend life acting on truth against destruction's whiteness; to spend life working with our people, searching for paths to our way.
>
> This should be the lifework of spirits still open to the remembrance of the way, capable already of visions of its rediscovery, willing, determined to make it a living way again.
>
> Vision is the aim of this vocation: the clearing of

destruction's pale, thick-lying pus from eyes too long blinded to every possibility of the way. This lifework, its fruit should be the birth of new seers, other hearers, more numerous utterers. And the fruit of all our lifework together: that should be destruction's destruction. [5]

Nyansa nnsa da aids in the removal of the "thick-lying pus" of Yurugu from the eyes of Afrikan people. Limitless thought is necessary to envision "every possibility of the way" and "destruction's destruction."

Nyansa nnsa da is also of value for us to conceive of our ability to actually create on such large scales. Our creation will necessarily be a systematic redefinition of all aspects of our existence in conflict with the Afrikan Way. This systematic approach will be combined with the spiritual dimensions of our existence to articulate an old/new Afrikan consciousness, which can serve as a guide for our people on the road leading away from destruction. Kwame Agyei Akoto correctly frames what we are calling for, regarding an old/new Afrikan consciousness, with his reference to "re-Afrikanization."

Nationbuilding finally is the systematic and sustained effort to reconstruct the national culture in all of its dimensions. That effort must begin with the reconstitution of the historical nucleus, the fuel core of culture, whose dynamism radiates outward and energizes and defines the language, symbols, institutions and state apparatus of the national culture. [6]

Akoto goes further to share that

This nationbuilding, re-Afrikanization, process must necessarily follow the outlines of the cultural sphere elaborated earlier. It would entail three basic overlapping stages including;

(A) Rediscovery/Historical Recovery, (B) Redefinition/Cultural
Reaffirmation, and (C) Revitalization/National Liberation. It
must begin, as indeed it already has, with the systematic "exhuma-
tion and revivification" of Afrikan history throughout the continent and the diaspora, from antiquity to the contemporary. The
first stage must include the recovery and   revitalization of the core
values of antiquity, particularly as represented in the sacred works,
philosophy, language, and other symbolic forms. [7]

Included in Akoto's re-Afrikanization process is the
development of an Afrikan world ideology, as well as other steps that
are synonymous with and inform our development of an old/new
Afrikan consciousness.

A word needs to be said here about an Afrikan world ideology
or an old/new consciousness. There are many Afrikans, who reckon
themselves critical analyzers of the Afrikan struggle for liberation, that
would put forward the sentiment that because Afrikan people are not a
monolithic people we cannot speak of an Afrikan agenda or an
Afrikan World Order of the type Akoto proposes. They would suggest
such frameworks are too narrow for the diversity within the Afrikan
community.

To the degree these voices disparage the ability or necessity of
Afrikan people to come together on a *single* agenda, they must be
corrected and we must be very clear about what we mean by a "single
agenda," for the masses of Afrikan people. We do not mean to
proselytize and convert everyone to a single method of approaching
freedom. That is not our way. We do not believe in the missionary/
conversion model. Instead, there are very practical points of departure
that we must agree upon.

In *The Maafa & Beyond*, I approached this area of concern;
affirming that Afrikan people are not monolithic, but there are points
of consensus that we must be clear on as a people. The text went on to

elaborate on some of the areas of consensus, which were not unlike Akoto's re-Afrikanization process in that they were essentially areas based on the need for Afrikan people to SURVIVE, return to mental health and protect ourselves, among other things.

Survival, sanity and a return to health are ideological areas that are broad enough for Afrikan people to unify around, even as we acknowledge divergent definitions of what these areas represent and how to achieve them. We understand that, given the trauma of our existence there will be those who don't even agree that these are necessary areas to address, but nonetheless we make no apology for the call for a common direction for all Afrikan people.

For the purpose of clearly laying down an outline for some of the areas in which the brightest Afrikan minds must work their creation and redefinition, we will categorize these areas as "premises" of an old/new Afrikan consciousness, a consciousness which fulfills the Afrikan *asili*. The nature of Afrikan creation dictates that none of what is articulated here is static, but a dynamic outline capable of being changed, molded, improved, studied and articulated again to meet the needs of Afrikan people. In fact, in speaking of an old/new Afrikan consciousness, it is absolutely necessary and a given that what is laid down in this chapter is only a beginning, an imperfect sketch.

So, where to begin our creation? It is the belief of the author and activist, Oba T'Shaka, that a balance between the masculine and feminine principles *within* individuals is a necessary step in our return to The Way. The internal imbalance of these principles manifests in external conflict and degradation of females and the "cultural other." Looking back to chapter 1, we saw the articulation, in the ancient European philosophical writings (*utamawazo*), of this imbalance between the masculine and feminine principles. It is this imbalance which is a large part of what makes Yurugu, the incomplete being, what it is. This is a good place to begin our return.

SUGGESTED PREMISES OF AN OLD/NEW AFRIKAN CONSCIOUSNESS

PREMISE: Masculine and feminine internal synthesis and equality-
Masculine and feminine principles make up every complete human being and each is equally important to completeness. Individuals cannot be created without the union of the masculine and the feminine.

As is the natural order of the cosmos, we can see our purpose from the smallest elements of our bodies to the largest elements of the universe. In the physiological development of a human being, both a sperm and an egg are necessary for the formation of life, thus representing the masculine and the feminine. The sperm and the egg each have 23 sets of chromosomes to contribute to a complete union and creation. Each individual chromosomal set is composed of *two* chromosomes. Thus, the newly created human being has 46 *sets* or *pairs* of chromosomes. In addition, as the cell structures of the developing organism grow, dividing over and over again, each cell in the entire body contains a duplicate of the original 46 pairs of chromosomes given from the male and the female. Masculine and feminine synthesis and complementarity on the earliest physiologic levels are an absolute necessity within the human being and for the creation of life from two human beings, a man and a woman. Therefore, we see the physiological manifestation of masculine and feminine internal synthesis and equality.

It is the order of the universe for there to be harmony and equality between life giving forces that must come together internally and externally for life to happen. Internally, we have seen the chromosomal necessities and externally we know that the only way to create life is for man and woman to contribute equally of themselves to produce a new individual.

The Afrikan consciousness understands that based on such

signposts of male and female equality, we must be at peace internally with what have been assigned the titles of "masculine" and "feminine" principles. The intuitive, feeling, sensing, superconscious, nurturing, wise aspects of what have been called feminine principles are to be seen and used as complements and equals to the intellectual, reasoning, strong masculine principle.

Additionally and of extreme importance, Afrikan people must understand that there are no absolutes and these masculine and feminine qualities cannot be uniformly applied, one set to men and one set to women. In fact, because of the natural synthesis internally between masculine and feminine, men and women each have both masculine and feminine principles, as these principles have been defined. Differing principles simply tend to be more dominant in some women and men. Both masculine and feminine principles must be valued. We cannot buy the conceptual belief that those qualities represented by the masculine principles are divine and those represented by the feminine are base. Internal conflict and incompleteness is the result when there is imbalance internally. *Masculine and feminine internal synthesis and equality is the norm and imbalance is abnormal.*

We must value, nurture and cultivate sensitivity, intuition and emotion as much as we do reason, intellect and strength. All of these principles together are found in complete women and men.

PREMISE: Masculine and feminine external synthesis and equality- It is almost a given that once we accept masculine and feminine equality within each of us, it will manifest in healthy relationships and respect between individuals. Especially where men are concerned, the animus that our actions and thoughts tend to show towards women can be alleviated with internal balance and the understanding that comes with it. Believing in the Afrikan mother principle, we also see the feminine principles as a divine manifestation of the creator in their life giving potential. Thus, we can only respect, value and hold women as sacred, while additionally seeing the beauty of these same feminine principles in ourselves as men. The defiling and abuse of a women is akin to the defiling and abuse of one's mother and oneself, which is unacceptable for Afrikan people. By the same token we cannot extend negative conceptions of women to the assigning of value to "white supremacist capitalist patriarchy." [8]

There are also responsibilities that this magnified status of the feminine carries for those who are women. The woman must bear her sacred life-giving qualities, responsibilities and mother relationship (regardless of whether she has children) by carrying herself as divine, worthy of all respect and an equal partner in the just governance of an Afrikan reality.

Contrary to Plato's opinion, there is no greater love nor governance than the union between and governance by women and men in balance with one another and in balance with themselves.

PREMISE: *Nyansa nnsa da-* Our ability to employ thought without boundaries and conceive of Afrikan people doing anything and everything, just as the cosmos is without the limits of our conception, is a necessary part of the Afrikan consciousness. The cultural aggression of the European *asili* has done much to destroy the confidence Afrikan people have in themselves and their potential; a confidence that *nyansa nnsa da* can do much to replace and restore. There is so much creation to be done after so much destruction, that *nyansa nnsa da* is necessary for us to conceive of it all being done.

PREMISE: A return to The Way must avoid *Nyansa Yereketse-* *Nyansa Yereketse* is an Akan word of the Fante which means "distorted wisdom." [9] As we sift through the European *asili,* our Afrikan past and the present, it is important to distinguish *Nyansa Yereketse* from useful paradigms. An example of the distinctions that need to be made can be found in the modern practice of the West justifying its destructive behavior toward humanity and nature by pointing to all of its technological advances.

Afrikan people have to be more pragmatic than this. Afrika as an example, we tend to attribute technological advances and industrialization on the continent to European conquerors and their presence. Foolish people look at this as a benefit of colonization when it actually represents *Nyansa Yereketse* because it is wisdom, but wisdom distorted into aggression and brutality. It is wisdom that in the larger picture of life is ultimately more harmful and damaging than it's worth.

Chinweizu points out that "The conquest of Africa, it must be emphasized, did not have to happen for Africa to undergo industrial revolution." [10] He goes on to explain that,

> It is rather easy to make a case arguing that the invasion, by spreading literacy, by energetically planting an industrial infrastructure and opening up mines and new plantations, speeded up Africa's economic revolution. But this intervention did not merely speed up the process. It did so in the wrong manner and along the wrong tracks, the tracks of dependency. By destroying and at best hobbling and discouraging African initiative, it did fundamental harm to Africa's incipient economic revolution. If such a speeding-up of things by the already expert industrialists of Europe should be taken as satisfactory justification—and not merely a convenient rationalization—for the colonized character of the African economy, if this speeding-up is treated as an overriding good, then, by the logic of that argument, we should voluntarily relinquish whatever little control we have since won over our economy, return total control to the western colonizing experts so they can impose upon us the most rapid industrialization they can, or are willing, to impose upon us. On such a premise independence should then be reversed; it should have never

been allowed to happen at all, much less fought for by Africans...
the direction and character of our economic development must be
seen to be just as important as its mere quantity and speed, if not
more so. In that case the laudatory claims made for colonial
intervention in our economic history, like those made for their
intervention in our political and cultural history, must be repudi-
ated.

How fast and healthily Africa's industrial revolution would
have occurred in autonomy, what patterns of development might
have been realized had African rulers and entrepreneurs never been
subjugated, had they never lost charge of their history, is one of the
"might have beens" of history. [11]

It is *Nyansa Yereketse,* or distorted wisdom, that can plunge a
continent into despair through conquest, while introducing new
technology. That technology is useless. In fact, it is precisely because
of the *Nyansa Yereketse* of the European *asili* that we will never know
the heights that Afrikan people could have risen to, if allowed centuries
of harmonious development in the absence of the chaos and
destruction of The Maafa and the general thousands of years of
outside assault upon the continent.

People are grateful today for the quality of life of a
technological age, especially in America. However, this is a product of
Nyansa Yereketse when we realize that the annihilation of Native
Americans and The Maafa were necessary precursors. In a world free
of the *Nyansa Yereketse* of the European *asili,* we may have been able
to achieve a high enough elevation of the human spirit and harmony
with the cosmos that the type of technology that exists today would be
unnecessary to a large degree and we would have developed what was
necessary. Our ancient Afrikan cultures, like the Afrikans of Kemet,
show us that we would have been more than capable of profound
scientific advance. However, would we have seen a need to disrupt the

harmonious balance of humanity, destroy nature and all the other damaging consequences following the lines of the modern *Nyansa Yereketse*? Marimba Ani analyzes the European "Progress as Ideology."

> European "progress" has been made at the expense of the quality of human existence. Where is the progress toward greater spirituality, toward human understanding, toward tolerance, toward an appreciation of diversity and plurality, away from aggression? Obviously European "reason" has not performed well in these areas, because the template of the European asili does not include a model for the development of humanity, only of its negation, of technological efficiency and of greater capital gain: the tools of power. [12]

This type of so called progress is *Nyansa Yereketse*. An old/ new Afrikan consciousness should differentiate between real human progress and *Nyansa Yereketse*.

PREMISE: TRUE liberation is self-knowledge, self-definition, psychological health, self-determination and self-sufficiency- These are the defining circumstances of an existence that is truly free.

PREMISE: Afrikan people must make their life work TRUE liberation whenever and wherever we are oppressed. Comfortable captivity is unacceptable- TRUE liberation is a return to The Way through self-knowledge, self-definition, psychological health, self-determination and self-sufficiency. This must be our thrust and ultimate direction. Making our captivity and oppression more comfortable is not viable.

As has often been the case in the history of Afrikan struggle, our goals have not represented freedom, TRUE liberation. Retrospectively we find that we have often been about making our captivity more comfortable through legislation, government intervention, access and movement within the institutions of the European *asili,* etc. It is as though we have been in a cage and instead of trying to break free, we have repeatedly pleaded to our captors for pillows and blankets to put on the hard floor of our cells, so that we might be more comfortable in our cage.

Undoubtedly, our incarceration, psychologically and intellectually, must end before we can even be considered serious about TRUE liberation. Our misdirection has had us asking for things and when searching for ideas and concepts, we have traditionally looked no further than the European *asili.* TRUE liberation is the key. TRUE liberation is the fruit of a reality revolution.

PREMISE: The human being can only be understood in relation to the cosmos. The cosmos can only be understood through spirituality and not by science declared as reason devoid of spirit. We have examined the physiological basis for resistance in a previous chapter and see the examples of resistance in nature all of the time with the "fight or flight" experience. Because the universe is a whole which is manifested in its parts, resistance can also been seen in the larger universe as substances, especially gases, under too much pressure will explode. The explosion is the result of the rapidly moving molecules seeking space beyond the constrictions of whatever is binding them. We see and have heard the example of the mother having to give up the seemingly dependent child at nine months, as nature automatically severs the dependency to produce an independent functioning organism. These are examples of nature and the cosmos giving us hints about resistance to oppression.

There are many other lessons and parallels that the universe offers as a guide to our functioning. The sun rises and sets, there is a movement of seasons, there is life and death. All of these phenomena are complementary and dependent upon one another. Animals sleep and wake, with their bodies undergoing these rhythms of repair, rest, production, rejuvenation and spiritual connection. So, just as the sun setting and the moon rising are dependent upon one another in so many ways, including our ability to even see the moon by the reflection of the sun's light, our waking hours allow us to do things that are necessary for our body's work and functioning during the night. A good example is Melanin, which actually shows our interconnection to the universe.

Without getting into an in depth discussion of Melanin, we understand that the production of Melanin occurs through an interplay of hormones and chemicals which themselves tend to operate on a circadian rhythm (a rhythm governed by twenty-four hour time cycles). Melatonin and Serotonin, important hormones secreted by the pineal gland in the center of the brain, operate on this circadian rhythm and play a significant role in Melanin production. Melatonin seems to be more light sensitive and therefore is more active during the daylight hours, while Serotonin tends to kick in more at night or during rest. So, as with the rising and setting of the sun, as well as the waking and sleeping hours of organisms, we can see this same working on the biochemical level within us. Melanin also appears to be an absorber, conductor and transformer of light energy absorbed from the rays of the sun.

Crucially, Melanin is an important substance that is present in the brain stems and main organs of all people, even those who we call "white." Melanin is a key presence in the development of the fetus and has numerous other roles that are still being understood more everyday. It is Afrikan people who simply have a dominance of Melanin and the benefits of its concentrated activities.

The remarkable thing is that our Afrikan ancestors, as far back as Kemet many thousands of years ago, knew these things and their interrelationship to the cosmos. Not only did they express that "as above, so below," an expression of the interrelatedness of the universe and human beings that is probably the precursor to the "Lord's Prayer" phrase, "let it be done on earth as it is in heaven" (even though any understanding of this has been lost), but they were also more specific. Just as it is now known that we have hormones as important as Melatonin and substances as crucial as Melanin being influenced by sun light, our ancient sisters and brothers in Kemet depicted complex relationships in their complex and highly symbolic art. In the art of Kemet, one can see Afrikans with their arms extended to meet rays of the sun (Ra), which have hands on the end of them and are holding ankhs which touch all over the body of those extending themselves to greet the sun's rays. The ankh symbolizes life and so we can see the probable connection here between these symbolic renderings and the explicit ancient understanding of Melanin activity and the connection of humans to the cosmos in general.

This is especially remarkable concerning the pineal gland and its central role, which evidence suggests was known by our ancient Afrikan sisters and brothers. As recently as 1992, I asked a neurologist, at the prestigious Johns Hopkins University Hospital, what the function and significance of the pineal gland is. The response was that it was not a significant or functioning organ. This is at a time when conscious Afrikans who studied the knowledge of their ancestors were already talking about Melanin and having Melanin Conferences. They were being ridiculed and called racist and ludicrous by the European media and medical profession alike. Now, in 1996, the new craze is Melatonin and the life enhancing qualities of the hormone, as well as Melanin itself. Melanin shots and Melatonin pills are available to Europeans, and books with titles like *The Melatonin Miracle* have hit the market.

All of this is shared to show the relationship of the human's intricate workings to the larger cosmos. We must begin to better understand ourselves by understanding that the cosmos is a larger reflection of who we are.

PREMISE: The spiritual is an inseparable complement and unseen driving force to the material- With the premise asserting the connectedness of human beings to the cosmos and the cosmos to existence, the spiritual aspect of the cosmos means that spirituality is inseparable from materiality and very valuable as a necessary part of existence. We cannot begin to understand our world, not to mention the universe, based on demonstrable, material science. We must walk in the spirit.

PREMISE: We acknowledge and respect the *abosom* (manifestations of the supreme creative force), *nsamanfo (ancestral spirits)* and the supreme being, whether called *Onyame* (Akan), *Oludumarre* (Yoruba), *Amma* (Dogon), *Ngala* (Bambara), *Mungu* (KiSwahili)- The reason we have used Afrikan names for the Creator is partly explained by Kwame Agyei Akoto in *Nationbuilding: Theory & Practice in Afrikan Centered Education.*

> It is likely that our material impoverishment and depen-
> dency will continue so long as we subordinate ourselves to alien
> and imperialistic religious concepts. Our collective march toward
> true liberation and development will begin as we discard the
> "religious" shackles of two millennia, and reassert our connection
> with, and the centrality of the Afrikan creator-god force; a creator
> god force to be called by any name that is Afrikan. [13]

We have also spoken at length in this book about the power of language.

PREMISE: Balance, Order, Truth, Justice, Reciprocity, Compassion and Harmony, are the virtues of life and the most natural, desired state of human beings, national affairs and world relations- These virtues are the cardinal virtues of Ma'at. Ma'at is the path of righteousness. It is in effect the ancient Afrikan practice of The Way in Kemet. Ma'at is the guidepost of life, a framework in which balance, order, truth, justice, reciprocity, compassion and harmony are thought, spoken and practiced.

Similarly, Afrikan people must internalize other moral-philosophical systems that aid us in our return to The Way. The Nguzo Saba is a good example. These types of consciousness transforming endeavors must be thought, spoken and practiced.

PREMISE: The purpose of education is "the ritualized reaffirmation of the national identity. It is anchored in the real and idealized history of a people. The nation's education is shaped and given impetus by the cultural and ideological assumptions, dynamics, essential values, priorities and goals of the nation." Agyei Akoto- This type of redefinition of education's purpose is important if we are to significantly impact the future of Afrikan people. It is a redefinition that departs from the present thrust of American education, which is to find a job in order to acquire material comfort. This definition is an overall guide to those who would educate Afrikan people, while what might be passed on as a result of this guidance is information by which students are prepared to pick up the torch of liberation and run with it. Students will be produced who identify with and live the Afrikan Way, while being better human beings as a result of their education. These better human beings then form the foundation for the destruction of the destroyer and the building of a more sane and normal reality.

PREMISE: Afrikans must bear full responsibility for the nurturing, protection and education of Afrikan children - All that we have deemed necessary in the return of Afrikan people to The Way must be carried out by Afrikan people. We must cease the foolish practice of expecting others outside of the Afrikan community to change their ways in order to effect Afrikan liberation. Complaining and protesting the conditions under which Other People are miseducating, mistreating and terrorizing Afrikan children is lunacy. The question that should be asked is why are Other People participating in the lives of Afrikan children where we are supposed to be nurturing, protecting and maximally developing them?

PREMISE: Conscious resistance in a hostile environment of oppression is neither militant nor radical. It is sane, normal and desired behavior - Wherever people are oppressed, it is expected that they will rise and destroy oppression as the manifestation of sanity and a desire to re-establish the natural order of things; *Isfet* used to restore *Maat*.

PREMISE: We are a communal people and "I exist because and only if We exist."- Some of the aspects of communalism that must be adopted by the Afrikan Global Community can be taken from   Malidoma Somé.

1. **Unity of Spirit**. The community feels an indivisible sense of unity. Each member is like a cell in a body. The group needs the individual and vice versa.

2. **Trust**. Everyone is moved to trust everyone else by principle. There is no sense of discrimination or elitism. This trust assumes that everyone is innately well-intentioned.

3. **Openness**. People are open to each other unreservedly. This means that individual problems quickly become community problems. Being open to each other depends on trust.

4. **Love and Caring**. What you have is for everybody. There is a sense of sharing, which diminishes the sense of egotistic behavior. To have while others don't is an expression of your making up a society of your own.

5. **Respect for the Elders**. They are the pillars and the collective memory of the community. They hold the wisdom that keeps the community together. They initiate the young ones, prescribe the rituals for various occasions and monitor the dynam-

ics of the community.

6. **Respect for Nature.** Nature is the principle book out of which all wisdom is learned. It is the place where initiation happens. It is the place from where medicine comes. It nourishes the entire community.

7. **Cult of the Ancestors.** The ancestors are not dead. They live in the spirits in the community. They are reborn into the trees, the mountains, the rivers and the stones to guide and inspire the community. [14]

And to this we add that the community and its make-up will begin to define itself as Afrikan masses engage in reality revolution. Even wayward sisters and brothers will be included in this community to the degree that they have not shrouded themselves in Yurugu, refused help and aided in the destruction of Afrikan people. Additionally, because of the historic disruption of the Afrikan existence, our knowledgeable and sane elders who have been engaged in struggle will be the ones to guide and monitor the community, as well as assist our other beloved elders, who have not had the lifetime of sanity and positive knowledge necessary, in channeling their wisdom toward the benefit of the Afrikan Global Community. Finally, we acknowledge that the spirits of the ancestors are also "reborn" in those who are to come into this world as our babies.

PREMISE: Internal and external enemies of Afrikan people must be identified and held accountable - This process has already begun as we have identified the European *asili* and its destructiveness, while also engaging in Systematic Enemy Analysis. Also, we have realized the trauma and pathology that makes the victim of trauma unable to identify the perpetrator as the enemy. We must be able to identify the destruction of Afrikan minds and lives as the enemy, as well as those who carry out this destruction. This is the logical conclusion that sane people will always come to.

****

These suggested premises of an old/new Afrikan consciousness are only a point of departure as far as this author is able to see. The Afrikan *asili* is to be fulfilled through an old/new Afrikan consciousness that must be systematically and spiritually developed as a lifework and perpetuated in the nationbuilding activities and institutions of Afrikans around the world. It is paradoxically an old/new Afrikan consciousness itself that will make true liberation and nationbuilding possible and it is nationbuilding that will allow for the fullest expression, systematic articulation and living of the Afrikan consciousness, our return to The Way, and fulfillment of the Afrikan *asili*.

This is the extensive nature of the work that we have before us. Our future is one of hard work which breaks the circle of non-productivity and ineffectiveness that has plagued us as a result of an incomplete analysis of the problems inherent in the Afrikan existence within the European *asili*.

The table on the following pages is a summary of some of the principles, premises and concepts that have been dealt with in this chapter and in this book.

AFRIKAN OPERATION WITHIN...

EUROPEAN ASILI	AFRIKAN ASILI / NEW CONSCIOUSNESS	
ENVIRONMENTAL CONDITION	ABNORMAL BEHAVIORS AND CONSTRUCTS	NORMAL, SANE AND DESIRED BEHAVIORS AND CONSTRUCTS
The Maafa	Lack of resistance; self-hatred; adoption of the European cultural aesthetic; lack of unity; inactivity; adherence to European asili /\ rape, murder, kidnapping, lynching, torture, psychological mutilation of "cultural other"	Resistance (Nat Turner, Boukman, Marcus Garvey, Gabriel Prosser Queen Nzinga, Yaa Asantewaa, etc.) self-knowledge, self-love, self-definition, rejection of Yurugu, etc.
Contemporary U.S.	Proliferation of prisons as "big business"	Incarceration of human beings not seen as "financial opportunity"; preventative measures taken as a priority (food, clothing, psychological health, self-knowledge, etc.)
Contemporary U.S.	Education not profit based, therefore not a priority; "manageable democracy" requires unenlightened masses [15]	Education a priority based on creating better human beings and civilization (balance,order, harmony, etc.); enlightened masses necessary to advance civilization
Present world reality	Devaluation of women	"Harmonious Twin-ness" Parallel Complementarity (Oba T'Shaka's concepts for male/female equality)

AFRIKAN OPERATION WITHIN...

EUROPEAN *ASILI*	AFRIKAN *ASILI* / NEW CONSCIOUSNESS	
ENVIRONMENTAL CONDITION	ABNORMAL BEHAVIORS AND CONSTRUCTS	NORMAL, SANE AND DESIRED BEHAVIORS AND CONSTRUCTS
Present world reality	Failure to recognize or assign value to the spirit, therefore being out of balance, confused, insecure and incomplete (Yurugu)	Synthesis of the material and the spiritual; balance, harmony, completeness, and complementarity
Distorted reality becomes apparent (Yurugu recognizable)/ insanity and social decay	Acceptance of distortions, failure to move or react, attempts to assimilate into distorted reality, visualization of liberation within European *asili*	Creation of new reality, visualization of liberation with the destruction of European *asili* within Afrikans and creation of old/new Afrikan consciousness *Nyansa nnsa da*
Oppression and white supremacy (Yurugu and the aggression of the European asili	In Afrikans there may be amnesia which is "total or partial loss of memory. A dissociative reaction, occurs when an individual represses from consciousness the recall or remembrance of entire periods or episodes in his life in order to deny, escape, avoid the re-experiencing of certain painful feelings associated with those periods or episodes. Amnesia therefore results in the loss of pre-trauma identity..." [16]	Cultural consciousness and ancestral memory. Afrikan *asili*

AFRIKAN OPERATION WITHIN...

EUROPEAN ASILI ⓿ ❂	AFRIKAN ASILI / NEW CONSCIOUSNESS ⬇

ENVIRONMENTAL CONDITION	ABNORMAL BEHAVIORS AND CONSTRUCTS	NORMAL, SANE AND DESIRED BEHAVIORS AND CONSTRUCTS
Oppression and white supremacy...	Delusions defined as "false beliefs held by an individual which are stubbornly retained and defended despite their logical inconsistencies with objective reality and valid evidence to the contrary. Not only do such beliefs persist in the face of contradictory evidence, they persist in the face of continuous negative consequences resulting from their being held." [17]	Objective reality is identified as oppression and a clear recognition of Yurugu

CHAPTER 9

OOOOOOOOO

IN OUR IMAGE

As we seek to return to The Way, there are so many areas that we must address. This being the case, we as Afrikan people should not under estimate the importance of symbols and visual imagery in our creation of a new reality. Symbols can relate meaning that we are unable to articulate through the spoken or written word. They are another means of conveying information about our experiences, such as The Maafa, as well as directions for our future that reach different and perhaps deeper levels of thought than a book or a lecture. In this capacity, imagery and the symbolic are a necessary part of liberation. This is true whether we are speaking of video production, movies, memorials and monuments, photographic and artistic compilations, or any other means of relating on the symbolic level.

We should not fail to analyze the ways in which things such as motion pictures have been an integral part of idealizing the United States and its heroes. The images we see on the silver screen, especially those of the early and middle parts of this century, glorify European values and norms by presenting these images with all of the music and special effects that wow audiences and stir up butterflies in one's stomach. War movies show the images of America as a superior force physically, but more importantly, morally and philosophically. We see films like "Rocky" with inspiring music and the "champ" draped in an American flag, fighting enemies of the country and wearing trunks with the American flag design. These images and symbols are power-ful.

One only needs to watch the emotion of fans at sports events as they humble themselves to the American flag and the "star spangled banner." Why would these images be presented at a sporting event? What does the American flag have to do with a college football game? All of this is being said to illustrate the enormous importance that symbols and images are assigned in everyday life. We as Afrikan people need to begin to make sure that our images are controlled by us and speak to our collective consciousness. We need to make sure our images are out there to be seen, so that the only monuments, movies, etc., to be viewed by our children are not those which are in the service of other people's consciousness.

One of the areas that our lack of positive and profound symbolism and imagery is most evident is with regard to monuments and memorials to our experiences and to our people. In building monuments and memorials we not only force the acknowledgment and remembrance of experiences such as The Maafa and liberation movements, but we also touch subconscious levels of thought that contribute to *nyansa nnsa da* and our ability to break through the constricting barriers of the European *asili.* Our images need to be erected wherever we exist.

Francis Cress Welsing, being an expert on the effects of symbols on human consciousness, relates to us that,

> These complex symbols are usually related to the deepest
> cultural themes of a people and have significant messages to
> convey about the people's and culture's reasons for being. Further-
> more, these reasons are passed uncensored in the unconscious, via
> the total environmental experience, from the beginning of 'people
> time,' generation to generation. In this manner, the symbols act as
> a stirring rod that agitates the unconscious, sending out energy
> responses in the form of thought, speech, actions and emotions. [1]

It is clear that erecting our images in monuments and memorials is more than an egotistical dawdle. It activates our consciousness on deeper levels. Monuments and memorials also serve to perpetuate and validate our aesthetic, the Afrikan cultural aesthetic.

Therefore, for our purposes the African cultural aesthetic is both creative production, as well as physical and mental standards of health and beauty that relate to a people's experiences and aspirations. [2]

With this definition of the Afrikan cultural aesthetic, we can begin to understand how it affects our consciousness, specifically relating to our move toward liberation.

The African cultural aesthetic and our embrace of it is extremely important to the movement towards African liberation. If a person and a collective group assign value and beauty to themselves and their creations, any repression of these things they hold valuable is unacceptable. Such repression is for all intents and purposes a repression of the people themselves. The natural reaction to this situation is to free oneself from this repression. [3]

Monuments and memorials will concretize the Afrikan cultural aesthetic and in this way contribute, on yet another level, to liberation. We are not without many examples of the deep meaning and impact symbolism and the erecting of a people's images has had throughout history. Our ancient Afrikan ancestors in Kemet erected some of the most awe inspiring edifices to the images of Afrikan people. These edifices appear in the form of sphinxes, megalithic statues, temple wall inscriptions and magnificent funeraries. Even structures such as the Great Pyramid at Giza and the tekhenu (obelisks) speak to the beauty, experiences and capabilities of Afrikan people on deeper levels. The spiritual and ritual functional elements of these images and structures is also not lost in their beauty and expression of the Afrikan aesthetic.

Colossal structures can also be found in ancient cultures around the world. The Chinese left their aesthetic mark in beautiful temples, inscriptions, statues, etc. There is also a tremendous tribute to the culture in the form of the Tomb of Emperor Qin Shi Huang at Xian, an ancient capital of China, which has a legion of life size soldiers sculpted. [4] The Greeks and Romans both left their mark in terms of their sculpture and art in ancient times, as well as in the present design of many memorials and monuments in the United States and Europe.

Even in modern times there is perhaps not a better example of the power assigned to images than Washington D.C. The nation's capitol is replete with images. There are monuments, memorials and statues which serve any number of different purposes. In a book entitled *Outdoor Sculpture of Washington D.C.*, there is an indication as to the nature of the District's monuments.

> Indeed, we can all learn from the stories each sculpture has to tell, such as the allegorical statue *Heritage*, by James Earle Fraser at the National Archives, which bears the inscription: "The heritage of the past is the seed that brings forth the harvest of the future." [5]

There are also other statues outside of the National Archives building; one is called *Past* and the other is called *Future*. *Past* bears the inscription, "Study the past," while *Future* bears the inscription, "what is past is prologue." Afrikan people who are constantly talking about forgetting the past and have a problem with what they consider to be militant Afrikans should pay close attention to what is being shared here. These types of Afrikan people are usually the type who believe in assimilation and see working within the structure and ideological matrix of Europeans as a possibility. Such sisters and brothers should

Statue outside of the National Archives which bears the inscription, "Study the Past."

be able to see that the country and culture which they are trying to love and defend against Afrikans who are resisting is itself telling them why they should study the past and understand how they have come to be who, what and where they are; thus the symbolism of the nation's monuments is encouraging them to behave more like those Afrikans they currently consider militant. However, the message in the aforementioned monuments is symbolic and directed, through imagery, toward European people.

It is significant that the inscription on *Past* says "study the past." This means that a rudimentary understanding of your history in the form of trivia is not sufficient for liberation. Study is necessary for Afrikans who dismiss consciousness and transformation because they "have already heard all of this slavery stuff" or "are tired of talking about the white man." Whether tired or not we need to study and understand the nature of our existence and stop being lazy and lost about liberation. The very European *asili* that has sucked the life out of many Afrikans is tipping its hand to expose its lies and contradictions in the inscriptions on its monuments which say things like study the past and emphasize how important heritage is.

So, the erecting of our Afrikan images takes on extreme importance. When we talk about naming, defining and creating an old/new Afrikan consciousness to return to The Way we should keep in mind an inscription on the National Archives building that reads "The glory and romance of our history are here preserved in the chronicles of those who conceived and built the structure of our nation." Just as we are in the process of conceiving an old/new Afrikan consciousness, we need to chronicle the glory of this process in the erection of structures to Afrikan liberation. Our children need to be able to gather strength from the work that Afrikan soldiers of the reality revolution are doing and see the concrete reminders of its worth and purpose. The unconscious liberation messages of symbolism need to be relayed to our children and to the masses of our people who may not be direct participants in this reality revolution. The hearts and minds of the people need to be captured with our purpose and paramount return to The Way. As we build and create this new reality, or ideological and cultural matrix, we need to send "powerful and subtle messages about how and why the culture came into being, and what the people must do to survive and maintain itself." [6]

Washington D.C. has still more to teach as to the importance of building and creating in our image. In *The Maafa & Beyond*, there was allusion to the need for remembrance, mourning and healing from the horrendous experience of The Maafa. This necessity can be seen as more than theoretical and conceptual by looking at the examples of The Vietnam War Memorial and The Holocaust Museum.

Of the Vietnam War Memorial, we learn that, "The memorial is a way back and a way forward. A pass through Constitution Gardens and a walk along 'the wall' makes us think of the future in the language of the past..." [7] Of those soldiers and families traumatized by the experience of war, we find that "They come to mourn and to remember, memory mixing with grief, making an old ritual new, creating in this time another timeless moment." [8]

The return to The Way has been and certainly will be a war. The Maafa has crushed the spirits of many and taken the lives of so many more. We are searching for a means of healing and therapy for the masses of Afrikan people, unable to consider the logistical impossibility of sitting every Afrikan down on the psychologist's or psychiatrist's couch.

One of those many men and women who go to gain strength and rekindle spirit from the Vietnam Veteran's Memorial was quoted as saying, "If I could, I would lead each person in hand past the monument and make them read each name and imagine each life that was cut short." [9] The question here is why? What purpose is served? To witness what war does to grown men, women, their families and subsequent generations, and then to see the effect of the memorial on these people is nothing short of amazing. The emotion, the tears, the peace of mind that it brings is profound. This is all being done by symbolism and imagery, and in this case imagery in the form of a wall with names written on it. It conveys deeper meanings that touch deep levels of consciousness. The Vietnam Veteran's Memorial even elicits emotion and responses from those who have never seen or been involved in war. This is a form of therapy.

On the topic of therapy and symbolism, European Jewish people give some of the more clearly articulated examples of the importance of this type of work. A book called *Preserving Memory: The Struggle to Create America's Holocaust Museum*, is informative in the title alone, but has profound insights clearly stated within its pages. The therapeutic goals of Holocaust remembrance are clearly articulated in statements like, "Perhaps a repository of Holocaust memory, symbolized in part by this museum, could prove to be therapeutic for nations as well as individuals." [10] The need to remember and be in charge of how the memory of the Holocaust is kept is also stated with clarity.

> When one was speaking of the Holocaust, it was unwritten etiquette to   begin by saying that no one could understand the Holocaust, but it needed to be spoken of so "it" would not happen again, or be forgotten. The Holocaust was not only a transcendent event, it was unique, not to be compared to any other genocidal situation, and its victims were Jews. Any comparison of event or linkage to any other victim group could be, as often was perceived as, if not the *murder of memory {italics* mine}, at least its dilution.[11]

This claiming of memory by European Jews is significant and a large part of the motivation for erecting monuments and a museum. The reference to the "murder of memory" is also very profound. Might

European Jewish Holocaust memorial in Baltimore, MD. The memorial occupies a city block. The statue depicted is on one side of the memorial visible to a main city street and features a mottled mass of naked human bodies enduring suffering and seemingly going up in flames. The inscription reads, "THOSE WHO CANNOT REMEMBER THE PAST ARE CONDEMNED TO REPEAT IT."

it be that Afrikan people are participating in murdering the memory of
The Maafa, not only by allowing it to be considered in the generic light
of "slavery," but also by not having monuments and memorials that
reclaim, validate and distinguish The Maafa from any other historical
process in the history of the world.

> ... wrote historian Robert Azbug, "an almost unbearable
> mixture of empathy, disgust, guilt, anger and alienation" engender-
> ing the urge both to remember and bear witness to the horrors
> encountered, and to forget, to distance oneself from unacceptable
> images and inconceivable realities, to turn away from what seemed
> to be the futile task of communicating this to a war-weary Ameri-
> can public. Consequently, what came to be known as "The
> Holocaust" was often indistinguishable, in immediate postwar
> years, from the millions of noncombatant casualties due to terror
> bombing of civilian populations, epidemic illness, or starvation. It
> was considered by most as simply part of the horror of war. [12]

European Jewish people were faced with much the same
situation as Afrikans, in terms of their historical experience of
genocide being viewed as simply a generic part of war tragedy; Afrikan
people see The Maafa viewed simply as "slavery," an institution that
has always existed in many of the world's cultures. However,
European Jews claimed their memory and have redefined it despite
initial conceptions of it. A large part of this has been the writings,
films, memorials and the museums filled with photographs and other
remembrances. Again, they have made use of imagery and
symbolism.

The import of Afrikans building and creating in our image
would be difficult to show more vividly than in the experiences of people
who have already done what we need to do and explained why. We
need to erect memorials and monuments to our suffering and our pain.

Even the AIDS epidemic has seen this move to evoke symbolism in moving the masses. A book called *A Promise To Remember* points this out in the sharpest way expressing that, "We chose the symbol of the Quilt in a deliberate effort to evoke and recapture the traditional American values that had yet to be applied to this apparently 'nontraditional' situation..." [13] Additionally,

> For those who have lost someone they loved, the Quilt is a place to put the memories, and a place to do something in the face of an awful helplessness. It touches the suffering, the bereaved, the fearful. And it touches those who had previously felt unaffected by AIDS. [14]

A group of individuals collaborated to build this quilt, a blanket of tremendous proportions, to symbolize and activate some things they felt were missing in the fight against AIDS and the remembrance of its victims. Afrikan people certainly could use symbols, memorials and monuments to touch the fear, confront helplessness, inspire *nyansa nnsa da* and affect those who feel unaffected by The Maafa, our return to The Way and the trials and obstacles of those Afrikans who are already involved in a reality revolution.

So, just as in *The Maafa & Beyond* we touched upon the importance of the Afrikan Aesthetic in liberation struggle, the erecting of our images wherever Afrikan people are is also a part of liberation struggle. If we could come together as a people in America to do no more than give one dollar each, we have sufficient funds to build memorials and monuments, as well as institutions. And, one dollar from each member of the populace is only a beginning to what could be a substantial endeavor in all areas of nation building.

****

Who controls Afrikan images today and who will control them tomorrow? If it is not Afrikan people then we can be assured that the interests of Afrikan people are not only failing to be met, but that the falsification and destruction of Afrikan consciousness continues.

CHAPTER 10
OOOOOOOOO
THE CONCEPT OF "RACE"

As we have seen, our engagement in a reality revolution and our return to The Way is a systematic process. We will have to be vigilant because, as Chinweizu says, this is the price of liberty. We visit the concept of "race" precisely because of its failure as a tool for clarity and analysis in the liberation struggles of Afrikan people. Additionally, "race," as a means of classifying the human family, is ambiguous, problematic and often times confusing. It has generally failed to mediate any understanding or provide any meaningful information between so called races.

We are left with saying, bringing us full circle to the first scientific classification of the human species 200 years ago, that a race is a phenotypic grouping of human beings, no more and no less. It has no particular genetic significance. Since all *H. sapiens sapiens*, living or dead, belong to the same species, genetic differences among them are infinitesimal, making racial classifications based on these differences extraordinarily problematic. [1]

In as much as the word "race" is used to refer to groups of people and their cultural, ideological and political worldviews, the concept of *asili* is preferred as a more clear and precise concept for analysis. Terms like "cultural group" better describe "racial groups" in the capacity of identification based on the phenotypic differences that go along with cultural/ideological differences that distinguish "racial groups." The confusion, emotionalism and lack of precision that often accompanies the use of "race" to describe groups of human beings stems from many things. Perhaps the best place to begin clarification is with a historical, anthropological, archeological and biological glance at the *human family*.

From the perspective of evolution, the prehistoric biological origins of all human beings are in Afrika. Australopithecines, which are thought to be the primate ancestors of humans are thought to have evolved to *Homo habilis*, the first recognized species of *Homo*, the human family. Specifically, *Australopithecus aferensis* and *Australopithecus africanus* are the two species which are considered to be the ancestors of the *Homo* species to which *Homo sapiens sapiens*, or modern human beings, belong. So, the Australopithecine fossils were found predominately in the Southern part of Afrika and East Afrika's Rift Valley. Olduvai gorge in Kenya, East Afrika is where "the most important fossils of *H. habilis...*" [2] have been found. *Homo habilis* species are thought to have existed until about 1.5 million years ago. *Homo habilis* is followed on the evolutionary time line by *Homo erectus*. *Homo erectus* is thought to have appeared around 1.6 million years ago as the predecessor to *Homo sapiens*. The evolution and appearance of *Homo sapiens* occurred around 500,000 years ago in Afrika.

It is undisputed by Western science that *Australopithecus*, *Homo habilis* and *Homo erectus*, the ancestors of modern humans, originated in Afrika. However, there are two lines of thought as to how and where *Homo sapiens* developed. By some it is believed that in Afrika *Homo erectus* evolved into *Homo sapiens* and then migrated throughout the world. Others believe that small local populations of *Homo erectus* evolved separately in different parts of the world, but in a parallel manner, into *Homo sapiens*.

It is important to understand that regardless of which evolutionary theory is accepted, both point indisputably to the Afrikan origins of human kind. The second theory of the separate development of *Homo erectus* to *Homo sapiens* has traditionally been used by Europeans to dilute their direct descent from Afrikan *Homo sapiens*. The suggestion of separate evolutionary paths has been used by people such as Carlton Coon, to suggest the superiority of "races" such as the European, who supposedly, according to Coon, underwent this evolution to *Homo sapiens* before everyone else. However, there is evidence to suggest that the theory of a singular evolutionary process occurring in Afrika and the Afrikan *Homo sapiens* migrating to different parts of the world, is the most viable.

Given the theory of an Afrikan evolution of *Homo erectus* to *Homo sapiens* and the subsequent migration of this Afrikan to different parts of the world, the question arises as to how the so called "races" of human beings came to be so diverse having all come from Afrikan ancestors. This is a question often left unanswered and unapproached by those who have an interest in keeping gaps in the origins of humankind so that it is not realized that Afrika is the mother of humankind. The late Cheikh Anta Diop asserts that Grimaldi man, the Afrikan *Homo sapiens*, migrated to Europe around 42,000 years ago and underwent a process of "racial differentiation" over a period of 20,000 years. This racial differentiation of the Afrikan Grimaldi man was facilitated by the Afrikan *Homo sapien* being isolated in Europe during the ice age of the Wurm Glaciation for 20,000 years.

The theory of racial differentiation, or the mutation of Afrikans to Europeans in this case, is viable and far less spectacular than many people think. The following points give validity to such a scenario.

1) During the European ice age, and in many parts of Europe in general, there was not an abundance of intense sunlight and cloud cover tended to be the norm. If we simply look to nature we find that there exist animals referred to as troglodytes, which are cave dwellers. The interesting and informative thing about these animals is that in

their environment of complete darkness with no exposure to sunlight, they have no pigment. You find that some of these animals are completely white, while others are translucent or partly "see through." Animals of the same species, that exist outside of caves and are exposed to sunlight, have pigment. Interestingly enough, "troglodyte" is a term that has been used to refer to cave dwelling prehistoric humans.

2) The general weakness of sunlight, and often the lack of sunlight, in ice age Europe was not conducive to the dark skin of Afrikan migrant *Homo sapiens*. In Afrika, deeply pigmented skin offers protection from the intense ultraviolet rays of the sun. Light skin or the "white skin" of Europeans is highly susceptible, not only to sunburn, but also to skin cancer. However, in an environment where sunlight is scarce or weak, the dark skin that Afrikan *Homo sapiens* would have had is a liability; dark skin blocks the ultraviolet rays of the sun which are necessary for Vitamin D production which aids in healthy bone formation.

> A deficiency of Vitamin D in the growing child can lead to skeletal deformities called rickets. There is some evidence that prior to the introduction of Vitamin D-enriched milk, rickets occurred more frequently among black children than white children of similar socioeconomic status living in cloudy northern cities. The inference is that in areas where sunlight is weak—especially in winter, when most of the body surface is covered—dark skins have more difficulty absorbing enough ultraviolet radiation to produce the needed amounts of Vitamin D. [3]

So, if we take the extreme in the lack of and weakness of sunlight in ice age Europe, as well as the necessity to have most of the body surface covered year round in the ice age, we can see how the dark skin of the Afrikan *Homo sapien* migrants becomes detrimental as rickets can render one unable to support the weight of one's body and certainly the inability of a pregnant woman to support the weight of carrying a baby. Dr. Charles Finch shares with us that,

> Under these conditions of drastically reduced sunlight, the melanized dermis, i.e., black skin, becomes a liability. In northern latitudes, the protection melanin affords against skin cancer becomes nearly superfluous while it screens out sunlight, already severely reduced, which is necessary to produce Vitamin D in the skin. Simply put, black skin in a northern ice-age environment becomes an adaptive liability. We see this today in the two-to-threefold higher susceptibility of Blacks to rickets in northern latitudes compared Whites. White skin, lacking the melanin barrier, can more efficiently utilize the limited northern sunlight to produce VitaminD than can black skin.[62] White skin therefore has two adaptive advantages in an ice-age northern clime: more efficient Vitamin D production and greater cold resistance. [4]

Eventually it would seem that those with lighter skin live, while those with darker skin are unable to survive and reproduce themselves. Add physical adaptation, the survival capacity albinism would represent and mutation over a **20,000** year period, and it is more than conceivable how, with regard to skin color, Afrikans with dark skins were transformed to Europeans with "white skins."

3)

Indeed, there are Celtic and Viking reports of "little Blacks" still living in northern Europe as late as 1000 A.D.[63] These little Blacks could survive here because they had access to Vitamin D-laden northern salt-water fish and therefore escaped the kind of selection pressure seen further inland. [5]

The existence of indigenous dark skin Afrikan people throughout Europe and Asia is astounding evidence of the theories of racial differentiation occurring in Afrikans who migrated from their home continent to Europe.

4) Just as there are physiological explanations for skin color changes in the differentiation of "races" or the change of Afrikan *Homo sapiens* to all the other peoples of the world, there are explanations for changes other than skin color.

The distinctive facial structure of "Orientals" has long fascinated Westerners. (If physical anthropology had been a Chinese discipline, anthropologists might be more concerned with explaining the interestingly "beaky" noses and "rounded" eyes of Europeans.) The distinctive components of the Oriental, or "Mongoloid," face are (1) high, prominent cheekbones combined with a low-bridged, nonprominent nose, which together make the face appear flat; and (2) the so called epicanthic fold, a fold of skin covering the inner corner of the eye, which, together with a fatty eyelid, makes the eyes appear slanted. It has been claimed, with little experimental justification, that this facial configuration is more resistant to extreme cold than other facial types. In any case, it is found most highly developed in the coldest regions of Asia—northern China, Mongolia, and Siberia. However, some of its features, in more or less diluted form, are seen in Southeast Asia, in central Asia as far West as the Urals and the Himalayas, and throughout North and South America. [6]

We can see many of the same facial features in the Eskimo populations in the Western Hemisphere who obviously exist in extremely cold environments.

5) The research of Rebecca Cann has made a serious impact in the way the world views the origins of all people.

Cann's preferred minimum-length tree is rooted squarely in Africa, meaning that it is an African *Homo sapiens* ancestor who generates all later African and non-African types. The African mtDNA's diverge from each other by an average of .057 percent, making them by far the most varied, and therefore the oldest, mtDNA's in the world. With a mutation rate of two-to-four percent per million years, Cann postulates that the common ancestor of all surviving mtDNA's in the world, hence of   all surviving human beings, lived between 140,000-290,000 years ago in eastern or southern Africa.[54]   In published interviews, Cann gives a mean date of 200,000 B.P. for our first common human ancestor who was female and whom Cann has nicknamed "Eve."[55] Since the oldest mtDNA in Cann's sample came from a Bushman or San individual from the Kalahari Desert, we can say that these people are representatives of the oldest living branch of the human race. Says Allan C. Wilson, "Basically we are all! Kung."[56] Remnants of them, and other "Negrito" or "Pygmoid" peoples, can be found as aborigines in India, southeast Asia, Australia, and the South Pacific. [7]

In this context of the prehistoric biological origins of humankind, all of the world's people would be considered Afrikan people based simply on Afrika being the birthplace of humankind. And, of course, we are all human beings. Thus, all of the world's people are essentially Afrikan. However, there is more to being Afrikan than prehistoric biological origins, just as there is more to being Afrikan than pigmentation. It involves an internalization of a particularly Afrikan ideological and cultural matrix, or *asili*, of harmony, balance, order, reciprocity, compassion, justice, spirituality, communalism, masculine-feminine internal synthesis and any number of other principles.

Despite the origins of all people as Afrikans in the prehistorical biological context, including Europeans, Europeans specifically are far removed from both their beginning in Afrika and the Afrikan ideological and cultural matrix. The European despiritualized, material, aggressive, violent, individualistic *asili* has wreaked havoc on nature and humanity, while imposing its values on others. *The European has by this fact forfeited any rights that might have accompanied their Afrikan origins and we do not consider them Afrikan people.* For example, they have committed murder and psychological mutilation to take land and resources that their Afrikan origins and membership in the human family would have allowed them to share; this is speaking generally about the assault Europeans have waged on the world and the world's resources in terms of the colonization in Afrika, The Maafa, and the various other egregious events we have already dealt with in this book.

Keeping in mind all of the evidence that points to the Afrikan origins of humankind, and the general thrust of this book in terms of redefining and reconceptualizing the present world reality, one should ask the question of what all of this about the concept of race means to a reality revolution. Understanding the dynamics of the human family, we can better understand some of the misconceptions and distortions that have been perpetuated in Western society, as well as see more clearly the inadequacy of the "race" concept to reach any understanding of the problems that exist between people. Where the misconceptions and distortions are concerned, there are a great many in the images we are presented in history. As a single example of this, whenever we see images of the earliest human beings, we see cave dwelling European types living in the rough world of ice age Europe. This imagery is prevalent and conjured up almost automatically when it comes to ancient human beings or the earliest people. This false

This photograph comes from an exhibit in the Smithsonian Institution National Museum of Natural History and National Museum of Man. The exhibit is called the "Origins of Western Culture" and the problematic nature of the image represented is discussed on pages 290 and 292.

image is so pervasive that it is perpetuated even by the National Museum of Natural History and National Museum of Man, as seen in the photo on the previous page.

The photo comes from an exhibit titled "Origins of Western Culture," which would lead some to believe it is an accurate depiction since we are speaking about Western culture. However, in this same exhibit the Afrikan civilization of Kemet is referenced as part of the origins of Western culture (The mummies and their "coffins" which are on display are from the Ptolemaic period of Kemet, however, and fail to give an accurate picture of both the Afrikan character of Kemet and the precision of the artwork. The Ptolemies, being Roman invaders who attempted to emulate the culture of the then conquered Afrikan civilization of Kemet, were notorious for the poor quality of their artwork and architectural design. The only reason for this time period of Kemet being included in the exhibit is probably because of the European looking images, another distortion of the great Afrikan Kemet.) Given the inclusion of Kemet in the origins of Western culture, then the Afrikan early humans who predate cave dwelling Europeans by thousands of years, should be the image seen in the museum and in general. We would not see a cave dweller in animal fur, but more than likely the splendor of Kemet, or depending on how far back you go, matriarchal and agricultural Afrikan societies basking in the sun of Afrika in fertile valleys. We might probably and appropriately see images of the Twa people of Afrika.

The fruit of this discussion on the inadequacy and ambiguity of the race concept, as relates to understanding the human family, is a complement to our validation of Ani's *asili* concept as a more accurate tool for analysis. The discussion on "race" has often been well intentioned, but basically fruitless and misdirected in terms of long-term clarity and problem resolution. The *asili* concept brings a clarity that we have not seen before.

So, the major point here is that all humans not only have their origins in Afrika, but from Afrikan people. Consequently, the best way for us to approach the study of human beings and their behavior is not by the ambiguous and oft times intentionally manipulated race concept. The specificity and soundness of concepts such as Ani's *asili* is much more functional and clear for our movement forward in understanding, strategy and victory.

PART 4

REMEMBRANCE,
REVERENCE,
CLOSING THOUGHTS

CHAPTER 11

○○○○○○○○○

BEHOLD THE AFRIKAN QUEEN MOTHER-WARRIORS

This chapter is dedicated to Afrikan women. In general, it is to honor Afrikan women everywhere; Afrikan women who have performed the arduous task of nurturing families and raising children. Honor is due to Afrikan women living the dual struggle of being women and Afrikan. These are our mothers, wives, sisters and friends who have at least been there for their families in the most adverse conditions.

I honor these sisters in writing this chapter, but more specifically, praise and recognition is due to the Afrikan women who have been there for their immediate families, as well as having fought for the Afrikan community. These Queen Mother-Warriors have not only defended the Afrikan community, but have also gone on the offensive against our enemies when many of our men were afraid, inactive or comfortable with their captivity.

These women are not unlike the character of Abena in Armah's *Two Thousand Seasons,* the brave, wise, spiritual sister initiate from the town of Anoa. Abena was she who, after being captured by Maafa criminals and enslaved, was asked why she did not save herself since she was wary of the trap which she and her fellow initiates fell into. She declared that "there is no self to save apart from all of us." When all had given up, Abena went on the offensive and planned not only for liberation, but also for the destruction of the destroyers who enslaved her people.

Our Queen Mother-Warriors are also like Armah's Anoa, a

sister who was an utterer and proclaimer of truths that would prove prophetic. They are like Armah's Noliwe and Ningome who maintained vision and strength, leading their people out of despair and chaos when others were confused. It is to the Queen Mother-Warriors, who have often carried Afrikan people, that this chapter is dedicated.

Throughout time, the existence of such strong female figures has been verifiable. The titles of these sisters fill the pages of history. We can look to the *ktke* or *Kentakes* of Meroitic Kush. Kentake is a word derived from the Meroitic/Nubian/Ethiopian form of writing that is similar to the Medu Netcher of Kemet, but has yet to be well deciphered. Kentake means Queen Mother. [1] We can also look to the Akan hierarchy and see the *Ohemaa*. *Ohemaa* is "literally female ruler." [2] We also find the *Asantehemaa* who was the "Queen Mother of the Ashante union." [3] Agnes Akosua Aidoo makes an important point regarding Queen Motherhood, revealing that,

> The office of queen mother was not merely an elevated domestic position. It was a vital political office in the public domain and the occupant was an active political being. The queen mother's obligation to advise and guide the chief, including her right to criticize and rebuke him in public, was a constitutional duty.   It differed from the maternal responsibility towards children. [4]

So, Queen Motherhood has been an official position throughout history for Afrikan people and has existed in various forms in examples other than the two covered here. In addition to this very important official position, Afrikan women have carried on the responsibilities of Queen Motherhood and even the responsibilities of Manhhood wherever Afrikan people have existed.

Although this chapter is not meant to be an exhaustive history, we can see many Afrikan Queen Mother-Warriors throughout history. As far back as ancient Kemet we have examples of all that we have spoken of with regard to Afrikan Queen Mother-Warriors. Queen Tiye and her insistence on the respect due to her, as well as her defense of her Nubian homeland was admirable. Queen Hatshepsut took the reigns of Kemet in the 18th dynasty. Her rule was one of nationbuilding and returning Kemet to The Way.

> She adopted the spirit of Horus by taking responsibility for Maat (order), which included much new construction, eliminating the undesirables from the land, etc. Among her inscriptions are to be found the following statements: "I have restored that which was in ruins; I have raised up that which was unfinished." And, "I came as Horus, darting fire against my enemies." [5]

The list of Afrikan women to rule and contribute to the uplift and protection of Afrikans is long. It includes sisters like Makeda or the Queen of Sheba, an Ethiopian queen. It includes Kentakes of Kush/ Ethiopia who not only built in Kush/Ethiopia, but also went on the offensive militarily against the Romans. Queen Nzingha is also amongst the reknowned Queen Mother-Warriors for her fierce defense of Afrikan people against the Portuguese in Afrika.

Dr. Clarke informs us that during The Maafa and the subsequent colonization of the continent of Afrika, many Afrikan women waged offensives all over the continent.

> Among the most outstanding were: Madame Tinubu of Nigeria; Nandi, the mother of the great Zulu warrior Chaka; Kaipkire of the Hero people of South West Africa; and the female army that followed the great Dahomian King, Behanzin Bowelle. [6]

In Ghana during the early 1900's, Queen Mother Yaa

Asantewaa led war against the British invaders of that part of Afrika. She refused to allow the arrogant British invaders to defile Ashanti tradition by confiscating and sitting on the Golden Stool of the Ashanti. This Queen Mother-Warrior led her people into battle. She is said to have declared,

> I must say this: if you men of Ashanti will not go forward, then we will. We the women will. I shall call upon my fellow women. We will fight the white men. We will fight till the last of us falls in the battlefields. [7]

Queen Mother-Warrior Yaa Asantewaa is of a long line of Afrikan women who have stood for their people. Her declaration of war is a good transition into the recognition of two of the many sisters amongst us today who have declared war against the oppression and cultural/psychological destruction of Afrikan people.

Queen Mother-Warrior Francis Cress-Welsing and Queen Mother-Warrior Marimba Ani deserve our recognition and praise. These two sisters have taken the offensive against the destructive processes of Yurugu, both of them analyzing and attacking the pathology of white world supremacy and Yurugu. We truly need to acknowledge these and other sisters as we have acknowledged brothers who have done the liberation work Afrikan people need.

Our sister Frances Cress Welsing, in writing her book *The Isis Papers: The Keys to the Colors* and giving lectures around the country, was amongst those at the forefront of openly challenging the ideological and psychological structures of Europeans. Dr. Welsing gave us valuable insight into decoding the signs and symbols of European thought and behavior. She also helped to explain some of the psychological problems of Afrikans, resulting from white supremacy. In all of this, her declaration of war against the destructive psychological processes of white world supremacy was and is uncompromising. She is a practicing psychiatrist in Washington D.C. and is responsible for the *Cress Theory of Color Confrontation and Racism*, which is included in *The Isis Papers*.

Queen Mother-Warrior Marimba Ani has become a "point of departure" or leader of a movement of liberation from conceptual, linguistic and intellectual incarceration. Her book, *Let the Circle Be Unbroken*, was only a glimpse into her genius; a genius to be more fully revealed in her latest book, *Yurugu: An African-centered Critique of European Cultural Thought and Behavior.* Dr. Ani is truly ahead of her time as a scholar engaged in the arduous task of returning Afrikan people to The Way. She has approached the deepest conceptual levels of Europe's domination of Afrikan people and the rest of the world's people of color. It is her contribution to Afrikan liberation that has played such a tremendous role in the writing of this book.

With all that has been said about the Afrikan Queen Mother-Warriors, we certainly recognize that there are multitudes of women deserving of this title who are not including in this chapter. Women such as Ida B. Wells, Sojourner Truth, Harriet Tubman, Assata Shakur and many others, ancestors and living, that we may not even know of, deserve our praise.

As we speak of an old/new Afrikan consciousness, we should realize that the masculine-feminine synthesis and equality discussed in this work, dictates that we recognize the abilities of Afrikan women to lead Afrikan people. This very day we have Afrikan women capable of leading the liberation struggle of Afrikan people. The question is whether or not we are ready and willing to accept their leadership. Afrikan men, BEHOLD THE AFRIKAN QUEEN MOTHER-WARRIORS!

Conclusion
OOOOOOOOO

We have truly arrived at that point in our history where we will see the rise of a New Afrikan World, a new reality. I have every confidence that our reality revolution will be successful. It is simply a matter of time. I hope that this book has added a dimension to our struggle that serves to take it forward.

As each of us expand our knowledge and grow intellectually, our ideas mature, are more clearly developed and often change. In writing this book, I concede that I am in a state of continuous growth and evolution, with each new day, month and year bringing new insight and clearer vision. Therefore, in order to be able to write a book and have it published in my lifetime, it can include only my development up to the point of its writing. *Reality Revolution* is the best of my thought that I am able to articulate at this very moment, as I write this sentence. I can only hope that it has been pleasing to the reader and that, in time when I have matured beyond my 27 years and grown to another level, I can look back and proclaim this a quality piece of writing that positively impacted my people.

As this volume comes to a close, I remind the reader that there are many areas that I have not dealt with which will need to be further developed. An example is the concept of time. I was introduced to the Kemetic Kalendar by Abdul Aquil of the Detroit based Eye of Heru Study Group and of ASCAC. He has aided in my understanding of the importance of our concept of time and pushed the concept of time and the Kemetic Kalendar into the forefront of many people's consciousness.

Currently, because of the calendar we use, we are oriented temporally to European events and time continuums. The Kemetic

Kalendar, originally developed by Rkhty Amen Jones, reorients us to an Afrikan reality. It is a concept that we all need to better understand. According to this Afrikan time conception, we are currently in the year 6235 S.M. (Shemsu Menes or Following Menes). This kalendar and the time concept further developed will undoubtedly add to our reality revolution in a profound way.

Finally, it should be noted that when it comes down to it, I love life; and I especially love Afrikan life and I am not ashamed or apologetic for saying so. My heart is saddened when Afrikan life is lost or Afrikan life is full of suffering. Perhaps this is why the suffering of even the least conscious, most lost Afrikan people can often bring tears to my eyes. It is with this compassion and great love of Afrikan people that I write. This is why my critiques are often hard on my own people, not to mention the collective body of Europeans. In the final analysis, it is all because I love life and spirit.

As I finish this book, I redouble my efforts to fulfill what I have written about and work side by side with other Afrikan soldiers. As the Goodie Mob says...

I can't stop fighting for our spirits and minds!

NOTES

Introduction

1. Ayi Kwei Armah, Two Thousand Seasons (London: Heinemann, 1979), p. 17.

2. Erriel D. Roberson, The Maafa & Beyond: Remembrance, Ancestral Connections and Nation Building for the African Global Community (Columbia, MD: Kujichagulia Press, 1995), p. 5.

3. John J. Macionis, Sociology (Englewood Cliffs, NJ: Prentice Hall, 1993), p. 66.

4. Dwight Bolinger, Language--The Loaded Weapon: The Use and Abuse of Language Today (London: Longman Group Limited, 1980), p.vii.

5. Ibid, p. viii.

6. Kwame Gyekye, An Essay on African Philosophical Thought: The Akan Conceptual Scheme (Cambridge: Cambridge University Press, 1987), p. 29.

7. S.I. Hayakawa, Language in Thought and Action (New York: Harcourt, Brace and World, Inc., 1964), p. 260.

8. Ibid

9. John M. Ellis, Language, Thought and Logic (Evanston, IL: Northwestern University Press, 1993), p. 2.

10. Ibid, p. 55.

11. Bolinger, p. 89.

12. Ibid

13. Hayakawa, p. vii.

14. Alfred Korzybski, Science and Sanity: An Introduction to Non-Aristotelian Systems and General Semantics (Lancaster, PA: Science Press Printing Company, 1933), p. lxiv.

15. Ibid, pp. lxii-lxiii.

16. J. Samuel Bois, The Art of Awareness: A Textbook on General Semantics and Epistemics, 2nd Edition (Dubuque, Iowa: Wm. C. Brown Company, 1973), p. 158.

17. Amos Wilson, The Falsification of Afrikan Consciousness: Eurocentric History, Psychiatry and the Politics of White Supremacy (New York: Afrikan World InfoSystems, 1993), p. 117.

18. Ibid, p. 70.

19. Ibid

20. Haki R. Madhubuti, From Plan to Planet: Life Studies: The Need for Afrikan Minds and Institutions (Chicago: Third World Press, 1973), p. 13.

21. Yosef ben-Jochannan, <u>Abu Simbel To Gizeh: A Guide Book and Manual</u> (Baltimore: Black Classic Press, 1987), p. 8.

22. Roberson, pp. 5-6.

Chapter 1

1. Marimba Ani, <u>Yurugu: An African-Centered Critique of European Cultural Thought and Behavior</u> (Trenton, NJ: Africa World Press, 1994), p. 556.

2. Ibid, p. 12.

3. Ibid, p. 13.

4. W.E. Burghardt DuBois, <u>The World and Africa: An inquiry into the part which Africa has played in world history</u>, New Enlarged Edition (New York: International Publishers, 1965), p. 42.

5. Ani, pp. 14-15.

6. Ibid, p. 16.

7. Eric H. Warmington and Philip G. Rouse, eds., <u>Great Dialogues of Plato</u>, trans. W.H. D. Rouse (New York: Mentor, 1984), p. I.

8. Gunner Myrdal, <u>An American Dilemma: A Negro Problem and Modern Democracy</u> (New York: Harper & Row, 1944), pp. 13-14.

9. Ibid, p. 14.

10. Ibid, p. 21.

11. J. Samuel Bois, The Art of Awareness: A Textbook on General Semantics and Epistemics, 2nd Edition (Dubuque, Iowa: Wm. C. Brown Company, 1973), p. 2.

12. Warmington and Rouse, pp. 87-88.

13. Ibid, p. 107.

14. Ibid, p. 113.

15. Tom Reeves, "Reviving and Redefining Pedarasty," in Varieties of Man/Boy Love: Modern Western Contexts, ed. Mark Pascal (New York: Wallace Hamilton Press, 1992), p. 67.

16. U.S. Government Printing Office, Child Pornography and Pedophilia: Report Made by the Permanent Subcommittee on Investigations of the Committee on Governmental Affairs, United States Senate (Washington DC: 1986), p. 1.

17. Warmington and Rouse, pp. 78-79.

18. Thijs Maasen, "Man-Boy Friendships on Trial: On the Shift in the Discourse on Boy Love in the Early Twentieth Century," in Male Intergenerational Intimacy, eds. Theo Sanfort and Alex Van Naerssen (New York: Harrison Park Press, 1991), p. 66.

19. Ibid, p. 51.

20. John Addington Symonds, Sexual Inversion (New York: Bell Publishing Company, 1984), p. 67.

21. Ani, pp. 174-175.

22. Warmington and Rouse, pp. 103-104.

23. Ibid, p. 104.

24. Caroline Harlow, <u>Female Victims of Violent Crime</u> (Washington DC: U.S. Department of Justice. Office of Justice Programs, Bureau of Justice Statistics, 1991).

25. Haki Madhubuti, <u>Claiming Earth: Race, Rage, Rape, Redemption; Blacks Seeking A Culture of Enlightened Empowerment</u> (Chicago: Third World Press, 1994), p. 112.

26. Oba T'Shaka, <u>Return to The African Mother principle of Male and Female Equality</u>, Vol. 1 (Oakland: Pan Afrikan Publishers, 1995), p. 268.

27. Warmington and Rouse, p. 258.

28. Ibid, p. 259.

29. Produced by <u>Journal of Afro-Latin American Studies & Literature</u>.

30. Warmington and Rouse, p. 257.

31. Ibid, p. 258.

32. Ibid, p. 269.

33. J.A.K. Thomson, trans., The Ethics of Aristotle: Nichomachean Ethics, Revised Edition (London: Penguin, 1976), Back Cover.

34. Ani, p. 64.

35. Brian Fagan, Clash of Cultures (New York: W.H. Freeman & Company, 1984), p. 20.

36. Ibid, p. 18.

37. Urs Bitterli, Cultures in Conflict: Encounters Between European and Non-European Cultures, 1492-1800, trans. Ritchie Robertson (Stanford: Stanford University Press, 1989), p. 5.

38. V.E. Watts, trans., Boethius: The Consolation of Philosophy (London: Penguin, 1969), p. 1.

39. Ibid, p. 159.

40. Fagan, p. 88.

41. Ibid, pp.6-7.

42. Ani, p. 32.

43. Ibid, p. 36.

44. Howard A. Ozmon and Samuel M. Carver, Philosophical Foundations of Education, Fourth Edition (Columbus, OH: Merrill Publishing Company, 1990), p. 126.

45. Ibid

46. Ani, p. 298.

47. Ozmon and Carver, p. 126.

48. Edward Burton Levine, Hippocrates (New York: Twayne Publishers, 1971), p. 56.

49. Houghton Mifflin Company, The American Heritage Dictionary of the English Language, 3rd Editon (Boston, 1992), p. 856.

50. Erriel D. Roberson, The Maafa & Beyond: Remembrance, Ancestral Connections and Nation Building for the African Global Community (Columbia, MD: Kujichagulia Press, 1995), p. 170.

51. T'Shaka, p. 96. Hunter Adams III, "African Observors of the Universe: The Sirius Question" in Blacks in Science: Ancient and Modern, ed. Ivan Van Sertima (New Brunswick: Transaction Books, 1983), p. 28.

52. Ani, p. 448.

Chapter 2

1. Mose Pleasure, Jr. and Fred C. Lofton, eds., Living in Hell: The delimma of African-American survival (Grand Rapids, MI: ZondervanPublishingHouse, 1995), p. 10.

2. Russell Thornton, American Indian Holocaust and Survival: A Population History Since 1492 (Norman, OK: University of Oklahoma Press, 1987), p. 15.

3. Ibid, p. 23.

4. Urs Bitterli, <u>Cultures in Conflict: Encounters Between European and Non-European Cultures, 1492-1800</u>, trans. Ritchie Robertson (Stanford: Stanford University Press, 1989), p. 27.

5. Roberto Moreno de los Arcos, "New Spain's Inquisition for Indians from the Sixteenth to the Nineteenth Century," in <u>Cultural Encounters: The Impact of the Inquisition in Spain and the New World</u>, eds. Mary Elizabeth and Anne J. Cruz (Berkeley, CA: University of California Press, 1991), p. 28.

6. Herma Briffault, trans., <u>The Devastation of the Indies: A Brief Account</u>, Johns Hopkins Paperbacks Edition (Baltimore: The Johns Hopkins University Press, 1992), p. 59.

7. Bitterli, p. 23.

8. Alan Moorehead, <u>The Fatal Impact: An Account of the Invasion of the South Pacific 1769-1840</u> (New York: Harper & Row, 1966), p. 3.

9. Brian Fagan, <u>Clash of Cultures </u>(New York: W.H. Freeman & Company, 1984), p. 47.

10. W.E. Burghardt DuBois, <u>The World and Africa: An inquiry into the part which Africa has played in world history</u>, New Enlarged Edition (New York: International Publishers, 1965), p. 283.

11. Ibid

12. John G. Jackson, <u>Introduction to African Civilizations</u>, First Carol

Publishing Group Edition (New York: Carol Publishing Group, 1990), p. 311.

13. DuBois, p. 280.

14. Haki Madhubuti, Enemies: The Clash of Races (Chicago: Third World Press, 1978), p. 92.

15. Chinweizu, The West and the Rest of Us: White predators, Black slavers and the African elite (Lagos, Nigeria: Pero Press, 1987), p. 1.

16. Marimba Ani, Yurugu: An African-Centered Critique of European Cultural Thought and Behavior (Trenton, NJ: Africa World Press, 1994), p. 446.

17. DuBois, p. 25.

18. Chinweizu, p. 11.

19. Ibid, p. xv.

20. Moorehead, p. 134.

21. Ibid, p. 170.

22. Ibid

23. Ibid, p. 169.

24. Ibid, p. 135.

25. Edward Peters, Torture (New York: Basil Blackwell Inc., 1985), p. 18.

26. Ibid, p. 35.

27. Henry Charles Lea, Torture, 1st Pennsylvania Paperback Edition (Philadelphia: University of Pennsylvania Press, 1973), p. 90.

28. Nick Charles and Chrisena Coleman, "Black and Undercover: White officers see Black before seeing blue." Emerge Magazine, September 1995, p. 24.

29. Ibid

30. Ibid, p. 26.

31. Ibid

32. Sam Vincent Meddis and Deborah Sharp, "Prison business is a blockbuster: As spending soars, so do the profits." USA Today, 13 December 1994, 10A.

33. Sam Vincent Meddis, "Success of expansion a matter of debate." USA Today, 13 December 1994, 10A.

34. Charles and Coleman, p. 28.

35. Carol Innerst, "Male, female not enough for feminists: Hermaphrodites, transexuals are 'reimagined' genders." The Washington Times, 20, July 1995, A1.

36. Sam Vincent Meddis, "Report: ATF agents attended racist party."

USA Today, 13 July 1995, 4A.

37. Michael Abramowitz, "Early 'Roundup' Allegations Were Ignored by ATF Officials." Washington Post, 22 July 1995, A1.

38. Ibid, A11.

39. Ibid, A1 & A11.

40. "Alleged racism in ATF spurs call for hearing: Whites-only retreat under investigation." Baltimore Sun, 14 July 1995, 6A.

41. "California university board approves end to race-based admissions, hiring." Baltimore Sun, 21 July 1995.

42. Kate Shatzkin, "Life terms given in two slayings: Man bludgeoned his grandparents." Baltimore Sun, 18 July 1995, B1.

43. Sheridan Lyons, "Baldwin man gets life term in sex assault." Baltimore Sun, Howard Co., 11 May 1995, 8B.

44. Peter Herman, "Two children find body of man outside school: Victim was stabbed at least 50 times." Baltimore Sun, Howard Co., 11 May 1995, 8B.

45. "Suit filed over 50's radiation tests." Baltimore Sun, 11 May 1995, 3A.

46. USA Today, 11 May 1995, 3A.

47. Ibid

48. "26 at NIH unwittingly contaminated." <u>Baltimore Sun</u>, 18 July 1995, 3A.

49. Steve Marshall, "Name change denied, dad kills son, self." <u>USA Today</u>, 16 may 1995, 3A.

50. <u>USA Today</u>, 25 July 1995, 3A.

51. Anita Manning, "Lawmaker: Kids used in tobacco test." <u>USA Today</u>, 25 July 1995, 1A.

52. John Schwartz, "More Teenagers Smoking Cigarettes and Marijuana, Survey Shows." <u>Washington Post</u>, 20 July 1995, A11.

53. Linda James Meyers, "Expanding the Psychology of Knowledge Optimally: The Importance of Wordview Revisited," in <u>Black Psychology</u>, ed. Reginald L. Jones (Berkely, CA: Cobb & Henry Publishers, 1991), p. 19.

54. Ani, p. 332.

55. "Thomas Invokes Religion." <u>USA Today</u>, 24 August 1995, 15A.

56. C.P. Otero, ed., <u>Noam Chomsky, Language and Politics</u> (Montreal: Black Rose Books, 1988), p. 561.

57. Ibid, pp. 616-617.

Chapter 3

1. John J. Macionis, Sociology (Englewood Cliffs, NJ: Prentice Hall, 1993), p. 66.

2. Deepak Chopra, Ageless Body, Timeless Mind: The Quantum Alternative to Growing Old (New York: Harmony Books, 1993), p. 12.

3. Deepak Chopra, Perfect Health: The Complete Mind/Body Guide (New York: Harmony Books, 1990), p. 3.

4. Henry Skolimnowski, "The Scientific World View and the Illusions of Progress," in Social Research, Vol. 41, No.1, 1974, p. 53.

5. Ibid

6. Francis Cress Welsing, The Isis Papers: The Keys To The Colors (Chicago: Third World Press, 1991), p. 153.

Chapter 4

1. Dona Marimba Richards, Let The Circle Be Unbroken: The Implications of African Spirituality in the Diaspora, First Red Sea Press, Inc., Edition (Lawrenceville, NJ: The Red Sea Press, Inc., 1992), p. 53.

2. Ibid, p. 8.

3. Ibid, p. 9.

4. Malidoma Patrice Somé, Ritual: Power, Healing and Community (Portland, OR: Swan Raven & Company, 1993), pp. 97-98.

5. Richards, pp.25-26.

6. Some, p. 90.

7. Houghton Mifflin Company, The American Heritage Dictionary of the English Language, 3rd Edition (Boston: 1992), p. 303.

8. Ibid

9. Haki R. Madhubuti, From Plan to Planet: Life Studies: The Need For Afrikan Minds and Institutions (Chicago: Third World Press, 1973), p. 15.

10. bell hooks, Killing Rage: Ending Racism (New York: Henry Holt & Company, 1995), p. 14.

11. Ibid, p. 12.

12. Judith Lewis Herman, Trauma & Recovery: the aftermath of violence--from domestic abuse to political terror (New York: Basic Books, 1992), p. 51.

13. Ibid, p. 75.

14. Ibid, p. 86.

15. Ibid, p. 93.

Chapter 5

1. Amos Wilson, <u>The Falsification of Afrikan Consciousness: Eurocentric History, Psychiatry and the Politics of White Supremacy</u> (New York: Afrikan World InfoSystems, 1991), p. 101.

2. Citizens Commission on Human Rights, <u>Psychiatry's Betrayal</u> (Los Angeles: 1995), p. 5.

3. Ibid

4. Ibid, p. 8.

5. Na'im Akbar, "Mental Disorder Among African Americans," in <u>Black Psychology</u>, ed. Reginald L. Jones (Berkeley, CA: Cobb & Henry Publishers, 1991), p. 342.

6. Wade Nobles, <u>African Psychology</u> (Oakland: Black Family Institute, 1986), pp.95-96.

7. Akbar, p. 343.

8. Ibid, p. 344.

9. Ibid

10. Ibid, p. 345.

11. Kobi Kambon, <u>The African Personality in America</u> (Tallahassee, FL: Nubian Nation Publications, 1992), p. xiv.

12. Akbar, p. 345.

13. Nobles, pp. 106-107.

14. Bill Moyers, <u>Healing and the Mind</u> (New York: Double Day, 1993), p. 191.

15. Ibid, p, 94.

16. Ibid, p. xiii.

17. Judith Lewis Herman, <u>Trauma & Recovery: the aftermath of violence--from domestic abuse to political terror</u> (New York: Basic Books, 1992), p. 159.

18. Ibid, p. 172.

19. Charles L. Whitfield, <u>Memory and Abuse: Remembering and Healing the Effects of Trauma</u> (Deerfield Beach, FL: Health Communications Inc., 1995), p. 267.

20. Ibid

21. Ibid, p. 288.

22. Ellen Bass and Laura Davis, <u>The Courage To Heal: A Guide For Women Survivors of Child Sexual Abuse</u>, Third Edition (New York: HarperPerrenial, 1994), p. 65.

23. Ibid, p. 134.

24. Ibid, p. 65.

25. Kambon, pp. 177-178.

26. Maulana Karenga, The African American Holiday of Kwanzaa: A Celebration of Family, Community & Culture (Los Angeles: University of Sankore Press, 1988), pp. 95-96.

27. Kambon, pp. 189-191.

28. Ibid, pp. 193-194.

Chapter 6

1. Erriel D. Roberson, The Maafa & Beyond: Remembrance, Ancestral Connections and Nation Building for the African Global Community (Columbia, MD: Kujichagulia Press, 1995), p. 87.

2. Ibid, p.88.

3. Amos Wilson, The Falsification of Afrikan Consciousness: Eurocentric History, Psychiatry and the Politics of White Supremacy (New York: Afrikan World InfoSystems, 1991), p. 10.

4. Erriel Roberson, Awaken: Creating a Blueprint for Enlightenment, Organization and Freedom (Silver Spring, MD: Sea Island Press, 1993), p. 59.

5. Marimba Ani, Yurugu: An African-Centered Critique of European Cultural Thought and Behavior (Trenton, NJ: Africa World Press, 1994), p. 312.

6. Roberson, The Maafa & Beyond, p. 75.

7. Robert A. Wallace, Gerald P. Sanders and Robert J. Ferl, <u>Biology: the Science of Life</u> (New York: HarperCollinsPublishers, 1991), pp. 901-902.

8. Wilson, p. 10.

Chapter 7

1. Thomas Sowell, <u>Race and Culture: A World View</u> (New York: Basic Books, 1994), p. 189.

2. Chancellor Williams, <u>The Rebirth of African Civilization</u> (Chicago: Third World Press, 1993), p. 4

3. Sowell, p. 220.

4. Jonathan H. Turner, <u>American Society: Problems of Structure</u>, 2nd Edition (New York: Harper & Row, 1976), p. 43.

5. Williams, p. 153.

6. Oba T'Shaka, <u>Return to the African Mother Principle of Male and Female Equality</u>, Vol. 1 (Oakland: Pan Afrikan Publishers, 1995), p. 268.

7. Williams, p. 154.

8. Ibid, p. 170.

9. Amos Wilson, The Falsification of Afrikan Consciousness: Eurocentric History, Psychiatry and the Politics of White Supremacy (New York: Afrikan World InfoSystems, 1991), p. 94.

10. Aurthur Schlesinger, Jr., The Disuniting of America (New York: W.W. Norton & Company, 1992), p. 122.

11. Marimba Ani, Yurugu: An African-Centered Critique of European Cultural Thought and Behavior (Trenton, NJ: Africa World Press, 1994), p. 400.

12. Schlesinger, p. 127.

13. Robert Hughes, Culture of Complaint: The Fraying of America (New York: Oxford University Press, 1993), p. 138.

14. Shelby Steele, The Content of Our Character: A New Vision of Race in America, First Harper Perennial Edition (New York: HarperPerennial, 1991), pp. 5-6.

15. Ibid, p. 173.

16. Wilson, p. 125.

17. Ibid, pp. 102-103.

18. Kobi Kambon, The African Personality in America (Tallahassee, FL: Nubian Nation Publications, 1992), p. 154.

Chapter 8

1. Oba T'Shaka, <u>Return to the African Mother Principle of Male and Female Equality</u>, Vol. 1 (Oakland: Pan Afrikan Publishers, 1995), p. 428.

2. Robert Wright, "The Evolution of Despair." <u>Time</u>, 28 August 1995, p. 50.

3. Ibid, p. 52.

4. Marimba Ani, <u>Yurugu: An African-Centered Critique of European Cultural Thought and Behavior</u> (Trenton, NJ: Africa World Press, 1994), p. 570.

5. Ayi Kwei Armah, <u>Two Thousand Seasons</u> (London: Heinemann, 1979), p. 158.

6. Kwame Agyei Akoto, <u>Nationbuilding: Theory and Practice in African Centered Education</u> (DC: Pan Afrikan World Institute, 1992), p. 32.

7. Ibid

8. bell hooks, <u>Killing Rage: Ending Racism </u>(New York: Henry Holt and Company, 1995).

9. _____, <u>Akan Ethics: A Study of Moral Ideas and the Moral Behavior of the Akan Tribes of Ghana</u> (Accra: Ghana University Press, 1988).

10. Chinweizu, The West and the Rest of Us: White predators, Black slavers and the African elite (Lagos, Nigeria: Pero Press, 1987), p. 215.

11. Ibid, pp. 217-218.

12. Ani, p. 502.

13. Akoto, p. 30.

14. Malidoma Patrice Somé, Ritual: Power, Healing and Community (Portland, OR: Swan Raven & Company, 1993).

15. Erriel D. Roberson, The Maafa & Beyond: Remembrance, Ancestral Connections and Nation Building for the African Global Community (Columbia, MD: Kujichagulia Press, 1995), p. 89.

16. Amos Wilson, The Falsification of Afrikan Consciousness: Eurocentric History, Psychiatry and the Politics of White Supremacy (New York: Afrikan World InfoSystems, 1991), p. 120.

17. Ibid, p. 125.

Chapter 9

1. Francis Cress Welsing, The Isis Papers: The Keys to the Colors (Chicago: Third World Press, 1991), p. ii.

2. Erriel D. Roberson, The Maafa & Beyond: Remembrance, Ancestral Connections and Nation Building for the African Global Community (Columbia, MD: Kujichagulia Press, 1995), p. 149.

3. Ibid

4. Clifford Jolly and Fred Plog, <u>Physical Anthropology and Archeology</u>, Fourth Edition (New York: Alfred Knopf, 1976), p. 417.

5. <u>Outdoor Sculpture of Washington D.C.</u>

6. John J. Macionis, <u>Sociology</u> (Englewood Cliffs, NJ: Prentice Hall, 1993), p. 65.

7. Collins Publishers, <u>The Wall: Images and Offerings from the Vietnam Veterans Memorial</u> (1987), p. 15.

8. Ibid

9. Ibid, p. 25.

10. <u>Preserving Memory: The Struggle To Create America's Holocaust Museum</u>, p. 2.

11. Ibid, p. 4.

12. Ibid, p. 5.

13. <u>A Promise To Remember</u>, p. vi.

14. Ibid, p. ix.

Chapter 10

1. Charles Finch, <u>Echoes of the Old Darkland: Themes from the African Eden</u> (Decatur, GA: Kheti, Inc., 1991), p. 25.

2. Clifford Jolly and Fred Plog, <u>Physical Anthropology and Archeology</u>, Fourth Edition (New York: Alfred Knopf, 1976), p. 290.

3. Ibid, p. 462.

4. Finch, p. 32.

5. Ibid, p. 33.

6. Jolly and Plog, p. 455-466.

7. Finch, p. 27.

Chapter 11

1. Larry Williams and Charles Finch, "The Great Queens of Ethiopia," in <u>Black Women in Antiquity</u>, ed. Ivan Van Sertima (New Brunswick, NJ: Transaction Pulishers, 1988), p. 13.

2. Agnes Akosua Aidoo, "Asante Queen Mothers in Government and Politics in the Nineteenth Century," in <u>Black Women Cross-Culturally</u>, ed. Filomina Steady (Rochester, VT: Schenkman Books, Inc., 1985), p. 66.

3. Ibid, p. 67.

4. Ibid, p. 66.

5. Diedre Wimby, "The Female Horuses and Great Wives of Kemet," in Black Women in Antiquity, ed. Ivan Van Sertima (New Brunswick, NJ: Transaction Books, 1988), p. 46.

6. John Henrik Clarke, "African Warrior Queens," in Black Women in Antiquity, ed. Ivan Van Sertima (New Brunswick, NJ: Transaction Books, 1988), p. 132.

7. Ibid, p. 133.

Index

Finch, Charles 287

G

God 43, 152
Golden Stool 300
Good Ol' Boys Roundup 75, 76, 77, 80
Grecian sexism 39
Greco-Roman 29
Greek 16, 41
Greeks 51

H

Hapi 153, 154
Hawaii 61
healing 119, 122
Healing Models 138
Henrik, John Clarke xiii
Heru 153, 154
higher learning 199
higher level consciousness 50
Holocaust 216
Holocaust Museum 277
Holy Trinity 153
Homo erectus 284
Homo habilis 284
Homo sapiens sapiens 284
homosexuality 30–36

I

ideological matrix 22, 48, 82
ideology 163
imbalance 255
Imhotep 50
imperialism 81
independent institution 209
India 64
insane xv, 48, 81, 112, 191
insanity 15, 39, 49, 118
Institute of Independent Education 185
institution 186
institutionalized racism 23, 24

institutions 199
intuition 255

J

Jamal, Mumia Abu 111
Jim Crow 191
Judeo-Christian 29

K

Kambon, Kobi 68, 85, 133
Kemet 16, 49, 50, 51, 152, 258, 273, 292, 298
Kemetic Kalendar 303
Kentakes 298
Kenya 62
kidnapping 45
KiSwahili xiv
Kobi Kambon 147
Kongo 62
ktke. *See* Kentakes
Kush 298

L

language 3, 4, 9, 13, 151
language liberation 7
language theory 6
Legba 154
libation 148, 150
liberation 1, 115, 166, 273
linguistic xv
linguistics 4, 6
lynchings 71

M

Maafa 1, 18, 23, 24, 45, 61, 75, 81, 83, 85, 108, 112, 114, 116, 118, 120, 124, 128, 140, 151, 156, 158, 161, 187, 203, 209, 210, 216, 277, 280, 299
Maafa criminals 39